1/8/ P9-DMT-505

BELIEF

ALSO BY N. JOHN HALL

BOOKS
> Trollope: A Biography
> Salmagundi: Byron, Allegra, and the Trollope Family
> Trollope and His Illustrators
> Max Beerbohm: A Kind of a Life
> Max Beerbohm Caricatures

EDITIONS
> The Letters of Anthony Trollope
> The Trollope Critics
> Anthony Trollope's
>> The New Zealander
>> The Macdermots of Ballycloran
>> Barchester Towers and The Warden
>> Sir Harry Hotspur of Humblethwaite
>> The Struggles of Brown, Jones, and Robinson
>> The Three Clerks
>> John Caldigate
>> Doctor Thorne
> General Editor, Selected Works of Anthony Trollope (36 titles)
> Max Beerbohm's
>> The Illustrated Zuleika Dobson
>> Rossetti and His Circle
>> A Christmas Garland

BELIEF
A Memoir

N. John Hall

FREDERIC C. BEIL

SAVANNAH

2007

Copyright © 2007 by N. John Hall

All rights reserved.
No part of this book may be used or reproduced
in any manner whatsoever without written permission,
except in the case of brief quotations
embodied in critical articles and reviews.

Published in the United States of America by
Frederic C. Beil, Publisher, Inc.
609 Whitaker Street
Savannah, Georgia 31401
http://www.beil.com

LIBRARY OF CONGRESS CATALOGING-IN-PUBLICATION DATA

Hall, N. John
Belief : a memoir / by N. John Hall
p.   cm.
ISBN-13: 978-1-929490-34-9 (hardcover : alk. paper)
ISBN-10: 1-929490-34-8 (hardcover : alk. paper)
1. Hall, N. John.
2. Catholic ex-priests–United States–Biography.
1. Title.
BX4668.3.H35A3 2007
282.092–dc22
[B]

2006023770

Manufactured in the United States of America

First Edition

FOR M

Contents

PREFACE

FRIDAY September 1, 1967, was a bright sunny morning in New York City. I was thirty-four years old. Never could I remember such a sensation of freedom. From that day to this, now nearly forty years later, I have not ceased to rejoice in the decision, taken after years of struggle, to start a new life. This new life had begun less than twenty-four hours earlier, when I was driven by car from Paterson, New Jersey, some twenty miles to the west, and dropped off here at 27 East 13th Street. That evening I lay in bed, still weak from a just-ended hospital stay, and asked someone to be my wife. Now I came down one flight of stairs, walked across the lobby, and out into the sunshine. My decision seemed to take on a more palpable reality. What sort of life I had lived until that morning is what this book is about.

It is often said that while everyone's story is different, they're all really the same. I think mine is different enough, strange enough, to be worth the attempt to retell. And I know that, as Henry James said of characters in novels, we care about people only in so far as we know about them. And so I shall back up, tracing the years and endeavoring to set the stage for my resolution and independence, which culminated on 13th Street in Greenwich Village those many years ago.

I have read, thought much about, and taught many autobiographies—those of Carlyle, Newman, Mill, Trollope, Gosse, Mary McCarthy, John Updike, Muriel Spark. I have thought, too, of the great autobiographical novels, of Dickens' *Great Expectations*, of Butler's *The Way of All Flesh*, of Joyce's *A Portrait of the Artist as a Young Man*. I have read in the theories of autobiography, and am, I believe, sufficiently aware of the pit-falls involved in writing one's own life. I know, for example, that the child, the adolescent, the young man that I try to describe here no longer exists. I have been, for many years, someone else. I know how selective and deceptive our memories are. I know the temptation "to set the record straight." I am aware too that autobiography is inextricably tied to fiction. Some critics hold that all autobiography is in fact fiction—the story, the narrative, the lies we tell about ourselves. Other critics have it the other way around, insisting that any book with a signed title page is in fact autobiography. And yet, along with most others, I know that there is a difference between self-writing and fiction. The two are not as different as the man or woman in the street may think, but they are different. Part of the difference lies in the writer's intention, what one critic calls "the autobiographical pact," the intention on the writer's part to do his best to speak truthfully about his interior life. The result leads to autobiography being read in a manner very different from that in which fiction is read. And the reader wants to know if what he or she is reading is autobiography or fiction.

Much is made today of the difference between autobiography and memoir. The latter is often seen as focusing on a single aspect of one's life—"My Days as Cardinal Spellman's Chauffeur"—and as briefer, more essay-like, requiring less verification, less research. This seems sensible enough. Yet Trollope, for example, and many other writers use the terms interchangeably. In any case, whether this be memoir or autobiography, I try to tell the story as honestly as I can. I have invented nothing. To the best of my knowledge I have not improved upon events. I have tried not to skew reality (as I recall it) to suit my purpose, knowing all the time that such a goal is illusory, that everything here is seen from my perspective. Still, I have looked outside my present self by searching through old notebooks, papers, letters, and books, and also by recording interviews with dozens of people who knew me back then. Isak Dinesen tells us how while she was working on *Out of Africa* she would write to people in

Africa so as to get the spelling of the middle name of a servant correct, something that would have mattered not in the least to her reader. I have made similar efforts to get my facts straight.

For anyone curious about the aftermath, I provide a post-script.

NJH New York 2006

BELIEF

1

AT FIRST

I WAS FIFTEEN when I underwent the religious experience that put my life on a course that would carry it in one
direction for the next eighteen years. Catholic high schools
like the one I attended held annual three-day retreats. A visiting
priest, the retreat master, who was always a Jesuit, gave a series
of talks to the student body assembled in the church. Classes
were suspended, strict silence was observed, and we were urged
to curtail all worldly activities after school for these three days.
The students' cooperation was really quite remarkable. The
retreat master, following in outline *The Spiritual Exercises of St.
Ignatius*, held most of us spellbound. There was no hollering or
shouting on his part, nothing at all of the noisy revival spirit.
The talks were meditative and quietly mesmerizing. Many
people have read a version of the *Spiritual Exercises* in James
Joyce's *Portrait of the Artist as a Young Man*. These retreat talks
in all their incarnations revolve around the four last things:
death, judgment, hell—along with its cause, sin, which in Joyce's
days and those of my own youth meant sexual sin—and heaven.
Here, surprisingly little different from what I heard in 1948, are
some morsels from Joyce:

> Hell is a strait and dark and foulsmelling prison, an
> abode of demons and lost souls, filled with fire and smoke.
> ... [The souls of the damned] lie in exterior darkness. For
> remember, the fire of hell gives forth no light . . . while
> retaining the intensity of its heat, [it] burns eternally
> in darkness. It is a neverending storm of darkness, dark
> flames and dark smoke of burning brimstone, amid which

3

the bodies are heaped one upon another without even a glimpse of air.

The horror of this strait and dark prison is increased by its awful stench. All the filth of the world, all the offal and scum of the world, we are told, shall run there as to a vast reeking sewer.... Imagine this sickening stench multiplied a millionfold and a millionfold again from the millions of fetid carcasses massed together in the reeking darkness, a huge and rotting human fungus.

But the flames of hell are worse than the stench. Human torturers and tyrants use fire to subject their fellow creatures, but their efforts are no match for God's:

The sulphurous brimstone which burns in hell is a substance which is specially designed to burn for ever and for ever with unspeakable fury.... Our earthly fire again, no matter how fierce or widespread it may be, is always of a limited extent; the lake of hell is boundless, shoreless and bottomless.... And yet what I have said as to the strength and quality and boundlessness of this fire is as nothing when compared to its intensity, an intensity which it has as being the instrument chosen by divine design for the punishment of soul and body alike.

And this physical torment is only prelude to the spiritual pain, the loss of divine light and of God. Moreover, all this misery and suffering are eternal:

Imagine a mountain of ... sand, a million miles high, reaching from the earth to the farthest heavens, and a million miles broad, extending to remotest space, and a million miles in thickness: and imagine such an enormous mass of countless particles of sand multiplied as often as there are leaves in the forest, drops of water in the mighty oceans, feathers on birds, scales on fish, hairs on animals, atoms in the vast expanse of the air: and imagine that at the end of every million years a little bird came to that mountain and carried away in its beak a tiny grain of that sand. How many millions upon millions of centuries would pass before that bird had carried away even a square foot of that mountain, how many eons upon eons of ages before it had carried away all. Yet at the end of that immense stretch of time not even one instant of eternity could be said to have ended.

To give the retreat master his due, I should add that the final talks, on heaven and the joy of loving God, were pretty vivid too. But he made it understood that before entering into the favor of God's grace here on earth, before the Mass and Communion that would conclude the retreat, one had to be genuinely sorry for one's sins and make a new start with a "general confession" covering the whole of one's life.

Like Stephen Dedalus in Joyce's novel, I was dumbstruck and moved to sincere, extreme repentance, though I had on my conscience nothing like his very real sins. Would it have been better for me, I now wonder, had I had the courage to sin, at least a little, with another of my kind, as Joyce's autobiographical character had done? Would it have helped me to grow up faster? Some people are ready early for life, or, for that matter, for sex. In any case, the retreat master bowled me over. I determined not merely to make that general confession, but to begin life anew. And I did.

TO MAKE SENSE of what happened to me in 1948 and of what was to come, I must go back and see, as clearly as I can, what kind of person I was until that moment. My life had not been terribly different from that of many youngsters my age. And it had not been particularly troubled. Nor had I been markedly religious or irreligious. I was in most regards "average." Tolstoy wrote famously that all happy families resemble each other and all unhappy families are different. I have not the slightest hesitation in saying that my family was among the happy ones. Of course there are darker schools of thought, especially psychoanalytical ones, which see any assertion of a happy family life as a sure sign of repression. I am not of such a school. I take Max Beerbohm's view of his family life as being rather like my own: "I adored my mother, I adored my father, I adored my sisters and brothers. What kind of trauma would they find me victim of?" But if we were a happy family, it was in spite of or perhaps because of the fact that my parents came of such different backgrounds and brought to their marriage and to their three children such broad differences. That said, I can add that my father was different not just from my mother; he was different from anyone I ever knew.

Norman C. Hall—NCH—came of old Yankee stock. He was born in Newark, New Jersey, in 1899, and grew up in comparative luxury, the only child of a prosperous dentist. A picture he left me shows him at age eight posing beside a maid. He explained apologetically that they had a maid because his mother had to spend so much time crafting false teeth for her husband's dental practice. Young Norman got whatever he wanted. He began to learn to shoot a rifle and a pistol as a little boy of seven, and he was to remain enamored of guns always. He had piano lessons, singing lessons, and boxing lessons. When Norman was in his mid-teens, his father, who had owned one of the first cars in Newark, saw to it that his son also got one before most people did. Norman loved cars all his life, and you might say that in this regard he started at the top and worked his way down. The car his father got him was a Stutz Bearcat, a red, "souped-up" sports roadster, "my pride and joy," as he called it. I should think so. Rather like getting a top-of-the-line customized Mercedes two-seater convertible today.

He was sent for one year to a Presbyterian Sunday school, but religion didn't take with him. Radio and electricity were his religion. From childhood, he showed an obsessive interest in these subjects. When he graduated from elementary school, the class prophecy, preserved in a scrapbook, reads: "A second Marconi shall be Norman Hall,/ who will make many discoveries both large and small. / To him we give this roll of wire, and hope from inventing he'll never tire." This was all well and good at the time (or not so good, as poetry), but in years to come the mere mention of Marconi as the "inventor" of radio would drive him crazy. Norman got his ham radio operator's license at the age of fifteen, the youngest in New Jersey to do so at the time. At Newark Central Technical High he impressed some of his teachers as something of a genius; other teachers tried to take him down a peg because they thought he thought he was a genius. He himself would have considered such talk nonsense; he didn't much believe in anyone's genius, let alone his own—at most there might be one or two electrical geniuses a century, and "certainly not Marconi, or that crook DeForest." Norman knew that he was smart, that he had a special gift. In the evenings while still attending Newark Central, he was teaching radio at the Federal School, a place that later became the Newark College of Engineering. Just how he came to know all he did about radio and tubes, how he made himself into a prominent electrical engineer with nothing more than a technical high school education, is beyond discovery.

Norman joined the Signal Corps out of high school, but was disappointed when the Great War ended before his unit was scheduled to be sent "over there," as the saying had it in those days. Norman returned to civilian life and worked in supervisory capacities for various electrical concerns in New York City. For a time he was riding high. And then suddenly, in the early 1920s, his prospects dimmed. His father came down with rheumatoid arthritis and was soon confined to a wheelchair, unable to practice dentistry. His mother suffered the first of a series of small but debilitating strokes. They had no savings, not even a house since the "mansion" where they lived on Roseville Avenue in Newark was a rental. There was no such thing as Social Security. NCH, having to scrap all thought of returning to school to study electrical engineering at Columbia, would support his "two invalids" for the next ten years.

In 1926 he left the New York firm of Stanley and Patterson

to become production engineer at Westinghouse, which had its huge "lamp" or tube division in Bloomfield, just next to Newark. He prospered in his work, producing a string of new tubes, "automatic seasoning machines," and "water cooled bombarders," and becoming supervisor of X-ray, power, and special tubes. In one production area he had thirty young women putting glass bulbs into sockets. He was still a whiz kid, but having to support his parents and pay the Roseville Avenue rent, he barely made ends meet. He got by, working nights at second jobs in "the radio and tube game."

He seems to have led an active social life. NCH was a very good-looking man; he drove imposing cars and held impressive jobs. If told that he looked like F. Scott Fitzgerald, only more handsome, he would not have known or "cared a damn" to know who F. Scott Fitzgerald was. In the taped recollections he left me to find after his death and which constitute the source of the quotations attributed to him here, he rattles off a long list of names of the "girls" he went out with. He remarks that all the women he names were "only passing fancies" compared to "my one and only." This last was a beautiful young woman from (as he loved to joke) "down by Jersey City Heights," one of those thirty women putting glass bulbs into sockets at Westinghouse.

My mother came from a background very different from that of my father. Lucille Hertlein was the daughter of poor immigrants from Bavaria. Her parents had met aboard a North German Lloyd ship carrying such immigrants to America in 1895. Anna Markert was coming to live as an indentured servant in Milwaukee, and Georg Hertlein was a young sailor on the ship. Anna, after two unhappy years in Milwaukee, sent him a letter saying that she was returning to Germany. He wrote back that he would meet her train in New York and identify himself by wearing a flower in his button hole. The two were married in 1898, settled in Jersey City Heights, and had four children, of whom Lucy, the third child, born in 1903, would become my mother. Georg loved to tell the story how as a young sailor he had been shipwrecked off Cameroon, where for months he had been stranded and where the sun had permanently darkened his skin and in due course his daughter Lucy's skin. Of course heredity doesn't work that way, but, no matter, she was dark-complected like her father, and later she could pass for Italian during the two world wars she lived through in which the "Krauts" were America's enemies. This, she explained to me, was why she never mentioned things German or spoke the language: "We're always at war with them." She also took after her father in being mild-mannered and shy, just the opposite of her strong-willed and forceful mother. It was at the time of Lucy's birth that her mother put her foot down and forbade Georg's going to sea anymore. Henceforth he operated elevators at the North German Lloyd piers in Hoboken. He would walk to work to save the nickel trolley fare.

If Norman Hall, "for all intents and purposes," as he loved to say, grew up with no religion at all, Lucy Hertlein had enough for two. Her family were devout Bavarian Roman Catholics, and she, like her brother and sisters, was sent to St. Nicholas Parish School in Jersey City Heights. Here the Sisters of Christian Charity—German nuns from the old country—taught all subjects in both German and English. Girls who misbehaved in any way were beaten on the hands with a ruler. Lucy was once slapped about the face for playing with a piece of string during lunchtime. Boys who broke any rule were made to kneel on the floor and were whipped with a wooden pointer. An altar boy in her class was beaten about the head so violently by a priest, one Father Meyer, that for a time it was feared the boy would lose his hearing. And children kept quiet at home about their school beatings or there would be more of the same. The nuns and priests of St. Nicholas, as elsewhere in the country, were irrational when it came to anything connected to sex. Two neighbors of the Hertleins, both eighth graders, whose first names only survive here, Emil and Frances, were friends; and Emil, the smartest boy in the school, was reported to have carried Frances' books home from school. He was immediately expelled, just short of graduation. There was to be none of that. It goes almost without saying that Lucy's eldest sibling, her brother Charlie, a regular hell-raiser, was also expelled and never completed grammar school, though this did not prevent his becoming a Hudson County policeman. The three Hertlein girls persevered and in turn graduated. My mother, I see in retrospect, was to remain all her life a slightly frightened little girl, intimidated by her authoritarian mother and her Catholic upbringing.

In 1917, when Lucy was fourteen, her father died of Bright's disease. Why, she kept asking herself, had God taken her daddy? It was not meant as an anti-god question, but it was the closest she would ever come to questioning her religion or her faith. Nineteen-seventeen was also the year of her graduation from St. Nicholas Parish School. The newly elected mayor, Frank Hague, who would autocratically rule Jersey City for thirty years, addressed the school and gave each graduate an orange. Lucy was glad to be through with school, where she had done well in most subjects except reading. But after the eighth grade she was sent out to work to help the family. This was nothing cruel or unusual. It was the way immigrant families operated. The hope was that in due course a girl would find a husband, someone who would be good to her and support her. My mother, like her two sisters, never worked a day outside of the home after getting married. It was one of the reasons they got married. My mother used to say, "I don't have to work, I have a husband," and "I don't have to learn to drive a car, I have a husband." Lucy worked for a hatter, for a china manufacturer, and as a waitress. After her mother's death, she moved into the home of her married sister Elsie and brother-in-law Edward Ehrenberg, at 96 Ella Street, Bloomfield, and went to work at Westinghouse.

Norman Hall and Lucille, as she now called herself, were married on July 2, 1929, by a priest of Sacred Heart Church in Bloomfield. Since this was a "mixed marriage" (between a Catholic and a Protestant), requiring a dispensation from the bishop, a quiet little ceremony took place in the rectory, after both man and woman had sworn to abstain from practicing birth control and to bring up Catholic any children born to them. Norman would not enter the Church until three years later, a sequence of events that made his conversion the more legitimate. Many partners in marriage were known to "convert" for the sake of the spouse or the spouse's family. Here no pressure was exerted on Norman—not that it would have done any good. But he was impressed by the young and intelligent assistant pastor who married them and who would later receive him into the Church. Norman told me that reading Spinoza also had something to do with his conversion, though what he was doing reading Spinoza or how Spinoza figured in his becoming a Catholic, I cannot imagine.

The young couple struggled financially. While still maintaining his father and mother, Norman now had a wife to support, and of course there was the likelihood of children. In early 1929 he had made a move that in retrospect he considered "a hell of a mistake." He left Westinghouse and went to work as assistant chief engineer for a small "outfit" called Jenkins Television. People think of television as having arrived suddenly in 1939 at the New York World's Fair, but that of course is nonsense. As for the big names in the development of television, including Baird, Jenkins, DeForest, Farnsworth, Ruckleshous, and Du-Mont, my father used to tell me, with all the dismissive scorn he could muster—and that was plenty—"God help us, there was no god damned 'inventor' of television." Poor old Charles Francis Jenkins, an Edison in his own right, is now forgotten, yet he held some four hundred U.S. patents, and contributed many advances in fields as diverse as motion picture projection, automobile technology, and aeronautical science. In television, however, Jenkins was on the wrong track, developing mechanical "scanners" as opposed to electronic television. But in the late 1920s Jenkins was full of hope, as was Norman Hall. In November 1929 Jenkins sent him to Washington, D.C., to represent the firm at an electrical exhibition at the Mayflower Hotel.

Norman wrote to Lucille at midnight (I have the letter because my mother never threw out anything written):

> Before I go to bed I must tell you all the excitement. If you were listening on the radio perhaps you heard the Vice President of the U.S., Mr. Curtis, open the show. It was on the National Broadcast chain. Well, honey, what do you suppose? As soon as he finished his speech he was escorted over to the Television booth. A U.S. senator introduced me to him and he spent quite a while there as the crowd just piled up while I was talking with him.

This reminds me of the time when as a young teenager I asked my father to explain to me "how television worked," and for an hour he kept my head spinning. In his old age he was expounding something similar to a teenage granddaughter, Karen Clark, while both were standing. She listened to grandpa, all politeness, till she fainted. Presumably, he was more concise when talking to the Vice President.

If things looked good at the beginning of November, by the end of the month the Crash had come, and Norman was soon out of work at the expiring Jenkins Television and going from job to job as the Depression deepened. Norman and Lucille's first child, Audrey, was born in April 1930, nine months and a week after they were married. Soon Norman's own parents both died. Less than three years after Audrey's birth, on the ridiculous date of January 1, 1933, I was born, at the height of the Great Depression and the height of my parents' money problems. The young Hall family of four lived on the bottom floor of Eddie Ehrenberg's three-story house on Ella Street. But as times got ever more difficult, these larger rooms on the first floor had to be rented to people who could pay more regularly, and Norman and Lucille and children had to move to the attic-like top floor. My mother recalled moving upstairs as a terrible defeat for her.

My father had only sporadic work. He was employed for a time at the Marvin Tube Company and at Arcturus Radio, where he was charged with closing down companies. He had to let employees go, and then be let go himself. He had to tell people they had "one more week, or two more weeks' work"; he remembered "girls crying, 'But where will we go, Mr. Hall?'" He recalled a "fancily dressed fellow with a nice car coming up and asking for a broom. He can be a good janitor, he says." Norman estimated that of the three thousand members of the Institute of Radio Engineers, only about three hundred had jobs: "Prominent engineers were pumping gas or running soda fountains." But even such employment was hard to find. He himself installed electrical outlets in people's houses, worked shooting off fireworks, even played Santa Claus at a department store. More often than not he had no work at all. On the third floor at 96 Ella Street, every penny had to be budgeted. Going on welfare was out of the question. My father had too much pride—people like him did not go on welfare. On the tape Norman claims (an exaggeration because Eddie Ehrenberg, though terribly strapped himself, would never have allowed his sister-in-law's family to starve) that they "would not have made it" but for a friend, a "glass man"—glass blower—from Westinghouse, who insisted on putting four dollars weekly credit to Norman's name at a grocery store.

Then, through an influential friend of his father's at the New Jersey Public Service, Norman obtained entrance to the Training School in North Newark for trolley drivers. Not exactly electrical engineering or pioneering of television, but, as it turned out, my father loved the training course, "the damndest experience," as he put it. For one thing, the instructor "knew what he was talking about." NCH earned top marks and was scheduled to drive a trolley on the South Orange Avenue line. He received his numbered badge and the regulation hat, "a good one, though slightly second hand." My older sister, Audrey, remembers the hat, an army-officer-style affair with a shiny black brim. Lucille was in tears for him. But the job paid $40 a week, with a chance of advancement. Moreover, it was dependable, as good as a lifetime appointment. He figured he had struggled long enough to stay in "the electrical game." Then, on the eve of his first day's work for the Public Service, another glass blower told him that someone who had known him at Westinghouse had started on his own in Upper Montclair and wanted to hire him. Allen B. DuMont, or "ABD" as he came to be called in our house, offered Norman the job of chief engineer at $22 a week.

My father was the sixth employee in a company that eventually employed thousands. Sixty years later Edward Ehrenberg was still admiring Norman's decision to take a job at half the pay in order to stay with work he loved. It doesn't seem, as I look back today, like a wrenching choice. Norman returned to his "vocation," and I would grow up the son of an electrical engineer and not a trolley driver. I would learn to hate RCA, the big rival and enemy in our house. What Protestants and nonbelievers were to my Roman Catholic mother, RCA was to my father. Not that he was a great fan of Allen DuMont. Norman, annoyed over the years at ABD's being called "the father of television," loved say to that DuMont "patented a tube that was 100 years old." In the competition to bring affordable television into homes, RCA had distinct advantages in money and in publicity produced through its radio network. That publicity culminated with the demonstration of television at the RCA Exhibit at the 1939 New York World's Fair. But DuMont was also exhibiting and transmitting television at the World's Fair, and indeed, as T. T. Goldsmith, a DuMont colleague of my father's, pointed out in a 1973 interview, RCA was using for the most part DuMont equipment, and, off the fair grounds, its broadcasts could be received only on DuMont sets. I can hear my father saying, "You're damned right about that."

2

TROLLEY TOWNS

M Y EARLIEST memories date from Uncle Eddie and Aunt Elsie's house on Ella Street in Bloomfield, where we lived during the first four years of my life. But as I would visit there so often over the next eighteen years it's hard today to specify what I remember from which time. That our house lay less than a block from the great Bloomfield Avenue with its trolleys connecting to downtown Newark and, in the other direction, to Montclair and to Caldwell, I would learn only later. My clearest memories of those early days include the time I had my picture taken on a pony. An itinerant photographer convinced poor mothers of those Depression years to lay out a precious twenty-five cents for the finished product, which photograph I still have. Do I remember the event, or does the picture make me think I do? I don't know. I definitely remember the ice man, who was always coming by in his horse-drawn wooden cart. He would crack off a large block of ice and carry it by tongs to the kitchen icebox. To us children he would give shards of ice, which we deemed a treat.

Next, we lived for five years in a large rented house on Central Avenue in Caldwell, the outermost of Newark's suburbs to the west, the place where the trolley line ended. Our house was again a block from Bloomfield Avenue, but this time near the terminus where the trolleys looped around and headed back to Newark. Those trolleys never ceased to fascinate us children. We would put pennies on the tracks to see them flattened. Once we placed a large chunk of ice on the track and got the motorman to slow down before he smashed it to pieces. I had no idea my father had nearly become a trolley driver, though I would have found the idea appealing.

My Caldwell memories are naturally much sharper than those from Bloomfield, and they revolve around school and religion, but I must first mention one peculiar development. At Caldwell, around 1938, I mysteriously stopped eating. I just could not or would not eat, and for a few months I was seriously ill. My parents took me to a specialist, "some damn fool specialist" as my father would later call him, who ordered complete bed rest and that I be carried about. I was to eat some special diet of his own devising, which included an egg-and-banana concoction and brown sugar. I would eat none of the prescribed foods and grew still more emaciated. During the day I was to sleep as much as possible, and a couch was set up in the living room for me. I lay there faking sleep and hearing my mother's anxious discussions of my condition with her sisters.

My older sister, Audrey, tells me my parents feared that I was dying. Then the woman living in the other half of our two-family house, Mrs. Clover, a nurse, told my parents about a new doctor, Irving Gross, a young Jewish man just setting up practice in Verona, the next town down Bloomfield Avenue towards Newark. In fact this Dr. Gross had been driving on Central Avenue and saw me sitting in a lawn chair in front of the house and had debated whether he should notify the authorities that this child was being starved or abused. Instead he spoke with Mrs. Clover, who in turn advised my parents to take me to Dr. Gross. To him I was taken, and he prescribed iron shots for anemia, moderate and increasing exercise, and plenty of outdoor air. He said that I should be allowed to eat anything I wanted, even an entire bowl of white sugar. My parents credited him with saving my life. It's impossible to know today if my sickness had been that critical or not. In pictures taken in the aftermath of this period I do look as if I had just been released from a concentration camp.

It was Dr. Gross who saw my mother through her near fatal last pregnancy and safely delivered my younger sister, Sally, in January 1940. To our family Dr. Gross—"Gross" in my father's shorthand—was a princely figure, not quite infallible, but as close to that status as was possible. Somehow his being Jewish added to the aura of expertise we saw surrounding him. And that aura was enhanced when, for example, he told my father how he admired the nursing nuns' devotion to their work and how he would much rather trust some very ill person to their care than to a nurse distracted by an upcoming Saturday night date. This, coming from a Jew, was especially convincing testimony of the efficacy of Catholic sick care and of his own integrity—if indeed he ever said exactly that. How are we to know, so many years after the fact and given my father's penchant for improving tales in the telling? In any case, when my father liked or believed in someone, he did so wholeheartedly. He taught me to admire experts of any kind—car mechanics, shoemakers, carpenters, barbers, street cleaners, surgeons, and, of course, engineers. But if in his view someone did not measure up or was inadequate, a mere "so-called expert," my father's disdain was unbounded. Incapable specialists he despised as "perfect fakers" and "complete phoneys." He had always to make it emphatic—"fraud" was never enough, the person had to be "a total fraud." With him, appreciation was warm and excessive, depreciation unrelenting and harsh. I suppose this involved his missing the grays of life, the intermediatenesses, the interstices, but it did make for clarity, for himself at least. Perhaps this was part of his engineer's bent. The switch was either on or off. One of my friends who read this book in manuscript says that I myself have "a categorical temperament," as demonstrated in the strong opinions, the firm moral approbations and dismissals of the various characters and theological opinions that characterize the narrator of this book. Another friend and reader disagrees, maintaining that my absolutisms "are all on the surface." What can I say?

My early story keeps coming around to my father. He and his ways were so animated and, even over this vast distance of years, so memorable. My mother herself seemed to concede that his influence on me was stronger than hers when she said repeatedly that I "didn't take after anyone strange"—meaning that I took after my father. But of course I "took after" her as well. My mother's influence was equally strong, but it registered itself quietly and, as shall be seen, deeply. In the course of writing this memoir I have come to believe that I can sort out aspects of my personality which I "inherited" or which rubbed off on me from each parent. To say this involves a large simplification, of course, but I believe there is something to it. From my mother I see myself as taking whatever I have of common sense and of interest in other people. I also took from her, less happily, a tendency toward introspection and worry. From my father I inherited or copied a results-demanding skepticism and a tendency to narrow my focus and work obsessively in one direction at a time.

At Caldwell religion entered my life. Here my mother was in charge. She had strong old-world Bavarian Catholic roots, and was reared in that terrible St. Nicholas School—down by Jersey City Heights. My father was a devout enough convert, but never the real thing. Converts are different from cradle Catholics. Some converts do become fanatic, more Catholic, as the phrase went, than the Pope, but this was hardly the case with my father. But, in fact, even my mother did not force religion upon her children. We never missed Mass on Sunday and never ate meat on Friday. And there was always the formulaic grace before dinner, "Bless us Oh Lord and these thy gifts . . ." At Christmas, under the tree, we had a crèche with a tiny wax Jesus—true to scale, as my father made it a point of explaining—lying on real straw shaved very thin. But this was pretty much the extent of my parents' religious indoctrination of their children. They never had other family prayers or talked of religion. They didn't threaten God's wrath or hell and damnation at our misdeeds, but figured we would get all we needed of such things from the nuns in Catholic school.

They were right about that. At St. Aloysius School in Caldwell, where I entered the first grade, the nuns, although they did not skimp reading, writing, and arithmetic, drilled us in catechism as the first order of work each day. We children were to learn first things first: *Who made you?* "God made me." *Why did God make you?* "God made me to know, love, and serve him in this world, and to be happy with him forever in the next." At the end of the school year we first graders would be making our First Holy Communion, preceded by a first confession. "Bless me, father, for I have sinned, I got angry and I 'distobeyed' my parents" was usual. First Communion itself constituted a very grand occasion. The year-long build-up of catechism lessons was followed by endless rehearsals as the great day drew near. The clothes were uniform and special, white dresses and veils, white shoes and stockings for the girls; black jackets, ties, shoes, stockings and knickerbockers for the boys. Even the little prayer books and rosary beads we carried came in their respective white and black colors. The pressure to perform correctly was enormous. It is no wonder that many children made the mistake (perhaps most eloquently dramatized by Mary McCarthy in *Memories of a Catholic Girlhood*) of accidentally "breaking their fast" by drinking water or swallowing water while brushing their teeth on the morning of the big event. My sister Audrey did exactly this, and went to Communion guiltily and miserably. For a year afterwards she was tormented, making a long string of "bad" confessions and "bad" Communions, convinced that should she die she would go to hell, until she unburdened her eight-year-old self in confession. My own difficulties would come later.

We were still poor. Money was not spent on things considered frivolities. We didn't, for example, go often to the movies. For us movies were rare treats, and from those early days I can count them on the fingers of one hand. In 1938 my father took me to see my first movie, a double feature, *Snow White and the Seven Dwarfs*, followed by *The Lone Ranger*, the latter disappointing me by being in black and white. Later I saw an Abbott and Costello movie, *Keep 'Em Flying*, which I thought was hilarious; then, with Audrey, *Blood and Sand*, about which I can't imagine what I thought; and lastly, again with my father, *National Velvet*. On coming home, he was asked by my mother about the movie and said, "It had some nice morals." He was referring, I learned, to the scene where the doctor assures people that the fallen jockey—Elizabeth Taylor—was a girl.

Nor were we a bookish family. I was taken once or twice to the Caldwell Public Library, but books were not an interest to any of us. We were not a "cultured" family, and the understanding was always that the children would learn anything necessary along those lines at school. We got the *Saturday Evening Post* and, later, *Life* magazine. My father loved to read aloud stories from the *Post* to my mother, but that was late at night and after the kids were in bed. If you started him talking about his playing Laertes in Newark Central High's production of *Hamlet*, you would have thought he lived and died by Shakespeare, whereas I doubt he ever read another word of Shakespeare. On the other hand, he was curious. Later on, if I left any book lying around, say, an abridged version of Boswell's *Life of Johnson*, he would pick it up, read it, and remark, "Not bad." But he would not go out of his way to introduce books into the house. They were not his department, nor, for that matter, my mother's.

At Caldwell I was getting old enough to assist my father in his electrical work by "holding the light" for him, a task that was fun at first, but grew with the years to be a terrible bore. But there in Caldwell, watching him work was thrilling, especially as that work brought about an actual television set. By a nice irony we, who could not afford many new-fangled improvements like a refrigerator and were still tied to a messy, inefficient icebox, had something nobody else had. One night my father brought home a chassis and a mass of tubes and wires that he jokingly called his "homework." I stood by for hours one Saturday morning while he worked on this primitive television set. There was but one broadcasting band operating, shared by RCA in the good hours and by DuMont in the wee hours. My father ran an aerial up the side of the house onto the roof, and then patiently fiddled with the insides of the set and the long skinny tube with a picture area about the size of a postcard. Finally the lines on the screen turned into a picture. To this day I can see it vividly, a scene from a comic movie showing two men chasing each other around the outside of a house. On another occasion, in the evening, he and I were watching television when the set "went on the blink." In our house electrical apparatuses never had cases on them, but were always open showing all the electrical innards. He reached down into the works and received a shock that knocked him backwards off his feet. He got up and cheerily told me he "shouldn't have tried to fix the damn thing in the dark." Television astounded people who came to our house. Returning home one afternoon when my mother and sisters were not around, I met outside our house a young man, a complete stranger, who said hello, and I asked him if he wanted to see television. Of course he did, and I showed him, but I was glad to get him out of the house before my mother returned.

But the Caldwell years were coming to a crashing close. Late on Sunday afternoon, December 7, 1941, Audrey and I were called into our parents' bedroom where they were listening to the radio. The country was at war. The television set disappeared back into DuMont's, and the company converted full tilt to war production—Signal Corps equipment and radar. The day after Pearl Harbor my father went to enlist in the New Jersey National Guard. He was first given the rank of captain, but it turned out his credentials qualified him only as a master sergeant. He took the disappointment like a good soldier. Two weeks later, coming home from the National Guard late at night, he was driving fast, as was usual with him, and the car skidded on ice and rolled over several times. His left shoulder was "pulverized," and a transformer he had in the back seat rattled around inside the car giving him a severe concussion. A policeman got him out of the wreck and was taking him to the hospital, but Norman insisted on stopping first to show his wife that he was alive. Audrey heard a commotion below, and, sneaking halfway down the stairs, saw the cop in the living room talking with her

parents before Norman was whisked off to the hospital. For
a time his condition was critical. On Christmas day Lucille
dressed tall, eleven-year-old Audrey in high heels, a long dress,
a hat, and lipstick, so she could be smuggled into the hospital as
an adult to see her daddy. My mother feared he might die and
ought to see his daughter. But he recovered. He underwent a
shoulder operation performed by a specialist "who knew what
he was doing." For months my father had to sleep in an upright
position. The shoulder was "never any good again," and a great
scar remained with him always, but he got better, returned to
work at DuMont's, and in due course resumed training recruits
two nights a week for the National Guard.

Six months later we were in a house of our own, in the country, far from Bloomfield Avenue and its trolleys. My parents
considered the move part of his recuperation.

3

AT PLAY

TOLSTOY'S dictum about happy families resembling each other says nothing about unusually happy families. I think that for a time my life was unusually happy. In 1942 we moved to a place called Packanack Lake. We had been out on a house-hunting Sunday drive, saw signs posted for new homes, and followed them to Hillcrest Drive, a dirt road with nasty holes and bumps, and slowly drove down it. A big, heavy-set man came running out of the model home, jumped on the running board, and insisted we come in and look at the house. This man was Bob Alexander, "Mr. A," the developer and, as my father later said, "the best damned salesman I ever met." My parents bought 39 Hillcrest Drive for $5,900 on a twenty-five-year mortgage. This price included a discount for the house having been the model in the development. I don't know how they managed the down payment of $900, even with selling Christmas bonus stock from DuMont and borrowing money from the ever-helpful Uncle Eddie and Aunt Elsie, who, God knows, were not "made of money" themselves.

The house bordered on a thick woods, a regular forest to us. The lake itself was a body of water one mile long, half a mile across, and the beach was but four streets down from Hillcrest Drive. Next to the beach clustered the only non-residential buildings: a clubhouse, used for dances and meetings, and three small commercial establishments, Knops' bar/restaurant, Wendt's ice cream parlor, and a tiny version of a supermarket, a Stop and Shop, which my father, addicted as he was to word play, always called the Stop and Slop. A short walk from our house was a ball field, converted farmland, crude by today's standards, but just fine back then. Packanack Lake was country. It had no sidewalks or street lamps. The neighborhood was utterly safe. The police were Wayne Township cops, their headquarters so distant that we kids didn't even know where it was. The high school and the nearest movie theater were located ten miles away in Pompton Lakes—the town where Joe Louis trained. The closest city was Paterson, the place that would take over from Newark as "our" city.

We later learned that the road we lived on, Hillcrest Drive, was looked down upon by some of the old-timers at the lake because it was a "development," with houses too similar to each other and too close together. It was even referred to as Tobacco Road (after Erskine Caldwell's novel of that name about impoverished white sharecroppers in Georgia). My father "didn't give a damn what anyone thought." And that was a clear-cut difference between my parents. My mother cared very much what other people thought. But nothing could diminish their mutual fondness for that little house. It would be their home until my mother's death forty years later.

My mother had one great misgiving about moving to Packanack Lake. The nearest Catholic church was in the neighboring town of Mountain View (a strange name for so dreary a little place, one red light on Route 23, a handful of stores, a barber shop, and an elementary school). This church, Holy Cross, had no resident priest, evidence of its missionary status. And that meant no Catholic school. Indeed Packanack Lake, a private community of some two hundred homes, though not at all well-to-do, was almost entirely WASP. There were no Jews and only the tiniest sprinkling of Catholics. I know I can absolve my parents of deliberately buying in a restricted neighborhood. They just fell in love with the house and the lake, and Bob Alexander made them an unrefusable offer. My mother's hopes about Catholic schooling had to give way.

At Packanack Lake I started to catch up with other kids of my age. It was here, for instance, that I learned to ride a bicycle. But as usual my father had his own ideas, and I had to have an English "racing" bike, with thin tires, hand breaks, and no fenders—"just extra unneeded weight." The other kids looked on my bike as freakish. They had bikes with fat tires and coaster brakes, which my father induced me to scorn. Thirty or forty years later American tastes in bicycles would come around to his, but in 1942 his notions were strange. He also showed me—as if to prove he was right—a bike store on Main Street in Paterson, which displayed in the front window a bike frame rather like mine, along with a placard saying "This little bicycle won the World Championship Six-day Bike Race six times." The store owner, whose name I forget, was a Frenchman. My father always made me feel somehow different, somehow special. Even when it came to toys, mine had to be distinctive. Instead of an American-made Erector Set for building model cars and mechanical devices, he got me an English Mecano Set. "No comparison," he insisted.

The most important progress I made that first summer in the country was learning to swim. My parents, in spite of my mother's tendency to overprotect her children, allowed me to spend the entire day at the beach on my own, with fifteen cents lunch money for a hamburger and a soda. They did not know that I got my lunch sitting at the bar in Knops' restaurant. The price was the same as in the ice cream parlor, but at the bar you could have, with your hamburger, a bottle of Royal Crown Cola, twelve ounces, while the other place served only Coke, six and a half ounces. The bartender came to know me and would say, "I know, a hamburger and a Royal Crown." That summer I had a great incentive to learn to swim. A note pinned to the beach bulletin board announced for sale a small sail boat, a ten-foot metal tub on wooden ribs, its single sail gaff-rigged, its overall condition so bad that it was about to be junked. Twenty dollars. My father told me that if I could swim across the lake he would buy it for me. This was part of my parents' campaign to "build up" their still spookily thin child. I learned to swim from the lifeguard, a man in his thirties called Scotty and "world famous at Packanack." Under his patient coaching, I practiced

continually. Then, one gray morning, late in the summer season and before the beach opened, I swam, with Scotty rowing
alongside, across the lake. Doing so certainly made me feel good
about myself. My father bought the boat, and over the winter
he parked it in our garage and completely rebuilt it—the deck,
mast, rudder, rigging, centerboard, this last with help from
machinists at the "plant," as we always called DuMont's. For the
next three years, having learned to sail from an older boy, I was
the youngest kid at the lake with a sailboat of his own, even if we
lived on Tobacco Road.

As for my sailing alone at such a young age, my father used to
tell people, "I figure if he falls out of the damn thing, he can make
it to the shore from any point in the lake." By recording so many
of his damns and hells—he never used stronger language—I am
perhaps giving a false impression of his talk with us children.
His manner with us, even after we became adults, was always
to be joking, coining words and puns, using baby talk, making
deliberate and silly mistakes in grammar. He simply would not
talk straight: "Is you is or is you ain't coming with us?" A sick
neighbor had to go to the "Horse Pistol." The authorities were
building a road to be called the "Garden Snake Parkway." If he
came home from work and found one of us sick in bed with anything from a fever to a broken leg, his first words were always,
"What did you go and do that for?" He talked about the "World
Serious" and Philadelphia as "the City of Brotherly Shove." We
heard hundreds of times his favorite expressions: "What the
Sam Hill," "I'll be a monkey's uncle," and "Not by any stretch of
the imagination." He had his own version of my mother's German language: *Danke schön* transmuted, in the manner of Cock-
ney slang, to "Shame on the Donkey" and thence to "Donkey's
Embarrassment." A German was a "Heinegeplatzis."

In September 1942 I began fourth grade in the public school
at Mountain View. My mother shuddered at the prospect.
Would her son become a little pagan? As for actual schoolwork,
I did satisfactory but not outstanding work. My teacher, Miss

Rhodda, told my mother not to worry, that the switch from Catholic school to public school was coming along nicely, that I was ahead in some subjects, behind in others. Lucille would have nothing of this. Everybody knew, she told the teacher, that Catholic schools were ahead of public schools. My real problem was social. Coming in as a shy outsider, I had plenty of misgivings and had not so much to catch up as to catch on. One way into any group of young boys is sports, but, except for swimming, which could do me no good at school, I was terrible at sports. We had to play softball at recess, and I didn't even know the basic rules of the game, much less how to play it.

My worst day at school, or for that matter in my young life, was the time in the fifth grade when we little wretches were all picking on a fourth grader, Otto Kellerman, because he was German. The taunting took place in the school yard before school opened. Others were doing it, and I joined in, having a friend hold my books while I got in a few shoves on poor Otto. With me, Otto became enraged and struck out wildly and furiously. I froze, unable to respond, and he beat the daylights out of me and gave me a very black eye. Next thing I knew, the school nurse was patching me up, and I heard her say to someone that I deserved it, we all did, or words to that effect. Silently, I agreed. I felt overwhelmed with shame. I had been bullying a younger kid, and for a bad reason, and had proved unwilling or unable to fight back, a coward. "Why didn't you hit him?" a pal asked. "I don't know" was all I could say.

My mother that afternoon was having lunch with a Mrs. Trottier, and her son came home with the story of the big playground fight, how all the kids had stood around in a circle while Otto and I fought. But either because young Trottier was shielding me, or because my mother got it wrong, at the dinner table that night she told my father that she had heard all about it and that although I did get a black eye I had held my own admirably. This satisfied my father fine. I said nothing one way or the other. It was bad enough as it was. For the next two or three days I wandered about after school, wondering if I should seek out

Otto and fight him, but worrying that I might freeze up again and again get killed. But our paths did not cross, even though he lived near me. A year later he invited me to his house to look at some chemical experiment he was working on in the cellar, and we became friendly. Neither mentioned the fight. There, I have told it. Trollope in his *Autobiography* asks who, in recounting the events of his own life, could "endure to own the doing of a mean thing?" I, for one, have done so.

After grades four and five at Mountain View, students were shifted to Wayne Township Junior High School, on Valley Road in Preakness. Junior High proper included grades seven through nine, but the sixth grade was also lodged in this splendid facility, with its sunny classrooms, big auditorium, gymnasium, locker rooms, elaborate woodworking shop, and large expanses of playing fields. It was in the sixth grade that I realized that I was a smart kid, that I was good at schoolwork. (I was told there was another smart person, a girl, Frances Grudelbach, in one of the other three sixth-grade homerooms.) My teacher was a very elderly woman, or so she appeared to us. Miss Ruth B. Winters was well into her sixties. I have a few of her report cards before me now. Miss Winters did not hand out high grades readily, and I shudder to think what the weaker students took home. One of her archaic-sounding comments said, "John is a good Scholar." Yet in an "Autobiography" we had to produce for her, mine titled "Twelve Years of Good Luck," she wrote "Please be more careful of your writing." I was her star pupil, and here were words omitted, numerous misspellings, capital letters wrong, punctuation askew, childish phrasing. I know too much can't be expected of an ordinary sixth grader, but frankly I am surprised at how poor my writing was.

Next came actual junior high school, where, as in a high school, we changed rooms and teachers each period. By the ninth grade, my place as the "brain" among the boys, like that of Frances Grudelbach among the girls, was taken by everybody as a matter of course. Being smart and reasonably well behaved helped me get on with my teachers. But I suffered a setback in ninth grade Latin class with a teacher I admired and liked, Frank P. Warren. "Frank," as we affectionately called him, had one hand cut off at the wrist. No, not a war wound, he honestly told us, it happened when he was a boy, shooting rats in a dump with his brother, down in Texas. Frank directed the yearbook and fraternized in a good-natured way with the students who worked for him. He had a desk in a supply room, which served as his "office" and headquarters for the yearbook staff. But his chief task was teaching beginning Latin. The textbook he assigned us, *Latin Book One* by Harry Scott and Annabel Horn, published by Scott, Foresman and Company—Scott Foreskin to the irreverent—was widely used throughout the country. The first lesson got us off to an easy start:

Eurōpa nōn est parva. Europe is not small.

Frank Warren, however, was a rigorous teacher. He insisted, for example, that our written use of a Latin word was incorrect if it lacked any necessary long mark, such as was required in the o in *Eurōpa* or in *nōn*. I worked hard at Latin, and it was in Latin class, I believe, that we students learned English grammar. My trouble followed upon some improper assistance from my sister Audrey. Three years my senior, she had used the same textbook at Mount St. Dominic's Academy in Caldwell, but in her school the nuns didn't use the weekly tests included in the book. Instead, her Latin teachers distributed to their students the answer books to these quizzes for self-testing. Audrey gave me the answer booklet. Frank administered the tests to us with perfect regularity, and one Friday, sitting in the back of class, I had this helpful little key out on my desk during the test. Suddenly Frank swept down the aisle towards me. Too late, I attempted to hide the booklet. He picked it up, angrily ordered the class to discontinue the test, and commanded me to see him after school. This was a serious offense. I came to him at his "office" and blurted out that I was sorry. "Where did you get this?" he demanded. When I told him, he partly shifted the blame to "the nuns," who, although it was within their prerogative not to use the weekly tests, ought never to have supplied their students with the answer books. His analysis seemed to remove the cloud from around me. "We'll forget it now," he said. "You don't need that kind of help, you know." To say I was grateful is to understate the case.

At Wayne I moved at the edges of the "in-crowd" among the students. I worked on the yearbook and I became editor of a mimeographed monthly school paper. Not popular enough to run for student government, I helped write the speeches for those who did. I even made the school basketball team, my progress in sports having come that far, and in our first game I came in briefly as a substitute and made a team-high five points in a losing effort against the alumni. After that I just sat on the bench and never scored another point all season.

Meanwhile a new hobby was pushing everything else aside. In the sixth grade I had tried to learn the clarinet for the school band but, not being any good on the instrument, soon gave it up. Then, in the eighth grade, music came front and center in my life. There was no movie house in all of the vast area that comprised Wayne Township, and the school authorities, as if to compensate for this cultural shortcoming, occasionally showed "improving" movies on Friday afternoons. I saw *The Fabulous Dorseys*, starring the brothers Dorsey themselves, and came away from the movie believing I should form a little dance band. The saxophone, I knew, was similar to and in some ways easier than the clarinet. With a confidence that is hard for me to fathom now, but with a single-mindedness typical of my father, I went to work. I asked him to get me an alto saxophone, Jimmy Dorsey's instrument. I recruited another and very able saxophonist from the class ahead of me, Charlie Miller, and also Michael Miller (no relation), a talented classical pianist, and got my best friend, Bucky Frank, to talk his father into buying him a set of drums. My father dug deep into his pockets and bought me a good used saxophone. The purchase was arranged by the man I talked into being our mentor, teacher, and arranger, a wonderful person named Gordon "Pete" Padelford, a superb saxophon-

ist who performed frequently at Club House entertainments. I
went to Paterson and bought a teach-yourself-the-saxophone
book by none other than Jimmy Dorsey. Alone, I practiced for
hours at a time in our cellar. The band itself practiced in Pete's
basement—how his wife tolerated the noise is beyond me. We
bought professional dance-band music stands, called ourselves
the Star Dusters, and began playing for dances run by the Boy
Scouts at the lake. Our numbers expanded to three saxophones,
two trumpets and, at his own suggestion, replaced Mike Miller
with a boy two years ahead of me in school, a fellow named Jeff
Jeffries, who looked like a white Jelly Roll Morton. We tried to
sound like Glen Miller, whose band arrangements I was able
to buy in Paterson. Over the next few years we rehearsed dili-
gently and had our best gigs at high school dances, at Wayne,
Pompton Lakes, and Montclair.

After three years the band broke up. But back in the eighth
and ninth grades, I had a sense that I could, within reason, do
anything I set my mind to. Many modern psychologists, I am
told, don't accept as valid the concept of "overachiever," but I
think I was an overachiever. I had not enough musical talent
to have founded and played in that dance band. I didn't have a
good ear, couldn't play by ear, had no great sense of time—trip-
lets, for example, gave me no end of difficulty—but I went
ahead, and I suppose you could say, overachieved.

During these years two other phenomena, sex and religion,
came to play an important role in my mental life. That the first
of these should do so was natural and in no way singular with
me. Sex, which each generation seems to think it has invented,
preoccupies the minds of most young persons. It did so with me,
though in this as in much else I was a late bloomer. My naïveté
with regard to sex far exceeded that of my friends. In the fifth
grade I overheard my schoolmates talking about "jerking off." I
had no idea what they were talking about, nor did I ask, though
I knew it had something to do with sex. Some of us got a thrill
from looking up bad words in the dictionary and once found

what we were looking for only when some more knowing fellow told us it was spelled "teat." One of my classmates shocked
me during lunch with his little joke that TNT stood for "two
nifty tits," and another told me something so disgusting about
the stew provided in the cafeteria that I have not the stomach to
put it down here. I remember debating with myself while riding
my bike and delivering the *Newark Evening News*—I had become
a paperboy—whether the magical appeal of a woman's breasts
beneath a blouse or sweater would have the same attraction if
the breasts were fake. Was it the appearance or the actual items
that constituted the allure? A silly question, perhaps, but I will
say in my defense that to have posed it showed mild promise.
Then the same newspaper route provided a small but memorable incident, this time only slightly less theoretical. While
"collecting"—once a week, paperboys were expected to collect
thirty cents for the six days' delivery—I rang the bell at the
house of a woman who lived alone on Chestnut Drive. A well
built, zaftig woman of about thirty, she came to the door in bra
and half slip, and, hardly bothering to cover up, handed me the
thirty cents around the screen door. She plainly thought of little
boys as sexual nonentities and too young to notice anything.
She had no idea the delight, excitement, and wonderment she
aroused in me. I could, sixty years later, point out in a moment's
time the front door of that house on the next street over from
where I lived on Hillcrest Drive.

As a boy of eleven or twelve I had no knowledge of the facts
of life, unhelpfully referred to in those days as the "birds and the
bees." (I still cannot keep the sex life of bees straight.) I was unaware even that there was much to learn, so naive, so innocent
was I in those early 1940s. I knew I loved to look at sheet-music
covers with their mildly daring photographs of Alice Faye, Dor-
othy Lamour, and, most striking by far, Betty Grable. Saucily
posing in shots taken from movies like *Sweet Rosie O' Grady* and
Coney Island, Grable was glamorous, lovely, dangerous. I didn't
know why, but I knew I loved to look at her.

The ogling of sheet music went on in private. Actual talk of anything connected to sex was taboo in our house. My mother was altogether inhibited in these matters. Even talk of "going to the bathroom" was kept as limited as possible. (Years later she once told me over the phone that my younger sister, Sally, then thirty years of age and having some medical tests done, "had to bring something in a bottle" to the hospital lab. I was thirty-seven.) Only once did my mother explain any of the mysteries to me. I was living in a house with her and my two sisters, the elder sister being now a teenager, and she felt obliged to tell me about menstruation. She did well, I think, considering how difficult it must have been for her. She even managed to soften the blow, so to speak, by stressing that it was natural, that all women and female animals had monthly periods of blood flow, even, as God is my witness, the squirrels outside the kitchen window where we sat during this painful instruction. To this day I am not sure about squirrels, but at the time I thought it was a nice touch.

I don't know where my parents thought I would learn the basic information about sex. I can picture my father saying that he sure as hell wasn't going to tell me. Of course little boys tell other little boys things, but often get the facts wrong. Certainly the jokes, which were the vehicle for much juvenile learning about sex, could confuse matters further. One story I heard indicated that a man had to masturbate immediately before having sex with a woman. The man in the joke is a mailman or a milkman who thought that a scantily dressed woman of a particular house had been coming on to him, but on arriving there all "prepared" is greeted instead by her husband—but you know the story.

I was in the main a good Catholic boy and never did what some of my pals did. My friend Louie Larsen comes to mind. He was one of two sons of nonpracticing Catholic parents, who drank more than they should have and had money one day and were broke the next. For a while Louis senior went into the construction business, and Louie told me how his father cut corners wherever he could—for example, by forbidding his carpenters to use more than one nail when installing the risers for walls. I used to look at houses he had built and wonder if a strong wind might knock them over. But the Larsens had from time to time enough money to hire a live-in maid from a nearby institution for "delinquent" girls. Louie told a gang of us how in the middle of the night a maid had allowed him and his little brother to fondle her breasts and even put their fingers into her. He shocked our crowd, especially me. Later he and two other boys told a group of us how they had gone into the woods and jerked off in a competition to see who could finish first. I was never invited to such contests and would have refused to join in. And I suppose this is the place to confess that I never masturbated. I write it almost with shame, knowing how normal masturbation is, though back then it was condemned as not only sinful but dangerous to one's physical and mental health. The prohibition was by no means a strictly Catholic one. My official *Boy Scout Handbook* (1944) says a Scout must strive for "conservation" of the "seminal or sexual fluid," the fluid that deepens a boy's voice, broadens his chest, and "changes and enlarges his ideals." The *Handbook* concedes that some of this fluid is naturally released in nocturnal emissions, with or without dreams, and explains that such "experiences are natural." However, "No steps should be taken to excite seminal emissions. That is masturbation. It's a bad habit. Keep control in sex matters. It's manly to do so. It's important for one's life, happiness, efficiency, and the whole human race as well." So there you are. But handbooks, ministers, parents, and educators notwithstanding, the incidence of masturbation among teenage boys and young men—and mature men too, for that matter—approached, by one reliable estimate, ninety percent even in those buttoned-down times.

For my young self, girls represented a kind of human being quite different from boys, and this difference somehow or other constituted "sex." Like most boys I had from my earliest years crushes from afar on safely distanced girls or young women whom I would daydream about in an altogether unerotic fashion. Indeed, I would not have known how to daydream about them erotically. In Caldwell, in the first grade, the object of my worship was the girl across the street, Jean Shellhorne, three years older than I, a classmate and best friend of my sister Audrey's. In the fourth grade I was sweet on, again with a more-than-platonic abstractness, a little girl named Vivian Coon, who—the other way round from Jean Shellhorne—was three years behind me in school. I don't think I ever as much as said hello to her.

Next there came an older girl of about fifteen called Polly—her last name is gone—who helped me out when I was nine or ten. I had gone fishing with a drop line and bread crumbs to catch sunfish off the back-porch dock of the Club House, and a gang of teenage boys were mocking me, insisting that I didn't know what I was doing and that I was fishing out of season. They were ruining my first day of fishing. But this very attractive young lady, whom they all evidently admired, took my part, shooed them away, encouraged me, and even walked home with me and my sunnies that day.

In seventh grade a pretty redhead, a year older than I, Irene Donovan, who lived four houses from us, agreed to go to a Boy Scout party with me. These parties were excuses for kissing games. For two hours we played post office and spin the bottle and musical chairs, kissing all the time. I knew nothing of open-mouthed "French" kissing. Maybe my fellows did, though I doubt it. We thought of and talked about girls all the time, but we did very little. The kissing games were initiation rites that the scoutmasters and our parents—though not my mother, who knew nothing of what was going on—thought would help us grow up, I suppose. By this time, like all my pals, I went on Friday nights to dances held in the school gym for students of the seventh through ninth grades. The boys stood on one side, the girls on the other, while girls and some older couples danced. I had never danced a step in my life. I still can't dance, though there are few things I would rather be able to do. At my very first dance, just before the 11 o'clock closing and the playing of "Good Night Sweetheart," tradition called for a "Sadie Hawkins" dance, the name deriving, as my generation will know, from the Li'l Abner comic strip, where the beautiful Daisy Mae always has her cap set for Li'l Abner. Well, who comes over to where the younger boys are standing and takes me by the hand and asks for a dance but Judy Prickert, a year ahead of me in school, one of the most attractive and popular girls in the whole place. "But I don't know how," I protest. "I'll show you," she says. And she did her best. I assume she was trying to make older boys jealous or perhaps was keeping two rivals on a level. But here nonetheless was another act of kindness. Are girls, I wondered, much more decent and generous than boys?

Then, in the eighth grade, I "fell in love" with a girl who actually cared for me. This was none other than that other "smart" person, Frances Grudelbach. We danced a few times and may have kissed once or twice during some party game. That was pretty much it. I remember the boys talking about who might marry whom in years to come and deciding that Frances and I should get married because "You could cook scrambled eggs by algebra." We deserved each other. Our best moments came when the two of us were given time off from class for the painting of program covers for the presentation, by the ninth graders, of Gilbert and Sullivan's *Mikado,* an assignment that entailed our working together backstage. With Frances I watched so many rehearsals of that glorious operetta that its words and melodies remain etched in my brain. I know more lines by heart, I am ashamed to say, of Gilbert's *Mikado* than of *As You Like It, King Lear,* and *Hamlet* combined:

> My object all sublime
> I shall achieve in time—
> To let the punishment fit the crime—
> The punishment fit the crime.
> And make each prisoner pent
> Unwillingly represent
> A source of innocent merriment,
> Of innocent merriment.

and

> Three little maids who, all unwary,
> Come from a ladies' seminary,
> Freed from its genius tutelary.

and

> Ah, pray make no mistake,
> We are not shy,
> We're very wide awake,
> The moon and I.

This last is sung by Yum-Yum. The very names of the characters struck me then and still strike me as magically droll: Nanki-Poo, Ko-Ko, Pooh-Bah. Frances and I, backstage and working away on our programs, delighted in being in each other's company. We never said we loved each other, or exchanged a word on paper, or visited each other's homes, or went on a date. And by the next year, our ninth and senior grade, we were merely friends although in those years it was difficult for boys and girls to be friends—you were either a couple or, at least as a boy, you regarded the opposite sex as almost a different species. But those hours backstage, and the handful of slow dances we had together, especially once or twice to that most romantic of recordings, Bing Crosby's *White Christmas*, remain vivid to me almost sixty years later.

There is a point to all this—namely, that during this period I lived a normal and happy childhood, in semirural Wayne Township. But gradually, during junior high school, religion started to affect my life in a serious way. Earlier the influence had been mild and benign. When we first moved to Packanack Lake, I was, because of my three years of Catholic schooling, miles ahead of other students in Sunday school class, held every week in the basement of Holy Cross Church in Mountain View. The Catholic kids in Wayne Township could have been heathens or Taoists for all they knew about Catholicism. They

seemed, moreover, impervious to any teaching the missionary nuns from Paterson tried to drum into them. At best they
learned to recite the words of the *Our Father, Hail Mary,* and
to rattle off most of the Ten Commandments. I didn't blame
these children in the least—they figured five days of school
was plenty. My own boredom was worse than theirs because
I already knew the words. I forgot more of the catechism than
I learned during those half dozen years of CCD, the Confraternity of Christian Doctrine. The very letters CCD still send
a shudder through me. Then, too, my mother saw to it that
during Holy Week I went to Good Friday services, where I was
the only person in the church aside from two or three pious old
women. Of course Good Friday came along only once a year, so
this was not too bad. I also became an altar boy, which involved
memorizing many lines of Latin, of which the very first was *Ad
Deum qui laetificat juventutem meum,* "To God who gives joy to
my youth." My mother further insisted that on every overnight
weekend Boy Scout camping trip I be taken to Mass. No excuse
except illness justified missing Sunday Mass, and the long-suf-
fering scoutmaster had to drive me, all alone, out of the woods
to the nearest Catholic church.

Still, religion early on presented me with no special pain or
problem. On the other hand, my temperament may have left me
exposed. One episode from seventh grade seems in retrospect to
have presaged what might be in store for me. Wayne Township
Junior High School stood in a truly rural place, bounded by cab-
bage farms on every side for miles. All the students were transported to school from the surrounding communities by school
bus. One afternoon as we stood on line to board our respective
buses, there was a long delay. Restless and fidgety, I picked up
a handful of gravel, small stones about a quarter inch round,
and tossed them one at a time up into the air, higher and higher,
trying always to catch them. This went on for some time. Then
a disturbance near me arose. A girl had been injured by a stone
that struck her in the eye. Interrogations and investigations as
to who had thrown the stone went on for days, and rumor had

it that the damage to her sight might prove permanent. The authorities did not question me, but I began to fear that one of my tossed stones just might have done the deed. Some had misfired beyond my grasp. A month later I was walking in Mountain View with Louie Larsen. Here's a case where I recall the exact words of a conversation from those many years ago:

"Do you remember the stone hitting Diane in the eye?" Louie asked.

"Of course I do."

"Do you know what?"

"No, what?"

He turned and looked me squarely in the face:

"I know who did it."

It was as if I had been stabbed. He had seen me do it. Thank God it was Louie Larsen, I said to myself, he will never tell:

"You do? Who threw the stone?"

"I did," he said.

I can still feel the relief as I write out his words.

But—to be melodramatic about it—in the months and years ahead, religious worry lurked near the playground of my life. And these worries would become intertwined with sex, hitherto that puzzling but unhurtful phenomenon. My "unusually happy" days were about to be intruded upon. The distressing side of religion arrived quietly enough in 1945 in the person of the Reverend Edward J. Scully, who became the first resident pastor of Holy Cross Church, his appointment transforming the place from a Franciscan mission into a diocesan parish. Tall, thin, and "swishy"—such was the word, I learned later, used in clerical circles to describe his type—Father Scully was a devoted, earnest man of God, but second-generation pious Irish Catholic to the core, that is, deeply conservative, puritanical, woman-fearing, and deep down, woman-hating. You might say he arrived at the same time as did my adolescence, and he moved right in on his target. No matter what you confessed, he wanted to know if you had had "impure thoughts," and he always asked young boys about masturbation, even when they

didn't know what he was talking about. He came to mold and
form my Catholicism, the morality of which revolved around
"holy purity." It was he, who, in the confessional, explained to
me the facts of life, so that I would know what it was I was not
supposed to think about. Impure thoughts, which consisted in
"taking pleasure" in any thinking about sex, were "mortal" or
grave sins, while kissing, as at those Boy Scout parties, constituted still more serious sins, all of which had to be confessed to
him, the only priest available.

Catholic teaching held that in matters sexual, there could
be no venial or small sin. Any deliberate sin of impurity, in
thought or deed, however fleeting, was a mortal sin. To die in
mortal sin meant going to hell, forever. To hide a mortal sin in
confession, to "make a bad confession," was itself an even worse
mortal sin, the whole business cascading into a morass of guilt
and worry. The school parties and dances began to bother me
terribly. Scully had me always on the rack: dancing was not
absolutely sinful, but did constitute an "occasion of sin," and to
place oneself in an occasion of serious sin was itself a mortal sin.
And kissing, except such as one might give one's mother, was
mortally sinful, no mitigating circumstances allowed. He even
held up the example of St. Aloysius, who would not look at his
mother for fear of sin.

One time some ninth-grade girls invited a group of us boys
over to the house of one of the girls whose parents were away
for the day. It was in Preakness, a very long walk, but of course
we went. There was a lot of kissing and necking. I am not sure
if any serious petting went on. Certainly not by me. It did become clear to me that the girls, apparently so proper, were in
fact just as interested in sex as were the boys, maybe even more
so. We boys were mostly all talk. I recall standing, embracing
a girl and sensing her breasts beneath her clothes pressing ever
so slightly against me through my shirt. I tried my best not to
enjoy even that little. Scully's God was spoiling the fun. Then
would come confession and promises to do better and avoid
"occasions of sin."

During a kissing game at a graduation party, Frances Grudel-bach got angry at me for not being more ardent. I felt bad, but I was at that moment in particular distress from a session with Scully, who had warned me against graduation parties. How could I tell her that I was confused, worrying about mortal sin and falling from the state of grace? Next time the chair came around, I kissed her enthusiastically, but with tightly closed mouth, still being ignorant of the mechanics of the thing. I hoped she took my kiss as an apology, but I was not sure. Many years later I wanted to tell Frances that it wasn't her I was avoiding, it was mortal sin. I heard from people that she had done very well in Pompton Lakes High School, where she was the only sophomore ever elected to some national honor society, but I was unable to locate her. Perhaps, with a name like Grudelbach she was happy to take her husband's name. My hope was to explain myself to her, to tell her how Scully's Catholicism had held me back. A silly mission it would have been, for how could she have cared? At another graduation party, given by a classmate who quite openly bore my secret first name, Norman, the arrangement, to the chagrin of the more hesitant boys, was to have no games at all; you were just to take a girl walking and "make out," as the phrase went. All night I agonized. In the end I asked neither Frances nor any other girl to go walking. I was in the throes of a particularly Scully-troubled time. Was he saving me for Jesus?

When the junior high prom came, I hesitated to ask Frances. Don't be a damned fool, my friends told me, of course you must ask her. So I did, and Bucky Frank, the drummer in my band, in a halfhearted way also asked a girl. His parents—not mine, who never got involved in such things—took the four of us out to dinner at a place opposite Frank Daly's famous Meadowbrook in Cedar Grove. Then we went on to the school gym for the dance itself. There Frances and I hardly saw each other, and later she came across the dance floor to tell me she would go home with some other parents, so that Bucky's parents would not have to drive all the way to Pines Lake, where she lived. I agreed

it was a good idea. This was to be my only prom. *Ad Deum qui laetificat juventutem meum.*

Frances Grudelbach and I were pictured together in our 1948 junior high yearbook as "Most Likely to Succeed," on the simpleminded premise that highest marks predicted most success. (I'm sporting the then fashionable bow-tie and boy's pompadour.) My parents were pleased about the yearbook, but disappointed when for graduation I was not chosen male valedictorian. Frances, naturally, was the female speaker. But my good friend Harry Dowell received the boy's assignment. Harry, who had decent grades but nothing like my straight A's, was chosen because his conduct reports were better. My lapses in conduct were never anything more serious than talking in class out of boredom. I had not unreasonably expected the honor, which most of my classmates, including Harry Dowell, presumed would be mine on the scholastic record. But, as my homeroom teacher, Myra Kamp, explained to me, the authorities had a policy that high grades in deportment formed a *sine qua non* for being named valedictorian. It's no big deal, I tried to tell myself.

4

FERVOR

M
Y MOTHER knew nothing of the sexual temptations to which her son was subjected, but, if she had, she would have tried to cut them off at the pass. From the time we moved to Packanack Lake, she made it clear that I could go to public school only until high school. Later she conceded I could stay through my ninth grade and graduate with my friends from junior high school, but thereafter it was to be Catholic school for her "sun, moon, and star." Her deep-rooted Catholicism demanded it. That I was to go to a Catholic high school had been dinned into me for so long and with such finality that when the time came I put up no resistance. She was not trying to make me particularly religious, she just wanted to keep me out of trouble and to obtain for me a Catholic education, which, she was convinced, would be a far superior education all around.

During my eighth grade I had had a narrow escape from another course of education that would have been catastrophic. My father, fanatic military man, would have loved to have sent me to LaSalle Military Academy, a Catholic boarding school on Long Island, run by the Christian Brothers. I think of James Joyce's father, with his admiration for Jesuit education and loathing for the Christian Brothers' school, where his son would meet Paddy Stink and Mickey Mud. For months the glossy brochure for LaSalle Academy lay about our living room at Hillcrest Drive. Two things saved me. First, this school was too expensive. Second, my mother objected that I was too young to be away from home. My father, who might have been able to overrule her, believed that military school would "make a man" of me. But it was financially impossible, and LaSalle dropped out of sight. However, ordinary, inexpensive Catholic high school did not. To my friends I kept quiet about the change right up until the last moment. When they heard, they were flabbergasted. You're not going to Pompton? Not going to the school we so admired, the home of our beloved football Cardinals, whose every home game we had seen for the past three years? Pompton Lakes High School was the aim of all us Wayne kids. Many signed my junior high yearbook "Good luck in Pompton" or "See you in Pompton." It was not to be.

Instead I was to go down to Montclair, to Immaculate Conception High School, a parish school accommodating students from half a dozen Essex County parishes, some six hundred students in all, smaller than Pompton Lakes High School, but larger than many parochial high schools. The commute to school was arduous. No bus ran past my home neighborhood, and I had to get a ride and be dropped off five miles away in Mountain View, whence I took the 114 Bus through Wayne, Singac, Little Falls, Cedar Grove, and on to Bloomfield Avenue at Verona and thence eastward into Montclair. Returning from school, I took the 114 to Mountain View and hitched a ride up Route 23 to the entrance of Packanack Lake, where a walk of a mile and a half brought me home. By my second year I hitchhiked home the entire distance from Montclair to Packanack. I was forever being asked, "Do you get a ride?" "Of course," I would cheerfully reply, "or else I wouldn't be here now." The real difficulty was not the travel, but changing schools, not an easy thing for a shy, tall, gangling boy from the sticks. Additionally, I was not starting out with other newly arrived freshman. I was coming in as a sophomore, when friendships and the inexorable social order among high school students were already established.

Looking back, I wonder how, even with years of warning, I made the switch, not easily, but without much pain. There were some saving factors, especially in that I would not be alone down there with the city kids. My cousin Richie Ehrenberg, youngest son of Uncle Eddie and Aunt Elsie, and an exact contemporary of mine, was in my year. His older brother, Bob, had just graduated—he was pictured in the yearbook as having the "Best Personality" in his class. Richie had not that surely, for there was a sullen streak in him, but he was a football star, strong as a horse, a lineman who every year was named to the New Jersey Catholic All Star Team. So I had the Ehrenberg connection, and although I was not placed in the same homeroom with Richie, he was there at the school for me. That first year I would often stay over weekends in my aunt and uncle's house at 96 Ella Street, Bloomfield, in what amounted to a revisiting of my earliest roots.

A break came my way when I got to know two boys in my class well, Jim Crowther and Jimmy Appice. Crowther came from money, was enormously tall, suffered under the nickname "Goon," and goofed around a lot. He had plenty of brains, but didn't use them. He later went to St. Peter's College, had a seat on the New York Stock Exchange, lived in a posh area of Montclair, and had seven children. Appice, who came from a poor Italian background, was the smoothest basketball player of his age I had ever seen, the only freshman on the previous year's grandly successful team. He was always in academic trouble, but he had an ingratiating way with the nuns, and everyone else. Tragically, three years later, just after graduating, Appice would be stricken with a paralyzing disease that left him in a wheelchair for the rest of his none-too-long life. But in 1948 Appice and Crowther, two of the most popular of my classmates, befriended me. By the end of that sophomore year I was able to repay Crowther somewhat. He took the Latin college prep course and struggled with it, not putting in any time on the subject. When the day came for the exam that June, he seemed bound to fail. As for my helping him with the test, it was too late for preparation of any kind. We would have to resort to outright cheating. The problem was that a single Latin exam—a translation of a page-long passage—was administered simultaneously in the various homerooms, and Crowther was in a different room from mine.

But with the aid of a fellow named Jerry Walsh—himself not in the college prep curriculum—we managed it. Walshy, as he was called, did various housekeeping tasks for the nuns in all four sophomore homerooms, and one such job was going down the aisles collecting paper trash. Into his wastebasket I deposited a translation, which he rolled up inside an empty fountain pen. He then visited the other homeroom, went down the aisle collecting paper, where, according to plan, Crowther called out "Anyone got an extra pen?" and Walshy obliged. I wonder that it worked so well. I wonder, too, that I did it. By the next year such cheating would have been against my conscience.

I was a bit of an oddity at Immaculate, coming from the country, commuting all the way from another county, another diocese, and living at a lake. I worked hard at being a normal, regular student, made some friends, attended not only football and basketball games, but dances, both at Immaculate and at Our Lady of the Valley parish in nearby West Orange. I caught on quickly to the unofficial dress code for winter wear as inspired by the school's heavy Italian influence, decent but tough-looking boys, who always seemed older than their contemporaries; and I had my parents buy for me that first winter the fashionable long gray overcoat, of which the collar *had* to be worn turned up. Still, my struggle to fit in advanced slowly. At my Wayne school I had been near the center of things, but at Montclair, I was—despite Crowther and Appice—nowhere near the inner circle. Moreover, I discovered that, in a way difficult to put into words now, everything I did was just slightly askew. Protocols of all kinds were different. How one spoke to the nuns or to girls. Trying to dance, I held my left arm incorrectly, and one popular girl, Barbara Brown, gently changed the way I was attempting to hold her, or at least to hold her arm. When I played pickup basketball, my every move seemed out of kilter, and I could not play up to my Wayne level, low as that was. My companions must have thought this was the first time I played basketball. Small examples, these, but going to Montclair meant encountering a very different world. The whole place, not merely the high school, seemed more citified, sophisticated, and worldly than anything I knew in Wayne Township. But not more intellectual. Immaculate was a working-class school, and grades were not a compelling force in student life. I recall having sundaes at Grunnings, a big ice cream parlor on Bloomfield Avenue, along with Richie Ehrenberg and his older brother Bob and two friends of Bob's. At one point I used the phrase—how could I have slipped?—"I dare say" and set the table on a roar. It was as if I had lapsed into attic Greek. The older fellows kept repeating "I *dare* say" until Bob, himself a large football player, told them to lay off his cousin.

In time, however, I came to accommodate myself to Montclair. I even became sweet on a girl who also lived a good distance from the school, though only half as far away as I, in a town called Little Falls. She and I occasionally took the 114 Bus together. Her name was Diane Banks. Popular, pretty, and a tease, she turned down my overture to go out. With Diane Banks I was aiming too high in that firm and awful pecking order that obtains in all schools of adolescent boys and girls. But she was friendly, and years later, at our class's tenth anniversary reunion, she kiddingly said in front of a group of us that if I behaved that night she would let me carry her books on the bus. It was a good line, and I laughed with more feeling than the others who did not know the history, slight though it was, of her remark. Forty years later I met her again, at our fiftieth class reunion. Some of the girls, now women in their late sixties, looked very fresh and well preserved. Diane Banks did not. I tried to remind her of her little joke, but she didn't seem to comprehend what I was talking about.

By my junior year, had I remained normal, I'm pretty sure I would have been, not exactly popular with the girls but not unpopular either. I even knew the girl I would have been keen on, Lou-Anne Smith, who, like myself, came to the school in the sophomore year and was considered a "brain." Soft-spoken, kind, and pretty, she sometimes served with me on committees.

Of course she might not in any way have reciprocated my interest. At the same fiftieth reunion, I meant to tell her jokingly about my feelings back then, but she left early and will never know of my secret, distanced fondness for her. With her I had suffered an embarrassing high school moment. During our senior year, when I worked on the yearbook staff, Lou-Anne was editor, and she did most of the work, including counting the votes for the "outstanding" designations. Lou-Anne called me aside and asked me confidentially, "Which would you rather be named—if you could have only one—'Did Most for Immaculate' or 'Most Likely to Succeed'"? Whereupon I, not realizing she was speaking hypothetically, told her I had not done much for the school. No sooner were the words out of my mouth than I realized my mistake, and she just as suddenly understood that I, as runner-up in the Most Likely category, was the last person she should have sought advice from on the matter. We both blushed and rushed on to some other subject. As things turned out, she gave Pete Groeschel Did Most for Immaculate and me Most Likely to Succeed, though I realized he had won the vote in both categories. Mine was a somewhat diminished honor, but I trusted she wouldn't tell anyone.

In grades I did well. For the first marking period I received all A's except in physical education and religion. In the former, I got a B as did everyone except the varsity athletes, who were excused. We had to have, by a state rule, one hour of gym a week. Our "instructor" was a bald-headed Italian-American, a decent fellow who did no more than keep reasonable order and get the boys back to the nuns without serious injury. He simply sent us out into the playground in good weather and into the gym in bad weather and let us play pickup games or just sit around talking. No gym clothes or sneakers were required. You took off your jacket and tie, obligatory at all other times, and did what you pleased. My C grade in religion was no worse than I deserved, because the grade at this point was predicated upon class participation, and I had not participated at all. I soon discovered that the nun who taught me religion that year, Sister Louise Mary, "LuMay," was criticized by the other nuns for not taking into account my almost unheard-of public school background. She as much as apologized to me and urged that I speak up. No more C's in religion. A year later she placed me and one other classmate on the staff of the newly formed newspaper, the only juniors so appointed. I recall her horror at a typo in the large black-letter headline for the first issue of the school's first student newspaper, CLARION MAKES IT'S DEBUT. I doubt any of the students caught or cared about the mistake. In class LuMay tried to interest her students in things cultural. She pressed on us the name Evelyn Waugh and his latest novel, *The Loved One*. Amid much laughter, fully half the class refused to believe Evelyn could be a man's name, and no one gave the slightest consideration to her suggestion that we read him, or anyone else. Hers was an uphill and losing struggle. For although the atmosphere at Immaculate was not anti-learning in a nasty way, it was decidedly indifferent to learning. What counted were sports and social life—"girls" as far as we boys were concerned. In this it was not unlike most other high schools, including Pompton Lakes, where I had longed to go.

We were taught French by an elderly nun, my homeroom moderator that sophomore year, who had difficulty keeping order, much less imparting anything of the language to us. We used to say, with some slight exaggeration, that over the whole year we never learned anything beyond the sentence *"J'entre dans la salle de classe"* and, for the more advanced students, one additional sentence, *"Dans la nuit tous les chats sont gris."* On one occasion this teacher demanded that the entire class stay after school. The boys agreed to defy her and walk out. We were immediately suspended until our parents appeared with us at the principal's office, where we were given stern instructions to stay in line or be expelled. But we had rightly surmised that there was safety in numbers. The principal, Sister Grace Benigna, could hardly expel half an entire class. This suspension did me good with the other boys, and I remember overhearing one of the popular students telling some others he was happy for me that I had been involved. I thought him rather patronizing, but in fact I silently relished getting into trouble along with my classmates.

In Latin, thanks to Frank Warren, I was ahead of everyone taking the course. The Latin teacher, Sister Josephine William, "Jo Bill," at first thought me insufferable. I was again on the wrong wavelength. One time, for instance, she had written a number of Latin words on the board and I raised my hand:

"Yes?"

"Sister, shouldn't there be a long mark over the second *a* in *tabernaculum*?"

She snapped her head back toward the board.

"Yes, there should be a long mark."

I had embarrassed her in front of the class. I was showing off. How could I help it if Frank had been such a fanatic about long marks? I hope that I went to Jo Bill after class and lamely explained this to her, but I was probably too shy. In any case, she forgave me, although once, before the forgiveness set in, she caught me acting bored in class and announced that I was the most *supercilious* boy she had ever taught. I had to look up the word. But by the end of the semester we were on excellent terms. In my senior year she escorted me and Barbara Brennan, the leading female "brain," on a train trip into New York, to NYU, for a national Latin competition, where I did no better than a weak honorable mention, along with what I assume were hundreds of others. In 1951 New York was a strange world to me, but I recall distinctly that the test was given in the Main Building of NYU on Washington Square Park in Greenwich Village.

My favorite nun was our math teacher and my junior year homeroom moderator, Sister Mercedita, a cheerful, upbeat, sympathetic person, not yet twenty five. She was a beautiful woman, with a tall, perfect carriage, and a lovely face that was there if you made the effort to see past the nearly impervious costume of the Sisters of Charity of Convent Station, New Jersey. This community of nuns wore, by consensus, the most obscuring and ugliest nuns' habit in the Catholic world. An accordion-like fluted white frame boxed in the face. Still, you could tell the pretty ones, and accordion boxes and yards and yards of black cloth could not entirely hide attractive bodies, and of course could in no way diminish laughing eyes, quick movements, sympathetic attention, womanly grace. I had to be on the *qui vive* lest I should develop a crush on Sister Mercedita.

Just the opposite in height was Sister Catherine Grace, who taught science and was called "The Mouse" for her short stature. At one difficult moment of my high school career, a group of boys locked themselves in the boys' room into which she could not continue chasing them. I happened to be passing by in the corridor and she commandeered me to stand with her outside the door. "Knock on that door," she said. "Tell them it's you." I had to do as ordered, whereupon one of the boys inside kept saying to me, "Is the Mouse out there? Is the Mouse out there?" I could have died. She let me leave.

Another nun, very ancient indeed, taught us junior year religion from an even more ancient textbook, which said in small print that in former times the sacrament of extreme unction involved anointing with holy oil all the senses, including the reins. A smart but lazy boy named Leo Bennis, "The Ben," raised his hand, and what followed remains in my mind the most embarrassing student-teacher exchange I ever witnessed: "Sister, what's reins?" Completely flustered, she kept saying that in times long past all the senses were anointed. And The Ben kept saying, "Yes, but what's reins?" He must have repeated the question six times. Finally, all blushes, she said, "Well, it's the middle leg, isn't it?" Actually, it's the kidneys, thought at one time to be the seat of the affections and feelings.

As I settled into this new environment, the religious atmosphere at Immaculate started to register with me. I was much impressed, for example, with tough football players going to optional Communion on First Fridays. I was touched by the humanity and devotion of the nuns and of the parish priests who taught senior religion classes and served as yearbook advisers and as athletic directors. I liked the prayerful church assemblies that closed with the ringing and martial Sodality Hymn:

> An army of youth
> Flying the standards of truth
>   . . . dare and do,
> 'Neath the Queen's white and blue
> For our Flag
> For our Faith
> For Christ the King
> (the last word on so high a note
> I could never reach it).

Most importantly, I liked the young man who sat near me in the alphabetical seating used in the school. This was Peter Groeschel, whom I nicknamed "Bird," or "Birdie," a name that pleased him because he cultivated the persona of a character or "bird." Pete made no secret of his desire to become a priest. He never addressed any of the girls by her first name. It was always, "Now, Miss Smith, don't you think . . ." The girls loved him for it. At school dances he would sometimes be the ticket taker, but the very notion of him dancing or dating seemed inconceivable. My earliest memories of Pete include one of his flying into a fit of anger, the only one I ever witnessed from him, because some boy had said that Pete had had an erection. It was just his ill-fitting trousers. Like many of us, myself included, he had only one (much used) suit for school, and I could see how the student got the idea. I also felt like interjecting—if that is the word—had I not been so reticent in such matters, that an erection of itself can be involuntary and hence no sin or fault. But Pete went at the fellow with a rage so ferocious it amazed me. He closed by saying that if he were to die at that moment he would be buried in the habit of the Dominican Order, by virtue of his being a member of the Third Order of St. Dominic, an association of laymen within the Dominicans. The bit about being a member of the Third Order was a fabrication that came to him in the heat of rhetoric.

Pete was openly religious, so to speak, but also funny, sarcastic, outspoken, and smart. After he and I became close friends, he, with much pain and shame, asked me if I could remain a friend of someone who had told him a colossal lie. I said of course I could. He then confessed that although he was thinking of joining the Dominicans, he was not in fact a member of the Third Order. Nothing could have troubled me less. He lost interest in the Dominicans when in his senior year he went to see the Dominican Fathers read the Holy Office in a New York City priory. The Fathers seemed bored, inattentive, and one of them swatted a fly. Pete, disgusted with the Dominicans, looked around for what he thought was the most strict, most rigorous of the active orders, and settled on the Capuchin Franciscans. After his ordination he served fourteen years as chaplain to disturbed, impoverished youngsters at Children's Village in Dobbs Ferry, New York. At that time he earned a doctorate in psychology from Columbia; he also developed an intense concern for the poor.

In time Pete left the Capuchins to form his own order of Franciscan Friars of the Renewal, whose primary mission is to work among homeless and AIDS-infected people in the South Bronx. While the rest of the Catholic Church is losing "vocations" to the priesthood, so much so as to reach crisis proportions in the U.S. and around the world, Pete—Benedict is his religious name—often has more men ordained to the priesthood in a given year than the huge Archdiocese of New York. Many regard him as the American equivalent of Mother Teresa, who was his good friend and inspiration. He has founded shelters for homeless persons, homes for unwed mothers, and hospitals for the poor in Central America. For many years he also ran the Trinity Retreat House for Priests of the Archdiocese of New York, and he is often spiritual adviser to the Cardinal Archbishop. Pete gives talks and retreats all over the world, taking in stipends to defer the costs of his order, where the big money problem is health insurance for his priests, seminarians, brothers, and religious sisters—he also founded an affiliated order of nuns. He has remained very traditional in his beliefs and has his enemies within the Church, largely because he appears regularly on the TV network of Mother Angelica, whom the Catholic intelligentsia regard with a combination of disgust and horror. I recently asked Pete to give me an instance of the doctrinal differences between him and, for example, Father Edward Ciuba, a later classmate of mine who became a liberal scripture scholar. "Well," says Pete, "I think Jesus actually multiplied the seven loaves and three fishes so as to feed thousands of people, whereas Ciuba thinks the men's wives all packed tuna fish sandwiches for them." To people familiar with him only from television Pete—Benedict—is a histrionic and facile Catholic evangelist; but to those who know his work among the poor he is about as close to a saint as anyone they will ever meet.

And thus the move to Montclair, once I adjusted to the procedures of the place and made new friends, worked out fine. Strange things were to come, but there had been no foreseeing that. A pious person would repeat here the formula that all things work unto good for those who love the Lord. I have not found that a person's loving or not loving the Lord has anything to do with whether things work out well. In my case I just happened to have been born of a religiously-minded mother who insisted that I attend Catholic high school.

MIDWAY THROUGH my first year at Immaculate came that critical retreat. For three days I sat through the visiting Jesuit priest's spell-binding talks based on the *Spiritual Exercises of St. Ignatius*. Would it be sin and eternal hell or a virtuous life and eternal heaven? The retreat experience overwhelmed me. I resolved to change my life. The first step was to make the stipulated general confession of all sins committed since childhood. And, by way of making my repentance more intense, I made up my mind to confess, not to the retreat master or any of the four parish priests at Immaculate, but to Father Scully. I would punish myself. I would go, hat in hand, to that strict, forbidding confessor whose constant emphasis on avoiding sexual sin had so troubled me.

I got off the bus one stop early in Mountain View, right in front of the rectory of Holy Cross Church. Scully was at home and welcomed me into the old-fashioned and shabby front room, with its big easy chairs and walls lined with books. I told him about the retreat, how I intended to become a good Catholic, how I wanted to make a general confession, to clear up any past omissions, to be sure that I was in the state of grace. He listened sympathetically, and had me kneel beside him as he put on the slim purple confessional stole and heard my confession. It was not as if I had anything stirring to confess: vaguely impure thoughts and desires, glancing at improper pictures of women, listening to lewd jokes, the kissing games of grade school, the slightest pressure of the girl's breasts against me that time in Preakness, the fear of "bad" confessions and "sacrilegious" Communions. Everything, such as it was, came pouring out. I was saying to him: I concede, I give in, I have wrestled with you and your teachings all these years, but I will struggle no longer. You win, God wins, it comes to the same thing. There in the semi-dark parlor, I made my peace with God and with him, his appointed representative. Scully pronounced the words of absolution. Afterward he was all friendliness and encouraged me to come to him at any time day or evening to talk or to go to confession. I felt inexpressibly happy, released from worry or fret. The experience freed my mind and spirit.

I did not all at once decide to try to become a priest. That decision would follow after a few months of frequent confession and, whenever possible, weekday Mass and Communion. By the end of my sophomore year I decided I had a vocation. Half a century later, one is hard put to convey the magnitude of just what this meant in the hermetic Catholic world of northern New Jersey in the 1950s. To aspire to the priesthood at this time represented ambition almost beyond words. To hope to become a lawyer or doctor or senator was nothing by comparison.

To be a priest was to be Christ's—God's—vicar on earth, to be his anointed, someone endowed with supernatural powers of absolving sins and converting bread and wine into the body and blood of Christ. Neither the angels nor the Blessed Virgin Mary herself—as was later pointed out continually—had such powers. One approached the priesthood humbly. It was never "I'm going to become a priest," but "I am trying to become a priest."

When I told my parents, they showed themselves pleased but cautious, wary of seeming too enthusiastic. They made it clear that this was entirely my own business and was to remain such. They knew it would be ten years till ordination, a long haul. Something might go wrong, or I might change my mind. Quietly, almost somberly, they were, I knew, proud. My father was glad because he believed all along that I was not cut out for engineering—"He hasn't a mechanical bone in his head," he told my mother—and he was content to see me moving toward something that he thought I would be good at. My mother was too happy for words, but would not let it show. If everything worked out and I did become a priest, this would be the best news of her life. Her son, a priest. Nothing could have delighted her more. But she hid her pleasure and didn't go out of her way to encourage me, as if that might prove unlucky. My mother had a strong superstitious streak in her, including a belief that talking about things one wanted was to court disappointment. She wasn't going to jeopardize my chances (or hers) by seeming too excited about what she hoped would come to pass. My parents indicated that any material support I needed would be forthcoming, but for the rest, it was my decision, my life, and they took a hands-off approach.

At school I said nothing to anyone, but withdrew from its more worldly activities. And I drew nearer to Pete Groeschel, who didn't care a straw if people knew he was religious. When I told him confidentially of my hopes of having a vocation, he said, "For the love of Mike, who do you think you're fooling? Everyone knows." Pete became my sole real friend, as I obsessively narrowed my focus. When I was old enough to drive, I went to his house on weekends, and we traveled to churches, shrines, and monasteries. One of these trips was to the Maryknoll Seminary in upstate New York, and for a short time afterward Father Scully saw what he called an "oriental gleam" in my eye. Was I thinking of becoming a Maryknoll missionary and working to convert the heathen in Asia? Scully squashed that possibility and even tried to turn Pete from the Capuchins to the diocesan priesthood, God's infantry, the men in the trenches of the war for his kingdom on earth.

While my parents stood aside, so to speak, Scully took control of my life. The man who in my younger days had been a joy-killing, guilt-inducing presence became not just my confessor, but my spiritual director and friend. Guiding young men to the seminary and the priesthood was a specialty of his, and now here I was, a new protégé. I was a fish that had jumped into his boat, into his very lap. He instructed and fathered me. He never let me out of his sight. We had long conversations about the spiritual life, commitment to God, and the priestly calling. In his car he drove me to parish churches, rectories, and religious events; he took me to visit the old nuns at the Sisters of Charity retirement home in Convent Station and to the Carmelite Monastery in Morristown, where the nuns saw no one, but spoke from behind a revolving wooden apparatus, a "turn," into which one could put donations and requests for prayers. He asked them to pray for me.

Under Scully's direction, I became progressively more serious and devout. I wanted literally—though I never used the word, even to him—to be saint-like. No halfway measures for Norman Hall's son. And I did become more and more dedicated and committed. My regimen included daily Mass and Communion, weekly Saturday confession, pious reading, the rosary at least once a day, attempts at meditation, and more conscientious work at school in preparation for the seminary. I practiced self-mortification as much as possible, denying myself little pleasures, letting pass some favorite dessert, not opening a hoped-for letter until the next day, refusing to scratch some bodily itch. Such practices were not of my invention, but were suggested in the literature and advice fed to me. I spurned worldly music and dissolved the band. I sold my saxophone. At the time Scully was building a convent for the nuns who taught in his new grade school. With the proceeds of the sale of the saxophone, I purchased a chalice for the convent chapel—a fitting swap, or so it seemed to me, of the worldly for the sacred.

Scully gave me a copy of Thomas à Kempis' *Imitation of Christ*. This book, a work written in the early 1400s, has over the intervening centuries remained second only to the Bible in its wide Christian readership and influence. Here's the kind of thing I took to heart as a teenager:

> My son, says the Lord, do not let fair and subtle words move you, for the kingdom of heaven does not stand in words, but in good, virtuous works. Give heed to My words, for they inflame the heart and enlighten the understanding; they bring compunction of heart for sins past, and oftentimes cause great heavenly comfort to come into the soul. Never read in any science to the end that you may be called wise. Study, rather, to mortify in yourself, as much as possible, all stirring of sin; that will be more profitable to you than the knowledge of many hard or subtle questions. Even when you have read and understood many puzzling things it nevertheless behooves you to come to One who is the Beginning of all things, that is, God himself; otherwise, your knowledge will avail you little.

The *Imitation*, as one can tell from almost any page, is harshly anti-intellectual, famously stated in the line, "I had rather feel compunction of heart for my sins than only know the definition of compunction." Its call is for self-denial and self-mortification:

> It is good that we sometime have griefs and adversities, for they drive a man to behold himself and to see that he is here but as in exile, and to learn thereby that he ought not

put his trust in any worldly thing. It is also good that we
sometimes suffer contradiction, and that we be thought
by others as evil and wretched and sinful, though we do
well and intend well; such things help us to humility, and
mightily defend us from vainglory and pride.

Heavy stuff for a sixteen-year-old. In retrospect, I think how
much better to have been reading Max Beerbohm to the effect
that only the insane take themselves altogether seriously.

There was fanaticism in Thomas à Kempis, but no real danger of psychic harm in Scully's having put me on to the *Imitation of Christ*. But another facet of Scully's guidance, arising
from his obsessive concern with sex, proved nearly ruinous
for me. Scully, a sincerely pious and religious person, was also
a prig and a prude. In retrospect, I believe he was probably a
repressed homosexual, though he may never have acknowledged this, even to himself. Homosexuality was in those days
so horrendous in the eyes of the Catholic world as to be literally
unspeakable. Scully's repressed sexual makeup seems to have
predisposed him to make avoidance of what he saw as sexual
sin—in thought or deed—the centerpiece of his teaching. To
his parishioners he unceasingly preached sermons against birth
control. For Catholics, only "natural" birth control was supposed to be permissible, and this consisted either in abstinence
or in the rhythm method, the drawback of the latter being that
it usually didn't work. Scully would drag in sins of birth control
even on Good Fridays while preaching the so-called Three
Hours Agony (the name is appropriate) commemorating Jesus'
crucifixion. Immodest female dress was another of his frequent
targets from the pulpit, and he denounced women who dared
to approach the altar rail in even slightly low-cut dresses. Distributing Holy Communion, he would bypass certain women.
I've seen him send an altar boy to the sacristy for a linen towel,
which Scully would place over the bosom of a mortified woman
kneeling before him waiting for Communion. He once got his
name in *Life* magazine for his letter canceling his subscription

because of a cover showing a scantily dressed woman. He was
quite proud of that. I was surprised he had a subscription, and
perhaps that part was a fib. Fixated as he was on sex, he couldn't
ignore any chance to introduce the subject. To us altar boys he
was forever speaking about holy purity—not just in confession,
but at meetings and Communion breakfasts. I remember—it
must have been just before New Year's Day—his asking me in
confession if I knew what circumcision was. I mumbled something about the Feast of the Circumcision being celebrated
on New Year's, the day when the Baby Jesus was presented
in the Temple. "Yes, but do you know what circumcision is?"
Then he told me. Though I did not know it at the time, I myself was circumcised, as were most newborns in my era, for
sanitary reasons. Isn't it strange—having been circumcised,
being unaware of that fact, and not even knowing what circumcision was until being told by a priest in the confessional?

It comes then as no surprise that Scully put the necessity of guarding holy purity by complete avoidance of contact with girls at the core of his direction of a future seminarian. The crowning event, the apogee of his drive toward keeping me pure, came when he "invested" me in something called the Angelic Warfare of St. Thomas Aquinas. Legend says that the young Thomas, by having taken the Dominican habit, so incurred the wrath of his wealthy family that they kidnapped him and held him captive in their castle. They attempted to lure him into sin by sending a prostitute into his chamber, but the future saint and doctor of the Church snatched up a burning stick from the fire and drove the woman from the room. He then scratched a cross on the wall and knelt in prayer, whereupon an angel appeared and girded him with a cord, the symbol of his purity in the warfare against sins of the flesh. This fantastic story formed the basis for the Angelic Warfare Society, a confraternity dedicated to preserving chastity among boys and young men, which had functioned briefly under the Dominican priests around the turn of the twentieth century. Scully tried in vain to get a pamphlet or any additional information about the Angelic Warfare from the Dominicans, but those he contacted had never heard of this "Society." Eventually, one of them, to prevent his pestering them further, dug up an old leaflet on the Angelic Warfare and sent it to him. Members were given a special cord, tied with thirteen knots—I forget what they symbolized—which was to be worn continually around the waist under one's clothing and serve as a reminder of the angelic warfare. As was to be expected but still to Scully's disgust, the Dominican priests had no such cord, whereupon he had to fashion one himself. This, accompanied by prayers of his own devising, he gave me to put around my waist as I knelt at the altar rail in the Church of the Holy Cross in Mountain View. That no one else was in the church at the time was a stroke of luck for which I thanked God. I was, at the time, surely the only member of the Angelic Warfare Society anywhere on earth.

Of course I followed my spiritual director's insistence on

absolute separation from girls, except unavoidable social contact at school. Besides, no one wearing that knotted cord around his waist would dance with a girl, much less go out on a date. I was to stay set aside for God. Even to be a receptionist at a school dance was out of the question. Girls represented not only to Scully's mind but to my own a distinct threat. There existed at this time two warring schools of thought about high school students who intended to study for the priesthood. One held that would-be priests should go to a minor seminary, completely segregated and isolated from the world and from girls. Scully would have favored this, but he knew my parents wanted me at home until college; and besides, he had me so under his control that I was as good as in a seminary. This approach, labeled the "hothouse" school by its opponents, saw girls and women as temptations so strong as to necessitate, during these formative years, a complete withdrawal from the world. The other way of thinking, which Scully considered as good as heretical, was that boys of high school age who hoped to become priests should during these years live a normal life, which included attending dances and going on dates. Future seminarians were to get a taste of the world and then see if they still wanted to sacrifice that for the priesthood.

Pete and I followed the hothouse tradition. I even denied myself the slight pleasure of having Lou-Anne Smith sign my yearbook, though we had both worked to produce it. Meanwhile, a third member of our high school class followed the "normal path" regimen to the priesthood. This was none other than my cousin Richie Ehrenberg. (I always felt that his decision to become a priest was motivated in part out of competitiveness with me.) His spiritual director was a newly ordained, handsome young assistant priest at Immaculate, Father Tom Davis. Davis belonged to the liberal school, and Richie attended dances, went on dates, and took a girl to the prom. Pete and I, on the other hand, during our senior prom week went to the Jesuit Monastery of St. Andrew at Poughkeepsie for a private retreat. Our act of difference and defiance was plain. While everyone else was living what for many were the culminating moments of four years of high school, we were hearing once again the *Spiritual Exercises of St. Ignatius*, interpreted for aspirants to the priesthood.

At St. Andrew's the old Jesuit retreat master slyly tried to interest the two of us in the Jesuits. To me he suggested how much more rigorous was the training both intellectual and spiritual in the Jesuits as compared with that of the diocesan seminary. But Scully had warned me to be on guard against such "propaganda." It was while on this retreat that I experienced a brief feeling of religious ecstasy. I had been walking outside meditating and stopped before a statue of the Blessed Virgin. The sensation lasted less than a minute. I was to experience another such feeling—of a similarly fleeting duration—while meditating at home from *The Imitation of Christ*. Such experiences are, as the mystics say, indescribable, but one does feel out of oneself and in touch with the numinous. (I do not now doubt the reality of these flights of religious experience, but I believe they are entirely subjective and self-generated and "natural.") To my chagrin, I was never able to reproduce such moments, and those two were the only ones I was ever to have. Pete, I believe, has such moments regularly.

The Jesuit Monastery of St. Andrew is now the home of the Culinary Institute of America, and the Jesuit motto, A M D G, is still visible on the dining room floor and elsewhere carved in stone on the buildings. The letters stand for *Ad Majorem Dei Gloriam*, "To the Greater Glory of God," and not, *pace* certain bonehead Protestants, "To Mary, Mother of God." Let us hope the food measures up to the motto.

But during these early days of my preparation for the priesthood and my drive for holiness, there arose a serious, almost fatal problem. Slowly and inexorably, catastrophe, or near catastrophe, came upon me. I slipped from care in avoiding sin into scrupulosity, the spiritual hypochondria that consists in seeing oneself as sinning always. I do not say my descent into this mental turmoil was altogether Scully's fault, though his own cautious, perfectionist cast of mind, coupled with his obsession with sex, doubtless contributed much to my mental confusion. Looking back now, I believe that he himself was scrupulous. But my predicament must also have arisen out of my own temperament. In any case, I gradually sank into scrupulosity, the dread disease among seminarians, priests, monks, nuns, and devout lay people. No amount of reasoning can help the victim of scrupulosity because the phobia does not respond to rational analysis. Scrupulosity is a psychological malady that can progress into a psychiatric disorder, a frightening prospect for an eighteen-year-old.

For the scrupulous person, his imaginary sins are very real. The conviction of having seriously sinned, of having fallen from the state of grace (to die in a state of sin meant eternal damnation) was bad enough; but the conviction of having offended the all-loving God brought with it also a devastating guilt. This guilt was many times more painful than the fear of punishment. It inflicted feelings of sadness, hopelessness, and helplessness, what today would be diagnosed as severe clinical depression, or worse. Scrupulous worry would descend upon me in a flash. After going to confession and unburdening myself, I would experience peace and elation in that I was again back in God's grace. Then, after a short time, usually a few hours, I would find myself again in despair; the whole black melancholy mood returned and menacing me terribly. As with some types of madness itself, a disconnect obtains between the subject's perception of reality and the way things are.

Scrupulosity comes fearfully close to insanity by virtue of the sufferer's inability to stay in touch with reality. The best place of operation for this particular lunacy has to do not with physical acts but with mental ones. I know I did not wield an ax on my neighbor, but I might have rashly judged him, or thought evil of him, or secretly willed ill for him, or failed to do some duty by him. I might, for example, out of timidity or embarrassment have neglected to warn him of possible black ice on the road ahead. Or, much more likely, I might, in the language of the Ten Commandments, have coveted or lusted after his wife. "Impure" thoughts and desires are the most common breeding grounds for scrupulous guilt. In my case impure thoughts did not reach the heights of imagining having sexual intercourse with a woman, but in taking, for example, mental delight in the fully clothed curve of her breasts or the shape of her body.

As my scrupulosity deepened, Scully and I had scores of longer and longer sessions in the confessional. I would wait and go last so as not to hold up other penitents. I saw myself as sinning in everything from not practicing "custody of the eyes" while talking with women to not looking away quickly enough from a women's underwear ad chanced upon in the newspaper. Occasionally my imaginary sins strayed beyond the sexual to other matters, such as not admonishing my father about "graft" because some company doing business with DuMont gave him a bottle of liquor at Christmas time. In some unsubstantial way or other I committed all the seven deadly sins: lust, of course, but also pride, covetousness, anger, sloth, envy, and gluttony. Medieval theologians—I was living in a medieval world—identify seven variations on the sin of gluttony, the "seven daughters of Gula," not just over eating, but "fastidious" eating, "ferocious" eating, and four others that I thankfully can't remember now.

Scully, intent on perfection, did not move quickly to cut off my scruples. Had he been a confessor like Father Edward Meagan, I might have been spared. This sensible, down-to-earth Jesuit priest had given the school's annual retreat in my senior year in a way that made many students take their religion more to heart. We dedicated the yearbook to him. He was opening a retreat house in upstate New York and doing the work of converting the building himself, and I organized a group of classmates who journeyed up to the country one weekend to help him. During the day we drilled holes and ran BX cable— probably contrary to code—and nailed up plasterboard. In the evening, as preparation for Sunday Mass, Meagan heard confessions. I told him how I wished to become a priest, how

I was suffering from scruples, and then made my confession. I shall never forget his almost angry reply to one of my "sins": while serving Mass, I had perceived what I thought were tiny fragments of the consecrated Host on the Communion plate, particles which the officiating priest had missed while cleansing the plate; yet I had not the courage to interrupt the priest and tell him. Hearing this, Meagan cut me short:

"Listen, you have to get over this."

"But what am I to do with the Communion plate if I think it still has particles of the Eucharist on it?"

"Put the plate under the carpet, for all I care. You must get over this."

But of course I did not get over it just like that. To Divinity School at Seton Hall I brought not just my straight A's and a compelling ambition to become a priest, but also a serious case of scrupulosity.

5

DIFFICULTY

ANYONE who attended Seton Hall in the early 1950s will recall the school's president, Monsignor (a strictly honorific title, usually conferred on older priests who had stayed out of trouble) John L. McNulty, addressing the student body and saying—he always said the same thing—"The immigrants came to South Orange and they dug deep. They had a dream. People said they couldn't do it, but they did it. They came up with Seton Hall. This school," he went on, "is founded on the principle that every Tom, Dick, and Harry should have a college education." Then he would lurch into a long non sequitur about the good work done by people in Alcoholics Anonymous. And indeed it did seem as if every Tom, Dick, and Harry among Catholic high school graduates in New Jersey were coming to South Orange. Like many other colleges, Seton Hall, in the wake of World War II and the influx of students attending college on the G.I. Bill, had grown at a rate disproportionate to its resources. By the time I arrived there in September 1951, the school, which had just become a university, was teeming with students, and many classrooms, offices, and student living quarters were crammed into army surplus Quonset huts and barracks. These buildings provided a somewhat informal look to a campus where everyone had to wear a jacket and tie. There were no women students, although we heard rumors of a class or two for nurses in the evenings. I myself never saw a female student on campus in my two years at the place.

The Divinity School formed a subset of the university, where we future priests took our freshman and sophomore years, after which time we were to move on to the seminary proper, a place called Darlington, miles away in Mahwah. As divinity students, or "divvies," we did not have to go through registration, that great headache of college students throughout the land. Everything was mapped out for us—courses, schedules, and room assignments. We were college students, but we were different, segregated, taking all our classes and activities together, with no intermingling with other students. Our main subjects were Latin and Greek—we were supposed to be classical language majors—together with the usual preliminary core subjects like English composition and American history, along with a string of what we called "Mickey Mouse" courses in education. All our instructors were priests except two or three devout Catholic laymen, including an elderly English teacher, a Mr. Rowan, "Rip Rowan," who decades earlier had taught my father at Central High in Newark. In addition to a five-day program of twenty-one college credits, we had noon-hour homilies in the chapel and special late Friday afternoon lectures on Scripture in the "Little Theater" in the basement of Walsh Gym.

To top it all off we were required, once a week, after a full day of college work and pious extras, to take a modern language, "in case we needed it in the confessional." Like most of my classmates, I took Italian. Our professor was a Father Monella, just over from Italy, alleged to have been slipped into the country as a member of the Brooklyn Dodger Baseball Organization. He had "Vincent Monella, Ph. Dr." handprinted on his office door. No one paid him any attention in class, and some signed the attendance sheet with names like Philip Morris and Chester Fields. It was late in the day, we were all wearied, most of us about to travel home, and here we were taking a non-credit course in spoken Italian from a man who despised teaching us. "I would rather," he said, "shine altar boys' shoes than teach this crazy stuff." In his broken English he would say he had had to leave Italy "on account of *this*"—and he would run his finger around his Roman collar—"because enemies of the Church were putting syphilis germs in my coffee." My classmate Joe Cassidy later claimed that after eight years of Italian all he could say was *Sono un prete. Faccia la sua confessione.* "I'm a priest. Make your confession."

There were some seventy divinity students in our freshman class, comprised primarily of young men from the Archdiocese of Newark. The archdiocese ran Seton Hall itself and the seminary; we seven Paterson lads were from a diocese too small to have its own seminary. The first new classmate I met at Seton Hall was Bill Giblin. He came up and introduced himself while I was standing on the lunch line in the cafeteria. We have been friends ever since. Fifty years on I asked him how I struck him in those early days. He took a while to think about it, before answering, "pious and smart, but most of all quiet and shy." Because he knew me as well as anyone back then, I pushed further and asked him if he realized at the time that I was going through a scrupulous phase. His firm answer surprised me: No, he had not sensed that. I offer here one example of my scrupulosity in connection with him. Bill, plenty smart himself but disinclined toward study and with no particular penchant for languages, found Latin and Greek difficult—he claims never to have learned the Greek alphabet. I sometimes helped him with the homework, but when he asked me for answers during a test, I told him I could not do that. Questioned now about how he could have put up with me, he replied that he thought my behavior admirable. At least that is what he says now about what he thought then. He insists he judged my actions "consistent with being a divinity student." And again, he did not suspect scrupulosity. If he did not, no one did. The episode prompts me to remark how cunningly the patient can hide certain diseases.

Our superior, the director of the Divinity School, Father William F. Furlong, was to many people a saint, though a somewhat forbidding saint, a man who strove continuously for what he urged on us—"spiritual perfection." He once told a friend that the only worldly thing he had not renounced was care in dress. His black suit was always immaculately pressed and his black shoes brilliantly shined. Furlong's reputation for holiness and for perfectionism earned him the nickname, predictable as coming from language students, of "Pluperfect," more than perfect. We circulated the rumor that when he made his way to chapel early on winter mornings he levitated, leaving no footprints in the snow. He gave us divinity students weekly spiritual pep talks, "feverinos," always urging "perfection." He was someone right out of the *Imitation of Christ*, of which, as I see now, I had already had quite too much. He told us of a seminarian who denied his vocation and left to get married and whose first child was born crippled: "I am not saying there was a direct cause and effect here, but such was the fact." Another case he expounded was that of the seminarian who dropped out, got married, and worked for the electric company: "At the very moment when his classmates were being ordained in the cathedral in Newark, this fellow touched a live wire and was electrocuted."

One peculiarity of Furlong's saintliness was the zeal with which he took to oddball devotions, like that to Saint Gemma Galgani, an Italian nun who was blessed with the stigmata (wounds, in the hands and feet, like those of the crucified Christ) that appeared every Thursday evening until 3 P.M. on Friday, the hour of Jesus' death on the cross. She also had visions of her guardian angel and the devil. The daughter of a pharmacist, she is the patron saint of pharmacists. Furlong also espoused the cause of Our Lady of the Rose Petals. He fell for the story that the Blessed Virgin had appeared to a Carmelite nun in Lipa City, the Philippines, in 1948. The Virgin hovered above a vine and caused showers of rose petals to fall, each petal bearing images of Jesus or Mary. A bluebird is also said to have appeared. The Virgin then proclaimed herself the "Mediatrix of All Grace," a notion closely allied to the belief in Mary as "Co-Redemtrix"—with Jesus—of the human race. Told that some of us divinity students were mocking this devotion, Furlong shouted from the pulpit, "I have *seen* the petals! I have *seen* the Papal Bull according them veneration!" (The Church apparently had a change of mind and hushed up the whole business. But in the 1990s rose petals were again seen falling from the sky above the convent in Lipa City, and reports told of a luminous female figure in prayer appearing on the leaves of a tall coconut tree. The ecclesiastical authorities are said to be investigating these phenomena.)

Furlong had an enthralling and melodramatic speaking style. He once delivered a sermon in which he recounted how at the wake for a young woman killed in a car accident, a Seton Hall College man broke down screaming, "She's in hell, and I put her there!" While some students thought Furlong the holiest of men, others believed him to be slightly batty. I expect that he, like Scully, suffered from scrupulosity, which in turn did not make him the ideal director for me.

AND HERE I ARRIVE at what could have been the climax of the story, or perhaps more honestly, the end of the story: I suddenly seemed to be losing my faith. I have since learned that age nineteen or twenty is often the time when one loses one's faith in things unseen, but I will let that pass, for the moment. It happened about halfway through the first semester while we were taking a course in Christian Apologetics, taught by Father Furlong himself. The text was a gray paperback in two slim volumes, *Christian Origins* by A. Patrick Madgett, S. J. I have that book before me now. It has not the dignity of real print, but is typewritten and reproduced in mimeograph. It purported to prove that God existed; that unaided reason could not but so prove; that all primitive peoples were originally monotheists whose religions became debased into various polytheisms; that the evidence was such that the Gospels were completely credible; that all rational men of good faith must see that Jesus was God; and so on. Everything about Catholic belief was "rational" and "intellectual" while all other thought was "irrational" and "absurd." Madgett was especially bellicose toward what he called "our modern anti-intellectualism," which, he explains, began with the Renaissance and was furthered by the Reformation, bringing a net result of "worldliness, pride, individualism, and low moral and religious life." Thenceforth came the "decline of reason" with villains like Descartes, Bolingbroke, Reimar, Voltaire, Kant, Schleiermacher, Hegel, Comte, Strauss, Sabatier, William James, Harnack. Not that such names had any meaning for me then. But every famous thinker was wrong on every count. All modern thought represented "the bankruptcy of human reason." Madgett asserts that the tone taken by modern-day atheists betrays "an interior admission of His existence who is verbally denied." Atheists may claim that theirs is an intellectual position, whereas in fact it is an "emotional stance," employing arguments that suggest "the small boy whistling in the dark to keep up his courage." Moreover, unbelievers "endeavor to erase the line dividing right from wrong"—that lovely old canard that atheists are by necessity dishonest, untrustworthy, and immoral. Agnosticism, Madgett contends, is if anything worse than atheism "in that it denies the very foundations on which all knowledge rests."

Everything is tied up neatly. When, for example, Madgett arrives at the Christian Gospels, he demonstrates how a document is credible if it can be established as "genuine, integral, and trustworthy." The Gospels are quickly shown to be genuine, integral, and trustworthy; therefore, they are historically credible. Their historicity in turn proves the divinity of Christ, who within the gospels claimed he was God and supported his claim with miracles rendered beyond doubt by the already established credibility of the gospels that recount the miracles. The circularity is stunning. All differences from Catholic teaching are dismissed as "errors," which are in turn "answered" by this little mimeographed book. It seems funny now, but it wasn't then. It was just plain unbelievable. I know my crisis of faith would have come upon me in any event, but Madgett's "apologetics" hurried on my distress. How could every philosopher, historian, and thinker of the last four hundred years be so utterly wrong and foolish, and this unknown Jesuit, quoting other unknown Jesuits ("See C. Ring, S.J., *Gods of the Gentiles*, Chapter 19") possibly be right? My difficulty was not with a particular piece of Catholic dogma, like the recently proclaimed doctrine of the bodily Assumption of Mary into Heaven, or with some question of the Church's moral teaching, like the prohibition of "artificial" birth control. My problem was more basic. It was the existence of God.

An agonizing struggle to believe ensued. I went to Furlong and told him I thought I was losing my faith. I broke down and wept. He listened to me sympathetically and in no way tried to argue. He told me that this was a cross I had to bear, that every believing man has occasional difficulties of faith, just as atheists have occasional doubts about their unbelief. But my difficulties, I protested, were more than occasional. Then Furlong quoted Cardinal Newman: "Ten thousand difficulties do not make a single doubt." John Henry Newman was a Catholic hero, the previous century's great intellectual convert, but someone more revered than read or taught in my day. These were the only words of his ever mentioned in all my many years of Catholic higher education. More to the point, this sentence, lovely as it sounds, is nonsensical if you look at it carefully.

I don't mean to compare myself or my lot with that of another Seton Hall man, the eminent polymath Will Durant, but parts of his story seem apposite. Famous and still publishing during my time at Seton Hall, Durant was a name scarcely mentioned on campus and then only in hushed and frightened terms, as if his case were too terrible to contemplate. He was a scandal to us, an apostate. In his autobiography, *Transition*, Durant tells how he had lost his faith while at St. Peter's College, Jersey City. After graduation he taught foreign languages for two years, and then, all aflame with socialism, he joined the seminary at Seton Hall in 1909. Durant's quixotic plan was to get ordained and then bring socialism to the American Catholic Church. He hoped that while in the seminary his faith would revive "by osmosis, by the contagion of the environment." His faith did not recuperate, and after a year and a half he dropped out of the seminary and went on to write his famous (infamous to us) *The Story of Philosophy* and *The Story of Civilization*, the latter in eleven huge and heretical volumes. Of his seminary days, he writes:

> The early twenties are the age of religious doubt; if a man does not learn to doubt then, he will believe to the end of his life. And doubt requires energy; it is unnatural, uphill work; acceptance is much easier. Most of us are as willing to let others think for us as we are to let others work for us; here it is the mass that exploits the few, and surrenders to them all the risks of innovation.

I had certainly learned to doubt, but I was driven by an overpowering will to believe. All my energies were poured into the doubly uphill work of making myself believe. My faith, or rather about half of it, revived by sheer effort of will. So desperately did I want to believe, to become a priest, to serve God and my fellowman, that I kept at it. Doubtless what Durant calls the contagion of the religious environment also worked on me. Catholicism seemed so marvelous a religion, so grand a phenomenon, with its striking and ancient rituals and liturgy, its cosmopolitanism, its catholicity. Here was no hole-in-the-wall religion headed by some Father Divine or other charlatan or crackpot, but rather a two-thousand-year-old institution with a glorious history (we heard nothing but good of the Church's past) and an indisputably high place in Western art and culture. Our Church could boast of the Lindisfarne Gospels, the stained glass of Chartres, the painting of Giotto, the glories of medieval cathedrals, the phenomenon that is St. Peter's Basilica. A catalog of Catholic art would be endless. In music "we" had everything from early Gregorian chant to Palestrina, from Pergolesi's *Stabat Mater* to Schubert's *Ave Maria*, even though the archbishop of Newark had just banned its singing at church services, explaining that it was "too beautiful" and might distract from the religious ceremonies.

The Church also seemed, by a bewitching slight of hand, coolly and staunchly intellectual. We were told of James Joyce being asked if he, having left the Church, might become a Protestant. He had lost his faith, he replied, not his reason. In our time we could boast of Catholic philosophers like Etienne Gilson and Jacques Maritain, Catholic novelists like Graham Greene, Evelyn Waugh, and François Mauriac. Moreover, Catholicism positively flourished in northern New Jersey, where it had churches and schools in every town. The Catholic grade school system was nearly equivalent in size to the public school system. We had Catholic colleges and a university, Catholic hospitals and nursing schools. The Church ran adoption agencies, orphanages, and homes for the aged. We had "our own" among doctors, lawyers, architects, and legislators.

We gloried in our accomplishments in sports: in basketball, for starters, Seton Hall, which during my time was a national power; in football, Notre Dame, admittedly not in New Jersey, but it might just as well have been, given its Catholic following there; in baseball, players like Joe DiMaggio, Phil Rizzutto, and Yogi Berra (even if they were Yankees). Only shallow people will think such considerations frivolous. Catholic sports teams and Catholic athletes were a highly visible part of our parallel culture within the culture at large—a subculture American to the core, we insisted, but different and distinctive. For someone to aspire to be a priest, to be at the center of this "universal" church, whose representatives were so revered in our corner of the world, was something very special indeed.

In one sense I was losing or half losing my faith in God, but not in religion. Most people in America have it the other way round: "I believe in God all right, but I don't go to church on Sundays. I just don't put much faith in organized religion." For myself, I could see the good that the Church was doing. Stanford Professor Robert Polhemus has written a book in which he tries to demonstrate that comedy is replacing religion— wishful thinking—and that comedy and religion share the same purposes: "to honor creation; to provide hope; to reconcile people to their harsh fates; to smooth over social enmity and to defend culture by authoritative moral sanction against selfish and destructive behavior; to make people feel important, part of a 'chosen' group; to institutionalize ways of getting rid of guilt; to allow people to identify with righteousness and let loose wrathful indignation and hostility in good conscience; to assure them of the possibility of future well-being; to lift them out of themselves, to free their spirits." It's a curious list—no mention of a God—but it makes persuasive points, and people who know the inside of religious communities will concur with Polhemus that religion does just these things. To this day I think that attendance at Sunday Mass is a good thing physically, psychologically, and socially—for those who can believe, however vaguely, in the magic.

Back in 1951 I was trying to balance unbelief, the result of thinking too much about the gratuitous assumptions behind religious thought, against belief, ingrained over many years and bolstered by the everyday realities of the religious atmosphere in which I moved. Without ever having heard of John Keats's "negative capability," I was in fact straining for it: the art of remaining "in uncertainties, mysteries, doubts, without any irritable reaching after fact and reason"; the art of negating the logical, rational part of the mind and being content with "half knowledge." Of course I *was* still reaching after fact and reason, but I was simultaneously doing my best to be content with half faith. Nonetheless, the question won't go away: Why didn't I get out in 1951? The will to believe, coupled with the desire to become a priest, doesn't seem an altogether satisfactory answer. Perhaps I should have left then. It's not as if I was or am proud of my staying on. But I still had a "sneaking suspicion"—a favorite phrase of my father's—that there was a God; that they, the Catholics, might be right; that my worries and doubts were a burden I had to bear, and that they were temptations or tricks of the Devil. A real and personal Devil was an essential part of the Catholic explanation of evil. These considerations, coupled with a strong desire to stay the long course, to achieve my goal, to serve people, prevented my leaving. Perhaps it was also cowardice, an unwillingness to face the world I had so fanatically repudiated. But my not having left the Divinity School does indicate, I think, something of the pull of 1950s Catholicism on an idealistic and impressionable youth.

Yet, by what was for me a terrible irony, my difficulties of belief did not in any degree lessen my scrupulosity. Instead, the doubts increased the sense of guilt. My mind ached from contending with opposing thoughts: that there was no God and that I was sinning against him at the same time, including the horrible sin of not believing in him, the sin against the Holy Spirit, the one sin that God will not forgive. (Theologians have argued for centuries over what precisely constitutes that sin "against the Holy Ghost," the "eternal sin" that God will not forgive, as mentioned in the Gospel of Mark. A maverick interpretation, one that might have served me well, is voiced by Anthony Quinn in the movie *Zorba the Greek*: "If a woman calls a man to her bed and he will not go—that is the one sin that God will not forgive.")

I was also studying too hard. And I wore myself down physically, driving to and from South Orange five days a week, in a long, congested, back-street commute. I had to coordinate picking up and returning home each day a couple of obnoxious Packanack Lake high school kids attending Seton Hall Prep, an arrangement that generated daily anxiety about meeting them in the parking lot of the college for the trip home—either they or I would arrive at the car early or late.

Then one day in the spring term I came home from South Orange, collapsed on my parents' bed—I don't know what I was doing in that room—and suffered a nervous breakdown. I felt I couldn't go on. Discouragement, sadness, and hopelessness bore down upon me. Everything seemed too much. I just wanted to lie down and give up and find some kind of oblivion. My sister Sally tells me—she would have been twelve at the time—that she came home that evening to find my father, her strong father, sobbing about me, the first and only time she saw him cry. That upset her far more than did my condition. She also remembers hearing Father Scully, who visited the house often during the following weeks, telling my father that if I had to be hospitalized, sent to a mental institution for rehabilitation, he should be sure that it was a Catholic place.

As it happened, no hospital was needed. Two things turned my life around, one psychological, one physical or, you might say, geographical. Scully, in what was his one sensible move in regard to my "spiritual life," told me that henceforth in confession, to him or to any other priest, I was forbidden to mention any specific sins of doubts about faith or of impure thoughts or desires. I was to use a generic formula only, expressing sorrow for any sins of my life. That was to be all. No details, no thinking about it. I was not to omit receiving Holy Communion for fear of being in mortal sin unless I had, for example, deliberately murdered someone. And, marvelous to say, it worked. I recovered my mental balance. My scrupulosity gradually disappeared, and I continued to try to believe through the stratagem of not facing up to, not thinking about, the "difficulties." I swept them under the rug. I wanted to believe, and this, I was told, was enough. Just how much I believed is hard to say. Years later, reading Trollope on religious belief, I quickly concurred with his assertion that we should not be surprised if we can't know what our neighbor believes since we don't know what we ourselves believe.

The other change was immediate. I became a boarder at Seton Hall, leaving off the long commute to South Orange and the attendant trouble of picking up those two prep schoolers. The move into the Divinity School Barracks at Seton Hall made life fun again. My Paterson diocese friends—Joe Cassidy, Dan Mahoney, Bernie Lebiedz, Jack Wehrlen, Bob Shelton—were all living in the same barracks, and they were amusing and diverting. Another classmate, Jim Kurpeck, a Paterson boy who had been sent to high school via the "hothouse approach" to a

minor seminary in Baltimore, lasted until one fateful day in
that freshman year at Seton Hall when he attended a movie,
fell in love with the actress—I forget which one—and dropped
out the next week. Bill Giblin also switched to living on campus
and soon became my barrack mate. I came to know new people:
Leonard Spanburgh with his love of all things English, including his red two-seater convertible Singer; Bob Richardson, who
was flippant and lighthearted and always joking; Donald Mc-
Cormack, a grave and serious man who had dropped out of the
Naval Academy to become a priest.

There was a tall, shy man with a name I can't recover—it began with "Vander"—who didn't mix with us and was at Seton
Hall only to study Latin and Greek prior to joining the Dominicans. He had been a Princeton undergraduate, and in one
of the few conversations I had with him he asked me why no
one on campus seemed interested in intellectual discussions,
which, he claimed, were the very bread of life among students
at Princeton. I didn't know what to say. What could I tell him?
That Seton Hall was a commuter school and a jock school?

Living in these same Divinity School barracks was Gerry
Breen, a smart, self-deprecating, and genial man, who was
somewhat older than the rest of us. His background differed
too. He had graduated from Yale, where he had starred in
basketball and baseball and been tapped for Skull and Bones.
(A Yale teammate and fellow Bonesman, George H. W. Bush,
when asked whether he had had any disappointments in life,
replied that yes, he had. Back in 1948, when he was playing first
base for Yale in the National Championship game against USC,
Yale, having trailed by many runs, staged a last-inning rally, had
the bases loaded, no one out, with George Bush on deck. Then
Gerry Breen hit into a triple play. We all have our frustrations.)
After graduating, Breen went to law school, but dropped out
to become a seminarian and was attending Seton Hall to learn
Latin. He distinguished himself at the Hall by a practical joke
that ended in nearly burning down the barracks belonging
to the older lay student who was in charge of our barracks. I

recently asked Breen how he remembered me, and I can hardly believe his analysis: he saw me having "an impish grin and looking laughingly at the world," someone who loved the world and its sillinesses, "a bright, modest guy" who harbored more liberal views than his friends, someone who liked asking questions, who was somehow always "out there, separate from this group." He could have been describing the man in the moon for all this meant to me. But whatever the exaggeration, it provides yet more evidence of how my troubled past was becoming past and how well I continued to camouflage the vestiges of my fading scrupulosity.

Now that I was living on campus, college life delighted me. I loved the camaraderie, the game playing in the late afternoons, the suppers together with friends, the study groups we called "ecumenical councils," the trips to the movies and to New York. I had missed a lot of class work, but Furlong helped. My greatest problem was a term paper due for English Composition, and Furlong contacted Rip Rowan about my case. The old man stopped me on a pathway and said I was to give him any notes that I had made for the project. I told him that I had nothing but a few scrawled lines and a pamphlet on what I see now as a creepy, cult-like lay organization called The Legion of Mary. "Hand them in tomorrow," he commanded. "But there is no paper," I protested. "As instructor, I can accept what I please. Hand them in." He gave me a B. In the Latin oral exam, which our instructor, Father Joseph Russell, held in his private quarters in the Administration Building, he presented me with a passage from Ovid that had been covered during my absence from class. "I can't do it," I blurted out. "Yes you can," Russell said. And with a little help, his giving me a word here and there, I did. I seemed buoyed up by kindnesses.

Dr. Gross also came to my aid. I suffered chest pains for a few months. With some lingering scrupulosity, I thought that playing pickup basketball in this condition was chancing a heart attack, even death. To gamble with one's life this way was a serious sin, allied to suicide itself. Gross insisted there was nothing

wrong with my heart. On my third visit he heaved a sigh and
told me to come into the back room. There, keeping the room
nearly dark so as to add to the solemnity of the procedure, he
gave me an EKG. It was negative, and the pains left me. Though
my parents would know nothing of it this time, that kind and
shrewd doctor had again done me a special service.

I admired and liked most of my professors at Seton Hall,
including the same Joe Russell, the very dry man who taught us
Latin. We were not supposed to use an interlinear translation,
called a "pony" or a "trot" (obtainable only at Barnes and Noble
on Fifth Avenue in the City). Whenever a student's translation
sounded as if it came from a trot, Russell would say, "Dixit the
Lord, Dominus said." *Dixit Dominus*, the most common phrase
in the gospels, means "The Lord said," but in Latin the words are
reversed.

Father Joseph Shea taught us Beginning Greek. We never
got very far, but it was good stuff as he presented it. The sim-
plest lessons included learning how to read and pronounce the
language. Shea loved to read Greek aloud, and I loved to hear
him read it. The opening passage of St. John's Gospel was a favorite of his. "Listen," he would say, "listen to the sounds and the
rhythms." And even if all one caught was one word, *Logos*, the
word for "word," as in "In the beginning was the Word, and the
Word was with God, and the Word was God," it *sounded* lovely.
Joe Shea, the poor man, as we campus boarders who served his
daily Mass knew, was scrupulous, at least about the words of
transubstantiation, the words in the Mass that change bread
and wine into the body and blood of Christ. Shea kept repeating, very loudly, very slowly, "*Hoc est,*" then starting again, not
stuttering, but saying again and again, "*Hoc, Hoc, Hoc est enim,
Hoc est enim corpus*" until he got through the words of consecration—"This is my body." The words have to be pronounced
clearly, Catholic teaching held, or transubstantiation would not
be effected. We lived partly in the world of the 1950s and partly
in a world of sheer magic. Most priests and seminarians took a
casual attitude toward this dual existence, but clearly Joe Shea

could not do so. In contrast, Father Jim Carey, the university's brash athletic director, would "knock off" a daily Mass, which customarily took half an hour, in ten minutes.

Professor Paul Jordan, one of the few lay teachers who were assigned Divinity School classes, a man in whose debt I remain to this day, taught us world literature. My high school "conversion" to religion had given me a desire to read, but only school texts and Catholic works. I read to do well in class and, more often, to deepen my devotion to Catholicism. Now Jordan gave me a taste for reading for its own sake, something altogether new to me. Through the example of the enthusiasm and the pleasure he took in literature, he started me on a desultory crash course of reading books, devouring them not for good grades—which, incidentally, I never achieved in college—but for the delight they had to offer. The first book I read for pure pleasure was a translation of Alessandro Manzoni's *I Promessi Sposi* ("The Betrothed"), and I asked Jordan about it. His reply seemed to proffer both surprise and approbation: "You have read an Italian classic." I valued too his wry manner. A student raised his hand and complained that it was dark in the room and would the professor please put on the lights. Wordlessly, closing the book that he was reading from, but keeping his place with one finger, Jordan moved to the side of the room and threw the light switch. Nothing happened. He walked back to the middle of the room, faced us, opened the book, and asked, "Is that better?"

My favorite teacher was Father William "Josh" Halliwell, a tall, thin, gray-haired, serious man. He looked to me like a doom-foretelling Old Testament prophet. In private life Halliwell was fanatically ascetic, and once told a few of us that for a priest to sink down delightedly into a soft easy chair was tantamount to a married man's committing adultery. He also asked us to pray for his sister whom he thought lost because she married into the family of "that apostate" Will Durant. But Halliwell, in teaching us "advanced" Greek, betrayed none of his religious extremism, and with him we arrived, after half a

year with Shea, at the first lines of the *Odyssey*. "Here we go!" I
scribbled atop the page:

> Ándra moi énnepe, Moúsa, polútropon...
> Sing to me, oh Muse, of that resourceful man...

Halliwell taught Greek with a peculiar sense of futility that
delighted me. I saw him as someone belonging to another
world, that of the questioning and critical intellect. He struggled to interest us in ideas for their own sake. I recall some of his
very words, which he would repeat endlessly, never seeming to
weary of the fruitless effort. As might be expected in a professor
of Greek, Halliwell was fascinated with etymologies. He kept
urging us to buy *Skeat's Etymological Dictionary*. Each week he
would inquire: "How many have purchased *Skeat's Etymological
Dictionary*?" Never once did a hand go up. He would shake his
head, "Too much stadium and not enough studium." He was
continually asking us what we thought of Homer's calling the
dawn *rhododáktulos*, rosy-fingered. And were we not thrilled
with the Greek word *spharagéunto*, describing the Cyclops' eye
as "crackling" when Ulysses puts the burning pole into it? Did
we not love the sentiments Plato has Socrates voice when he
says that he was indeed wiser than his critics because whereas
they thought they knew something, when in fact they knew
nothing, he knew he knew nothing, and hence was wiser than
they were? "What do you think of that, Mr. Jones?" he would
ask Giblin. "My name isn't Jones, Father." "Ah, yes it is, Mr.
Jones, yes it is." He put strange questions to us such as "What's
the meaning of meaning?" or "Why does the pencil end here?"
He seldom got answers, but he must have realized he was moving some of us along.

Halliwell thought just about all learning could be boiled
down to Greek language and literature. On the first day of a new
term a lay person mistakenly sat down in our classroom. Halfway through the opening lecture he raised his hand and asked if
this were American History II. Halliwell told him yes and went
on speaking. We had to attend a series of lectures by prominent

Catholic laymen on the theme "What Makes America Great?" and Halliwell, who suffered from a slight stutter, followed up every such talk with the question "Is is *is* America great?" One day the center of the basketball team, the All American Walter Dukes, came into the classroom asking to be allowed to make an announcement. Halliwell, like everyone else, recognized Dukes, the best-known person on campus—he was seven feet tall and black, at a school 99.9 percent white. The professor of Greek welcomed him but went immediately to work in his Socratic manner, while Dukes laughed good naturedly:

"Wha what do you do around here? Play basketball?"

"Yes."

"You you play basketball. And wh what is contained inside a basketball? Nothing?"

"Nothing."

"And what is contained inside a basketball rim?"

"Nothing."

"So so you go around here putting nothing into nothing."

"Right."

Divinity students, for some unremembered reason, had a priority in working as ushers at Seton Hall home basketball games. Maybe the authorities figured we would be more honest. Ushers got in free, made a few dollars, and saw the game. In the 1952–1953 season Seton Hall, under coach John "Honey" Russell, was hugely successful, with Dukes and Richie Reagan both being named to All American teams. For a week or two Seton Hall was ranked number one in the national polls, until they went West and got beaten twice, by Dayton and Louisville, the latter contest marred by racial attacks on Walter Dukes. For the postseason, Seton Hall chose to play close to home, in the National Invitational Tournament at Madison Square Garden, where they defeated St. Johns for the title. In those days the NIT was rated almost on a par with the NCAA tournament. I went to the big games at the Garden (then located on 8th Avenue at 49th Street), surely a sign that I was overcoming my religious perfectionism and scrupulosity. But it would have saddened though also amused me to know that Father Carey, the alcoholic athletic director, had taken the team, immediately after they won the championship, to a bar near the Garden and gotten himself soused drinking from the actual NIT cup.

Seton Hall's basketball championship in March 1953 led to what I consider the high point of my academic career at the college. On the day following the great triumph in the Garden, I was translating a Greek passage from Plato for Halliwell and got stuck on a word. I started to hem and haw over it:

"Wh What is the matter, Mr. Hall?"

"I don't know that word, Father."

"You you don't know that word."

"No."

"Di did did you look it up?"

"I looked it up but I can't remember it."

"You you looked it up but you can't remember it. Do, do you remember who won the game last night?"

"Who played, Father?"

"Ve very good, Mr. Hall, very good."

Devotion to the athletic teams of one's alma mater is a phenomenon mysterious to all who bother to think about it. I paid no attention to Seton Hall basketball for thirty-five years—occasionally hearing only that they were not doing well. Then in late 1988 I started to follow them again, the Cinderella team that the following March came close to winning the national title—this time in the NCAA. They lost in the final to Michigan in the last seconds of overtime on what New Jerseyans to this day think was a questionable foul call. I felt the defeat keenly. It depressed me, and at the time I marveled how this could be. I now believe that had the Pirates—as the team is called—won the national championship, it would have been a vindication of a peculiar sort. Seton Hall was, after all, my alma mater. The undergraduate schools of my closest friends today are Columbia, Harvard, Dartmouth, Oxford, Princeton, and the University of Connecticut (UConn does win national basketball championships). I think a victory in the NCAA would have given a kind of retrospective respectability to Seton Hall, to my past, to me. Silly, I know, but that is what I felt. On the other hand, when, some years later, Seton Hall Professor John Harrington and the provost of the university nominated me for an honorary doctorate as the school's most published graduate, they were turned down flat. All those books on Trollope and Beerbohm meant nothing, once my background was known. This was predictable, but I had secretly hoped that the place had become less parochial in such matters, but evidently it had not. Still, I so wish they had beaten Michigan.

I harbor no grudge against my alma mater. Like many of my fellow students I liked the place very much, while having no illusions about its being a particularly learned institution. We laughed at rumors that when the Middle States Association came to accredit the school, the library rented a multivolume Chinese encyclopedia, which was immediately shipped back once the inspectors left. Seton Hall tried to establish a Chinese Studies Program through the hiring of one Dr. John Wu, author of *Beyond East and West*, a brainy old fellow said to have been a chief justice of the Supreme Court of China, and more amazing still, a practicing Catholic with fourteen children. According to my classmate Jerry Pindar, Wu was regarded by the administration as an intellectual-in-residence and as an all-wise detective in the manner of Charlie Chan, to be consulted on all serious questions, including a recent campus burglary: "Dr. Wu say thief go out Ward Place [the side entrance]." Pindar also claimed that the Middle States team discovered a copy of *The Bobbsey Twins* which he, Pindar, had placed among the library's volumes of the *Dictionary of National Biography*.

Toward the end of our sophomore year we were preparing to go to the seminary, to withdraw from the world. I was about to leave my parents' home, and they who had been so supportive—my mother if anything almost too supportive—pass for the most part out of this narrative. I would continue to visit them on vacations and days off, but my home would be elsewhere. Like most parents, mine had exercised an enormous influence over their children, but at this point their direct impact on me receded and began to disappear. My mother did prevail on me to have my picture taken professionally, in my black suit and tie. I had these new clothes because they were included on a list of required clothing for the seminary. Other key items were cassocks and Roman collars.

We had to be voted on by the Seton Hall priest faculty as suitable candidates for the priesthood, and we had to undergo a medical examination by a doctor. The exam involved dropping one's pants and shorts, coughing, turning around and spreading one's cheeks, the last maneuver drawing from one gay would-be seminarian the quip, "Why, doctor, I hardly know you," a remark that came just short of debarring him. Another classmate, Bob Richardson, was not so lucky. His case revealed the real reason for the medical examination. We learned that he had undergone some mysterious operation at St. Joseph's Hospital in Paterson, and when some of us visited him there he told us that his testicles had not descended, and that the Church "wouldn't ordain anyone they weren't sure was a man. Isn't that right, sister?"—these last words addressed to an embarrassed nun who happened to be in the room. Whatever the explanation, Richardson was not admitted to Darlington Seminary. He later told us that his father, who was a high official in the New Jersey Division of Motor Vehicles, wished only that the authorities had told him this before he had invested so much money in a veritable wardrobe of black suits and cassocks for his son.

6

PICTURES FROM AN INSTITUTION

IT'S BETTER to laugh than to cry about what came next. At this distance there is no sense to recalling something with rancor, much less with spite. For six years my classmates and I were kept sheltered from the world at a place called Darlington, officially the Seminary of the Immaculate Conception, situated in the Ramapo Hills of northern New Jersey. Our term there ran from July 4, 1953—Independence Day, an irony that did not escape us even back then—to May 23, 1959. We "got out" for a week at Christmas and Easter and for a month or two in the summers. For me and for most of my classmates this time stretch coincided with our twentieth to twenty-sixth years, "the best years of our lives," as some used to say, and to which my classmate Vincent McCluskey would reply, "Yes, and that is the damn of it all." But then, he was bitter in a way I am not. I wanted to be a priest and Darlington was the route to that goal. And so here we were, this bright sunny July Fourth, saying good-bye to our families and walking around the grounds in regulation button-style black cassocks and Roman collars. For us students for the priesthood, wearing such clerical garb was exciting, at first.

The seminary was set amid 1,400 private acres. We had a river, swimming facilities, a lake, long hiking trails in the woods, athletic fields galore, all without going anywhere near the outside world. At the center lay an impressive four-story dormitory with three hundred private rooms (a toilet between every two rooms was shared with a "chateau mate"), a beautiful, high-ceilinged refectory, a gymnasium, lovely cloisters, and a large "genuine imitation" Gothic chapel. From here manicured formal gardens ran down to the classroom building, the former

Crocker Mansion, one of the finest re-creations of an English country house in America.

My father loved to call Darlington God's West Point. The military analogy was not far off the mark. Nor would it be a stretch to call the regimen Spartan. A wake-up buzzer sounded in each room at five-thirty in the morning, and by six o'clock we were in chapel for an hour and twenty minutes of morning prayers, meditation, and Mass, after which we had to clean our rooms, have breakfast, and be down at the "Mansion" or class-room building by eight. There we had four hour-long classes, until noon, Monday through Saturday. After class came chapel, lunch, twenty minutes of free time, private study from one-thirty to three, and two hours of recreation, the first of which had to be spent outdoors. Then chapel, supper, twenty minutes of free time, study from seven to nine, and finally evening prayers in the chapel, followed by the "great silence," which was in effect until you sat down to breakfast the next day. This arduous schedule, along with an emphasis on sports, served, I think, to tire us out physically and mentally. Perhaps, as Will Durant thinks, the wearying routine was intended to combat the youthful sexual drive. I do know that we spent so much time kneeling in chapel that we could, on summer vacations at the Jersey shore beaches, spot seminarians by their calloused knees.

Among seminarians in other parts of the country, Darlington was known as The Rock because of its prison-like discipline and all-around conservatism. Everything about the place reflected the intensity of its focused mission, the making of us young men into obedient, order-following priests. A free-standing semi-nary, unlike those associated geographically and intellectually with a university or college, Darlington was sufficient unto it-self. It had, of course, its own library, limited almost entirely to Roman Catholic books, although there was a large "cage," where anything disapproved of—including the French *Catholic Encyclopedia*—was locked up and restricted to faculty use. A tiny bookstore was open twenty minutes each evening. Book orders had to be cleared by the director of students. My classmate

Eugene Kasper, who knew Polish and Russian, tried to order Khrushchev's famous speech denouncing Stalin. Kasper was called in:

Director: "Is it true you're trying to order a book by Khrushchev? Is this Nikita Khrushchev, the Russian?"

Kasper: "Of course it's that Khrushchev."

Director: "Out of the question. He's a communist."

We had an elaborate infirmary, tended by an elderly nun, Sister Alice Benedict, who gave you an injection of penicillin for whatever complaint you had. For colds she also dispensed elixir of turpenhydrate with codeine, which we loved. More serious or chronic ailments were treated during the weekly visits of a local doctor, "Johnny" Petrone from Suffern, New York. His word alone could have you sent out to a specialist or a hospital, and he believed all of us were hypochondriacs or malingerers. Darlington also had its own barber shop, where seminarians cut each other's hair. Frank Hurtz, the sole black seminarian, insisted that his hair could be cut only by his own barber; and, to everyone's surprise, every month he would get an overnight leave to Bayonne for a haircut. A quite marvelous scam, which we all envied and applauded.

Contact with the outside world was kept to a minimum. In the woods, and straying occasionally onto seminary land, there lived the so-called Jackson Whites, a small band of inbred forest-dwelling people, thought at the time to be descendants of Revolutionary War Hessian soldiers and escaped black slaves. We were forbidden to have anything to do with them. (Today they are called "Ramapo Mountain People" and are believed to be descendants of Dutch settlers and their mixed-race servants.) Mail from our families was permitted, but packages were opened first by the authorities. Italian boys, especially, had food packages from their mothers confiscated. Newspapers were interdicted. Even the lay Catholic magazine *Commonweal* was forbidden, for its supposedly liberal bias. There were four radios, one each to the recreation rooms located on the several floors of the dormitory building, where listening was restricted to our very limited free time. Moreover, while the radio was playing, the "senior man" present (highest in year and in the arbitrary numbered ranking of students within the years) was supposed to change the station if the music being played was "too sensuous." "Rags to Riches" by Tony Bennett achieved this prohibited status. As for television, it was to arrive in the rec rooms only in my sixth and last year, when we were able to watch the Huntley-Brinkley Report and to follow the progress of Fidel Castro's Cuban revolution.

Our lives were at every moment guided by "The Rule," a printed set of seventy-seven regulations that the authorities alluded to constantly. Any trespass of the thirty-seven "major" rules called for immediate dismissal. These included the consumption, even while on vacation, of any kind of alcohol; the possession in the seminary of secular newspapers or magazines; leaving the seminary grounds, however briefly; having any contact "beyond what is called for by necessity or by the demands of Christian courtesy" with the nuns who cooked our food or the lay employees who tended the buildings and grounds; using the one public telephone; receiving visitors; entering another seminarian's room (with permission and for an urgent reason, one might "visit" another seminarian by standing at his door conducting business). The breaking of lesser rules, like talking in the hallways, being late for chapel or class, or not keeping one's room tidy with the bed neatly made up and the *darker* side of the reversible bed spread showing, did not carry the draconian sanction of expulsion; but such offenses, if repeated, were considered "negative signs" of a vocation to the priesthood. Even genuflecting improperly, "a three point landing," steadying oneself with the hand if the right knee had not come down aligned with the left heel, was a negative sign. Moreover, these and similar infractions were supposed to be voluntarily "reported" by the offender to the director of students. The Rule Book closed on a ringing note: any seminarian proving to be "incorrigible, refractory, or seditious" would be summarily expelled. Jerry Graziano, two years behind me in the seminary, known as "The Gra," a big fellow who looked as if he could have been a bodyguard and who grew up knowing several mob family members, recalls, "You could be a serial killer up there as long as you didn't talk in the hallways."

I won't trouble to set down any chronological account of my six years at Darlington, except to say that with each passing year, most seminarians, myself included, became more and more relaxed and cynical about the seminary routine and its rules, and more and more disillusioned about our education, both as to content and the method whereby it was administered to us: nothing but lectures, no discussions, no papers to write—a blessing—but long written exams at the close of each semester. My best hope of conveying the flavor of our schooling may lie in recalling some of our professors in their various subjects. It was a byword that bishops assign their very best priests to seminaries for the important job of forming new priests. All of our teachers were decent, hard-working men, and if it weren't such a terrible thing to say of anyone I'd say that they meant well. Here's a partial *dramatis personae*. First, the philosophy teachers:

Father Joseph J. "Prez" Przezdziecki, Ph.D. from the Pontifical Institute of Medieval Studies at the University of Toronto, was a keen scholar and completely dedicated to his field. In fact, he had become a kind of learned medieval man, altogether caught up in the philosophical terminology of that age—quiddities, essences, substances, accidents, forms, hylomorphisms, Latin and Greek texts, all scrambled together and of intense interest to him. A good thirteenth-century Thomistic Catholic, he hewed to the Church line. He considered all philosophers except Aquinas and a few of his followers as little better than "damned fools," and his denunciation extended to Carlo Boyer, S.J., author of our Latin philosophy "manual" (all textbooks were in Latin). Boyer followed the disconcerting system of "proving" theses: a "Question," a "State of the Question," "Errors"—a list of just about every authority, great and small, on the subject— followed by a "Solution" of the question. But for Przezdziecki, "the fact that Father Boyer teaches at the Gregorium in Rome [the central seminary in the Vatican] doesn't mean anything. We are going to take him down a peg or two." Prez taught us to disregard simple explanations and to question printed texts. "Cross out footnote 14 on page 38," he would say. "That note is foul ball. There is no such book." On the other hand, he seemed unable to make any headway. His circuitous thinking, deep but disorganized, took him hither and thither. He had not the ability to drive toward some stated objective. Thoughts would bounce off thoughts, ideas would provoke other ideas which provoked others, all of them calling for distinctions. When years later I read Carlyle's description of Coleridge and his listeners, I thought of Prez and his pupils:

> To sit as a passive bucket and be pumped into, whether you consent or not, can in the long-run be exhilarating to no creature; how eloquent so ever the flood of utterance that is descending. But if it be withal a confused unintelligible flood of utterance, threatening to submerge all known landmarks of thought, and drown the world and you!—I have heard Coleridge talk . . . two stricken hours . . . and communicate no meaning whatsoever to any individual of his hearers,—certain of whom, I for one, still kept eagerly listening in hope; the most had long before given up. . . . He began anywhere . . . but instead of answering [some question], or decidedly setting out towards answer of it, he would accumulate formidable apparatus, logical swim-bladders, transcendental life-preservers and other precautionary and vehiculatory gear, for setting out; perhaps did at last get under way,—but was swiftly solicited, turned aside by the glance of some radiant new game on this hand or that, into new courses; and ever into new; and before long into all the Universe, where it was uncertain what game you would catch, or whether any.

This was very like Przezdziecki's *modus operandi*. (We were forever being subjected to short Latin tags.) In a yearlong, two-semester course in the history of philosophy Prez began by telling us, "There are two ways of teaching the history of philosophy: to cover all of the philosophers inadequately or a few of them well. I am going to follow the latter method." He barely got started on Plato in the fall term and on Descartes in the spring term. We never had any discussion from the floor, but once, while he was catching his breath, I, from my place among the Paterson men in the back of the room, put up my hand:

"Father, we hear today so much about existentialism—could you give us a one-paragraph summary of just what existentialism is?"

Przezdziecki: "You are trying to waste the class's time. The subject is too large to say anything worthwhile about it here."

Later that year he stopped me in the hall, as if by way of apology, to tell me he was giving a course in existentialism that summer. I, being from Paterson, would be "out" teaching summer school, but he wanted me to know, and so forth.

Przezdziecki was the subject of numerous anecdotes. I was present when my classmate Jerry Pindar showed him an anthology of philosophy he had picked up in New York on vacation. Prez leafed through it: "Hobbes!—he's on the *Index* [*of Forbidden Books*]! Locke!—he's on the *Index*! "Hume! he's on the *Index*! Kant!—he's on the *Index*! I am afraid I will have to confiscate this book." And he did.

One Monday morning he told the class how over the weekend he had come upon a road accident. Thinking that he might have to administer the last rites, he stopped his car and found a man unconscious and in what looked like critical condition: "I asked his wife if this man were a Catholic. She said, 'Yes, but he doesn't go to church anymore and perhaps he wouldn't want a priest.' And I told her, 'Perhaps he is going to *hell!*'"

His brusqueness existed side by side with a shrewd wariness. He was a great qualifier. Once, when I was waiting on the priests' table at breakfast, I asked if he would have rolls or toast.

"I think perhaps I might have toast," replied that cautious philosopher. For all Przezdziecki's brilliance, we would laugh at his
locution "Let him be Anathema sit." *Anathema sit,* or "Let him
be anathema," was the Church's official formula for condemn-
ing someone who held an erroneous theological or philosophical position. In his eagerness to pronounce the damning phrase,
Przezdziecki always transmuted it into "Let him be Let him be
anathema." I liked Prez very much. The thought of him, in his
later years, after he became pastor of a suburban parish, sitting
in the rectory office and filling out five dollar Mass intention
cards, still brings a smile to the face of anyone who knew him in
his philosophical ardors at Darlington.

Father John H. Koenig, called "The Champ" because he was a
good tennis player, was a gentle, simple soul, who always called
us "fellers," and who as a teacher of philosophy was just the opposite of Przezdziecki. God knows what Przezdziecki would
have thought of Koenig's classes. Koenig, who taught logic and
cosmology, would doggedly translate from Boyer's Latin, that
"lightweight" textbook which so annoyed Prez. Classical Greek
logic was helpful in making one look at one's reasoning. The
eight general rules of the syllogism—for example, that, among
the three terms, nothing can be proved from two negatives, or
from two particulars, or that two affirmatives cannot generate
a negative—were straightforward enough, although the square
of opposition and the laws governing "logical figures" could be
involved and difficult. Still, the whole business seemed to make
good sense. It was, in a word, logical. But cosmology, in the parlance of the day, turned out to be another kettle of fish altogether. Here the view of the physical universe from 400 B.C. seemed
ridiculous. One of my classmates, the same Eugene Kasper who
tried to order the Khrushchev speech, would from time to time
ask Koenig a question from the floor and invariably draw the
same reply: "Eugene, if you'll be patient, you'll see that your
author has anticipated your question, and we will come to it in
due course in the text."

The Champ would seldom depart from translating the text, except occasionally to sum up, as when he reviewed the microcosm and the macrocosm: "So there you have it, fellers. The microcosm is the little things, like bacteria that you can see under the microscopes, down at Seton Hall. The macrocosm, that's the big things like the stars that you see through the telescope out at Mount Palomar, in California."

I remember his saying, after a paragraph from Boyer, "There you have it, fellers, the quantum theory." He also explained to us that there had to be ether (this was 1954, ether having been dismissed by science for about fifty years) because otherwise you would have *actio in distans*, a philosophical impossibility: "There has to be some medium between us and the stars, and that's ether." Following Boyer, Koenig spent a lot of time on "prime matter" and "substantial form," and he would sometimes address a question, naming always a particular student:

> Koenig: "Michael, can you give me an example of substantial form, of an *unum per se*?"
> Michael: "No, Father."
> Koenig: "Well, you see, Michael, it's a unity in itself, like a tulip, or a lump of coal."

Boyer, no help needed from Koenig, demolished human evolution, disproving it right there on the page in impeccable Church Latin. I can still translate him:

> The soul is either generated from itself or created by God.
> But the soul cannot be generated through itself or corporal transmission (as happens in brute animals), for from a potentiality with intrinsic dependence on material, nothing spiritual can be generated.
> Therefore, the soul of a man is created by God.

Countless doctrines and positions were labeled *de fide definita*, which meant that you had to hold this view, or you were a heretic and outside the one true Church. Thus, we had to believe, *de fide*, that each individual soul was a special creation of God—even when that creation accompanied an act of rape. Believing in this separate act of creation for every human who ever lived troubled me as much as, say, everlasting hell or guardian angels or indulgences, the last still very much in vogue back then.

Boyer went on to prove that even among animals evolution of different species "properly understood" is impossible. This last, happily enough, did not fall into the *de fide* category because it had nothing to do with religious belief "per se," and so I had no mental wrestling to do on that point. We were not primitive fundamentalists or Biblical literalists. We were—Boyer notwithstanding—perfectly free, for example, to believe in evolution as long as we held that God had devised the whole business, got it started, guided it to its summit in man, and thereafter created a separate immortal soul in each human being. Darwin would not have recognized this as evolution, but you can't have everything. One could sense too that not just Prez and Koenig, but all Catholic authors were just a little bit afraid of animals in this connection. There had to be preserved a clear difference, a real distance between the "brute" animals and ourselves with our "souls" individually created by God. Twentieth-century science seemed to be demolishing this distance, and Catholic thought had to keep retreating. For a while, for example, Catholic theologians held to the belief that only man could make and use tools, until it was shown that insects and animals, from ants to monkeys, make and use tools, and then the theologians had to backpedal—first into language, and then into abstract language, as distancing man from beast.

The attempt to allow for science while keeping at least half of one's mind in Thomistic medievalism would later on, in 1959, account for the amazing popularity among Catholic intellectuals of Pierre Teilhard de Chardin's *The Phenomenon of Man*. Teilhard de Chardin was a scientist, an accomplished and respected paleontologist (I think Stephen Jay Gould wrong in believing that the young Teilhard was an accomplice in the celebrated Piltdown Man hoax, the phony "human" skull that fooled experts for nearly forty years). But Teilhard was also a Jesuit priest, silenced by the Church, his works published only after his death. And in this book he set forth a synthesis of reportedly scientific cosmology, evolutionary biology, and Christianity. However unacceptable his ideas are to theologians and scientists today, when they sound like New Age gibberish, with their evolving "Noosphere" and "Omega Point" culminating in Christ, Teilhard de Chardin became a cult figure among progressive Catholics in the early sixties.

Catholicism had long surrounded itself with intellectual pursuits, like the study of the Greek and Latin classics; but in regard to theology, it was an intellectualism fettered to the Middle Ages and Thomas Aquinas, himself beholden to ancient Greek science and metaphysics. From my courses in philosophy the most useful thing I can recall had to do with medieval "psychology." Our professors, who didn't like talk about the brain, which smacked too much of philosophical materialism and science, believed that ideas came via the senses into our souls or *animae*, and made "impressions" thereon. The metaphor for this process has stayed with me fifty years. Minds were like wax or marble in their capacities to receive impressions and to retain them. There were four possible permutations: Some minds learned quickly but forgot quickly—they were "wax to impress and wax to retain," and I counted myself in this category. Others learned slowly but retained well—marble and marble. The brilliant mind was wax to impress and marble to retain. The saddest combination was of course the slow mind, "marble to impress and wax to retain."

My great problem in these early seminary years was the suspicion that William of Occam had it right. Occam was always listed under "adversarii" or "errores" in that he denied the existence of "universals," or "essences" as required by our mixture of Platonism, Aristotelianism, and Thomism. For Occam no such thing as "horseness" existed, only individual horses. I know this can be complicated stuff, and I have neither the inclination nor the patience to review the whole matter, but I do remember clearly that "our" Catholic position was tied to the ancient "hylomorphism" doctrine that corporeal things like bread and wine were made up of "prime matter" and "substantial form" or, from a different angle, substance and accident, and that we had to believe against the Occamite nominalists—almost everyone today is a nominalist if he or she gives it any thought—that there was in bread a "breadness," a substantial and real form or entity "informing" the prime matter. I had what I thought was the bright idea that the prime matter of the ancient Greeks might be the hydrogen atom, number one in the Periodic Table of Elements, and inquired privately about this to Przezdziecki, who dismissed it as nonsense. But "substance" especially troubled me because this notion was used to explain the Eucharist. It was *de fide* that in the Eucharist the substances of bread and wine were changed into the substances of the body and blood of Christ while the "accidents" of bread and wine—size, weight, texture, color, odor—remained those of bread and wine. I told myself that I could believe, or try to believe, in Christ's presence in the Eucharist, but I couldn't believe in transubstantiation because I didn't and couldn't believe in substance, the reality of "breadness" or "wineness." It also sounded to me a tad like DuPont's popular slogan of the day, "Better things for better living, through chemistry." I was a secret nominalist, an Occamite. I was calling down on myself, had I spoken my thoughts out loud, the words "Let him be Anathema sit."

Father John F. O'Brien taught courses in education and catechetics—how to teach religion. It was in his class that I scored my only triumph from the floor during my six-year career at Darlington. As it happened, O'Brien also served as the seminary liaison with Seton Hall. Our first two years at Darlington formed our junior and senior Seton Hall years, an arrangement that entitled us to receive college degrees. In May 1955, just before we were to graduate, O'Brien told us that there was some question as to whether our college degree would be in classical languages or in education. He added, "I don't see that it matters, really." Almost involuntarily, my hand shot up: "It might be nice to know, Father, in case somebody asked." Everyone laughed, including O'Brien.

After two years as "philosophers" we became "theologians" for four years. Our theology classes were more catechism than intellectual inquiries, because one had to believe whatever was taught. Past mistakes were explained away, usually by the introduction of clever distinctions. Over many centuries it had been undisputed Catholic dogma, for example, that there was no salvation outside the Roman Catholic Church: *Extra ecclesiam nulla salus.* But now the time had come to admit baptized Protestants to salvation and to elaborate on the invention of "limbo" for good nonbelievers, provided it was *no fault of theirs* that they remained in "invincible ignorance." One of my heroes at the time, Monsignor Ronald Knox, the English convert to Catholicism and Oxford chaplain, wrote in his half-joking manner that there were no Protestant children, that children baptized in Protestant ceremonies were in fact Catholics until they reached the age of reason and began to practice Protestantism. The special difficulty I had in "dogmatic theology" was believing that all these *de fide* doctrines were revealed to the Apostles. Things like the bodily Assumption of Mary into heaven were pretty unbelievable in themselves; but we had also to hold that such beliefs, although no record of them existed for hundreds of years, had been carried forward from Apostolic times through the centuries by an "unbroken, oral tradition" until eventually being written down. We lived firmly locked in what Monsignor John Tracy Ellis, a contemporary church historian, called "the American Catholic intellectual ghetto."

Our dogma courses were taught by Fathers William F. Hogan and George W. Shea, both of them dry, bored-looking, serious men. They were intensely conservative and dull. It was said of Bill Hogan that he was so strict and funereal because a number of his classmates had left the priesthood. In those days for a priest "to leave" was altogether horrific, a disaster worse than had he died early or turned murderer. We were taught that ordination changed a man "ontologically"—in his very being—and forever, while conferring on him irrevocable supernatural powers. As Hogan explained, the presence of an ex-priest in society made for potential sacrilege of enormous proportions. How, for example, would the Church cope with the situation created by a renegade priest who went about converting whole bakeries of bread into the body of Christ? This aside, neither Hogan nor Shea said anything memorable in my four years of theology. It was reported of Shea, however, that he attended a civic dinner and sat next to a minister with a beautiful wife and remarked to the man, "All this and heaven too."

Father John J. Dougherty, later a bishop and the president of Seton Hall, taught Scripture and relished his nickname, "The Prophet." Dougherty was a dark, handsome, stocky man who cultivated a deep mellifluous voice and frequently prefaced his sentences with a thoughtful and drawn out "Yaah," often with a hand to the forehead. He would say with innocent candor things like "Yaah, if I were three inches taller I'd be the perfect man." When shocked into immediate speech he would cry out, "Oh my *God*." Some of us saw Dougherty as a ray of light up there in the Ramapo Hills, for he encouraged seminarians to visit New York on vacations: "Yaah, I love that New York thing." He let a handful of us run an "Art Program," which during free time offered discussions of medieval religious painting, cathedrals, chalice design, and artists like Salvador Dali and Georges Rouault. Dougherty once invited jazz critic Barry Ulanov to address the Art Program, and introduced him with the words, "Tell these guys something about culture, Barry." He hadn't meant it to sound quite that condescending, but that's what he said.

Still, whatever his quirks, Dougherty represented a worldly and sophisticated side of Catholicism and the priesthood that many of us—given our cultural and intellectual deprivation

—deeply appreciated. There were those who claimed that as a scholar he was a faker. Others said that at one time he knew his Scripture, while working on his graduate degree about the Yahweh writer in Genesis, an approach he picked up from nineteenth-century Protestant scholars and adapted to Catholicism, but that, sadly, by the time he got to us he paraded a merely theatrical and surface learning. When he taught us Scripture in the first year, for example, he lugged into class a giant Bible and held it out before us saying that in the first term, Introduction to Scripture, we would talk *about* the book, whereupon he smacked it smartly; thereafter, he went on, we would in the next term *open* the book, which he did, slowly and dramatically. He appeared occasionally on TV, and we considered him the poor man's Bishop Sheen (whose "Life Is Worth Living" programs were all the rage among Catholics in the 1950s). Sometimes Dougherty gave retreats to movie stars: "Nice work if you can get it, eh?" he told us. The Prophet believed that he lived a charmed life—no credit of his, he would modestly insist—as, for instance, when in 1956 he was forced against his will, not being a great sports fan, to accompany a friend to a World Series game at Yankee Stadium, the one in which Don Larsen just happened to pitch the only perfect game ever thrown in a World Series. "Yaah," he acknowledged, "these kinds of things just keep happening to me."

His charmed life during the years I knew him had one sad public moment: while thinking of himself as a priest and Scripture scholar who was at the same time a knowing a man of the world, he wrote a review of Edmund Wilson's book on the Dead Sea Scrolls, in which he accused the eminent Wilson of catering "to the circle of those who can read but not evaluate." Dougherty charged Wilson with taking up the thesis of one scholar, André Dupont-Summer—an ex-priest, though the Prophet, in the interest of fair play, did not call attention to this—and "dressing it up in exciting diction." Dupont-Summer had held that the non-biblical texts among the Dead Sea Scrolls, discovered in 1948, those belonging to the sect of Jews called Essenes, proved that these Essenes were the precursors of Christianity and Jesus little more than an Essene who got into trouble. Dougherty's article was published in the obscure Jesuit weekly *America*, read by a handful of devoted Catholics. Wilson replied with a scathing diatribe in *The New Yorker*, sarcastically referring to Dougherty as someone who wrote for people who did understand what they read while the rest of the world had to be content with reading without guidance from the all-knowing parish priest or whatever Dougherty was. I felt terrible for Dougherty. Here was *The New Yorker*, an aspect of New York that he much admired and which he had dared to recommend to us, turning on him. Moreover, he was right. Dupont-Summer himself changed his mind, and fifty years of subsequent Dead Sea Scroll scholarship has come down collectively on Dougherty's side with regard to the originality of Jesus.

Dougherty's classes were for the most part flat and humdrum. I think he himself realized this, and he sometimes lightened up the study of Scripture by showing slides of his visits to the Holy Land and its deserts. "Yaah, that's I on the camel" he once explained, to the delight of the class. On another occasion, demonstrating how Bedouin people cover themselves, he threw his cassock up over his head, whereupon one of his hearers told him, "Father, your fly is open," prompting a quick "Oh my *God!*" Still another bad moment came when he invited Seton Hall's coarse athletic director, Father Jim Carey, who had been a chaplain in North Africa and Palestine, to address his scripture class. The purport of Carey's talk was as follows:

Carey: "The Holy Land is a pretty dirty place. You could slide all the way from Calvary to the Holy Sepulcher in camel shit."

Dougherty [sotto voce]: "Oh my *God!* Never again."

Father John J. "Jolly Jack" Cassels was a good-natured, optimistic man, who had so many students choose him as confessor that he had to set up a small electric marquee on the door of his room posting the hours he was hearing confessions each week. An amateur psychologist, he found plenty of clients to practice on among the seminarians, and he helped many of them through the six years. Long lines of "Cassels' boys" waited for their turn. It was said that he was a disappointed bishop. He did enjoy hobnobbing with judges and politicians, and once said to us, "You've heard of labor priests? I'm a management priest," this because he was chaplain to executives of the oil refining business. Cassels also had the unenviable position of teaching us homiletics—called "home electrics" of course—while suffering from the disability of being himself a terrible preacher, his performances made worse by a post nasal drip that made him continuously clear his throat with a strange "hrrumph" sound whenever he spoke. The Rector also assigned Cassels to teach the English novel and English drama, subjects in which he had no background. Even we realized that some of his statements were naive, such as "The thing about Jane Austen is her style of writing." At least he was more broad-minded in his tastes than his counterpart down at Seton Hall, who gave a course in The American Novel, which required the reading of seven novels, two of which were by Cardinal Spellman. Outside class Cassels asked my classmate Jerry Pindar, whom he knew to be a great reader, what he had read during the Christmas vacation:

Pindar: "Well, I've read *Oedipus Rex*, for one."

Cassels: "Hrrumph. Oedipus who?"

Pindar: "Oedipus Rex. You know, the play about the baby who grows up to kill his father and marry his mother."

Cassels: "Hrrumph. Doesn't sound like the kind of thing a seminarian should be reading."

Jolly Jack did me one real service. He stopped me in the hall and out of nowhere told me that I should not go around Darlington "apologizing for my existence." He suggested I come and see him sometime. I agreed, but never went to see him. However, his short, shocking advice alerted me to the fact that I was not overcoming or even disguising as well as I thought I was the timidity that had followed upon my scruples and breakdown. I would have thought that my past didn't show. After all, I was no longer scrupulous, I had recovered my mental balance, I was not overserious or bent on perfection. My friends suspected nothing. But evidently the effects of my past problems could be spotted by someone attentive and sensitive to such things. And of course I was still struggling with religious doubt. And so I determined, quietly and on my own, to throw myself more than ever into the effort to brush aside and to suppress and stifle worries about faith. I entered all the more wholeheartedly into activities that would keep me distracted from that worry—sports, reading, intellectual pursuits, music, friendships. With each year in the seminary I think I became less vexed by my doubts, less attentive to them, less inward looking. Jolly Jack with those few words probably helped me as much as he did those who came to him weekly for advice.

Moral Theology was taught by Father Aloysius J. "Uncle Al" Welsh. Al had a subtle mind and a quick tongue. "What are we holding this year on the Witch of Endor?" was his jibe at the Scripture scholars. Welsh was the only faculty member who made any reference, during my six years at Darlington, to social justice or civil rights. He was an advocate of black people and of a "living wage" for working people. His specialty, moral theology—what was sinful or not in human behavior—was less cut and dried than dogmatic theology, being replete with varying opinions held by recognized theologians. A huge issue hovered above the field: Could one, in moral questions, in good conscience follow a merely "probable" or minority theological opinion favoring liberty of action, or was one bound to follow the stricter, majority opinion as held among theologians? The schools of thought on this controversy numbered as many as seven, but they can be reduced nicely to three:

1. Tutiorism—one had always to follow the "more safe" or "most probable" opinion.
2. Probabiliorism—one had always to follow the "more probable" opinion.

3. Probabilism—one could follow any well-founded opinion, even though the contrary opinion was "more probable" and more widely held.

Naturally, all of us students were probabilists, for there was a probable opinion that it was permissible to be a probabilist. Al accepted this grudgingly. He himself was an "aequiprobabilist"—that is, one could follow the opinion favoring liberty of action only if it were "as probable as" its opposite.

It's easy to laugh at the thousands of distinctions our Latin moral textbooks made, but they were not all mere logic chopping. A case in point, and invariably a question asked on examinations, concerned the "two-fold" or double effect, a refinement of the generally held principle that in morals the end does not justify the means. But according to the doctrine of the two-fold effect, an action was morally correct if it resulted in two effects, one good and one bad, provided four conditions were met:

1. The action must in itself be good or at least morally indifferent.
2. The good effect must be intended, the evil effect only tolerated.
3. The good effect must follow from the action at least as directly as the evil effect.
4. There must be a sufficient or proportionate reason to allow the evil effect.

Thus, three men are on an ocean raft that will only stay afloat with two. Can one man deliberately jump into the water and meet his certain death? Yes: jumping into water is not evil in itself as would be the case if he put a gun to his head; he intends to save the others, not commit suicide; the good effect flows at least as causally from the act as does the evil; and two men are saved, a more than sufficient reason for the loss of one. Not all the examples had this fairy tale ring to them. For instance, everyone knows the Church's stand against abortion, based on the principle, with which nearly everybody agrees, that the end does not justify the means, and on the premise, with which most people disagree, that from the moment of conception the embryo is a human being into which God has breathed an immortal soul. Nevertheless, Catholic teaching held that certain ectopic or tubal pregnancies might be cut away. If the fetus attached itself to the fallopian tube and not to the womb and therefore endangered the mother's life, that section of the tube might be excised by surgery, provided all four conditions for the two-fold effect were realized. And indeed, the four conditions can be met. The doctrine of the two-fold effect, often maligned as all-too-subtle and "Jesuitical" casuistry, is in reality a rational and sensible approach to some complicated moral issues.

In four years of moral theology with Al Welsh we covered a lot of sins. Morality could be examined by way of the Ten Commandments, the Seven Capital Sins, the Church's prohibitions as set forth in Canon Law, or in connection with the Sacraments. We analyzed minute circumstances and were fed endless distinctions. For example, participation in or cooperation with non-Catholic worship came under the "strange gods" clause of the First Commandment. Such participation could be active or passive, proximate or remote. Might a priest who is refurnishing his church *give* his old pews to a Protestant church? No. But if he knew that a Protestant church congregation were buying old pews, he might, provided he received a fair price, *sell* his pews to them because his cooperation could be construed as more passive or indirect—they would get pews in any event—and the money from the sale would support the one true Church. But complicity in "illicit," that is, Protestant, religious activity drew close scrutiny: "Sisters in a hospital may not summon a non-Catholic minister for a dying person"; but if he were summoned by someone else, "It seems lawful for them to prepare a little table for his use in religious ministrations." (All quotations here are from Heribert Jone, *Moral Theology*, a work that became an indispensable aide of seminarians and priests in the years following its publication in English in 1955.)

Attendance at Sunday Mass fell under the Third Commandment. One had to attend the whole ceremony. It is a venial sin to miss an unimportant part of the Mass, for example, from the beginning to the gospel reading, but it is a mortal sin if you miss the consecration or if you "sleep soundly" through the entire Mass. If you are standing outside the church sixty feet from the door "even if you can hear the priest on a radio," you have not satisfied the obligation, although if you are part of a crowd—however large—attending Mass, you are "morally present" provided the crowd is unbroken up to and into the church and you do your best to follow the action. Sunday observance forbade all "servile" work, including the washing of clothes. But what if one used an electric washing machine? I cannot recall the answer.

The Seventh and Tenth Commandments embraced "Justice and Rights." Is a man who sets out to burn down his enemy's house, but by mistake burns down the wrong house, obliged to make restitution? Probable opinion, no. How much need you steal from a person to constitute a mortal sin? A day's wage? A week's wage? It depended on the wealth of the victim. A well-to-do person would not be seriously injured by the theft of a day's wage, whereas the same theft would gravely injure a poor person. One could not, however, rob a very rich man of a large amount of money without sinning mortally, for there was an "absolute" sum—usually put at a week's earnings of the average working man—the stealing of which constituted always a grave or mortal sin, regardless of the wealth of the victim.

The Eighth Commandment, which forbids lying, involved also mental reservations. These latter were divided into strict mental reservations, always forbidden, such as "I didn't steal it," while adding mentally "with my left hand," and broad mental reservations, allowable under certain circumstances and for a good reason, such as "I have no money," while adding mentally "for a loan."

An example of moral theology as pertaining to Church precepts was the prohibition against improper reading. At the top of the list came books specifically named on the *Index of*

Prohibited Books, which condemned the works of most philoso-
phers since the Renaissance, including (just a sampling) Bacon,
Hobbes, Locke, Hume, Kant, Descartes, and Spinoza, down to
Bergson, Croce, and Sartre; histories by non-Catholics, like
those of Gibbon and Goldsmith; the novels of Stendhal, Balzac,
Dumas *père* and *fils*, Flaubert, Sand, Sue, Hugo, Zola (to name
only some nineteenth-century French novelists). Montaigne's
Essais made the list as did all non-Catholic translations of the
Bible. The reading of books on the *Index* carried an excommunication. But the prohibition extended beyond named works to
all "obscene" books and those that in any way attack religion or
the Catholic Church, and books by non-Catholics that treat of
religion in any way. To read such books was ordinarily a mortal
sin, but here theologians such as Jone offer guidelines: If the
danger of "contamination" were remote, one could get by with
reading thirty pages and commit only a venial sin, but if the
book were very heretical or very obscene "even half a page may
be sufficient to constitute a mortal sin. . . . *To retain* forbidden
books is a mortal sin if one keeps them for more than a month.
It is not sinful to keep such a book for a short time because one
intends to surrender it to the authorities."

   In connection with the Sacraments, a priest might sin, for example, by distributing Communion while not wearing priestly
garb; by failing to have two beeswax candles lighted on the altar
during Communion; by breaking the Host (the small, round
wafer of consecrated bread) into more than three parts if the
number of Hosts proved insufficient for the number of com-
municants; by neglecting the sanctuary lamp, which had always
to be kept burning and fed from olive oil or beeswax; or by not
"renewing the species"—the eucharistic Hosts kept in the tabernacle—at least every four to six weeks. In this last matter
Pindar consulted the leading moral theologian in the country,
Father Frank Connell at Catholic University in Washington,
D.C., and proposed the case where the tabernacle was equipped
as a freezer such as would keep food fresh longer. Connell took
the question in earnest and told Pindar that in his opinion the

Hosts could be kept a good deal longer under such conditions. Meanwhile, we explored every possible circumstance—what to do if the Host were vomited or, worse still, were to fall into a woman's clothing? She was to extract the Host herself and hand it to the priest, who would re-administer it to her.

As might be expected, the commandment that received the most attention was the Sixth (in the Catholic numbering), Thou Shalt Not Commit Adultery, and, among the Sacraments, matrimony. We seminarians were all to become marriage counselors, in spite of our ignorance: "The doctor," it was explained to us, "doesn't have to have cancer to treat it." In matters of sex Al Welsh was a tutiorist—one had always to follow the strictest interpretation. He held it was *"at least* a venial sin" to read the *Daily News* three days running, because one was putting oneself in an occasion of sin on account of the girlie pictures featured on that paper's third page. His argument was undercut when it was learned that the newly appointed spiritual director of the seminary, old Monsignor George "Wee Bonnie" Baker, had the *Daily News* delivered to his room every day. But Welsh, in spite of this apparent setback, stuck to his guns. How, for example, might a married man collect his sperm so as to have it tested for fertility? Masturbation was out of the question, as was the use of a condom. The man and his wife should, under the auspices of a doctor, be supplied with a room near the laboratory, where they would have sex using a *perforated* condom, which, it was to be hoped, would catch enough of the sperm for medical evaluation, while still allowing the act of sex its "natural" purpose of depositing sperm into the vagina, for possible "procreation."

Adultery, we learned, came in two varieties: "imperfect" adultery if the third party were single, and "perfect" adultery if the third party were also married. The sin of adultery was twofold, a sin of impurity, but also a sin against justice, that is, against the rights of the injured spouse. We examined every possibility of sexual sin. If one committed fornication with a partner engaged to someone else, need this additional factor be mentioned in confession? Probable opinion, no. The bias in moral theology was decidedly male. For example, under *Rape* we read that this is a sin against chastity but also against justice; furthermore:

> A double injury is committed in ravishing a virgin, an unjust violation of her rights and the additional injustice of deflowering her of the precious possession of physical integrity. . . . To avoid sinning, a woman who is being ravished must offer internal and external resistance. She need not cry out when this cannot be done without danger to her life or reputation, unless she would otherwise consent to the sin. Rape is not so common.

As for sodomy, that also came in the perfect and imperfect varieties, perfect being between two men, imperfect being rectal intercourse between a man and a woman. It was a relief to learn that bestiality (regardless of the animal involved) is "the *worst* of all the sins of impurity."

The key to the Church's teaching in regard to sex was that sins of impurity—taking pleasure in illicit sexual activity, whether physical or mental—admitted no "parvity," no smallness, of matter. They were *per se* mortally sinful. A sexual sin could be venial only in the case of an action that constituted only a slight "occasion of sin," like reading the *Daily News* if it presented but a slender likelihood of sinning. Here are some excerpts from Jone:

> It is seriously sinful to touch the indecent parts of others (even over the clothing) without a reason, regardless of sex. Such touches are venially sinful only when done without an evil intention and in a hasty or casual manner or out of levity or in jest. Touching the less decent parts of a person of the same sex is generally a venial sin at most, whereas it is usually a grave sin in the case of the opposite sex. Even then there would be only a venial sin if it were done in a very perfunctory manner out of levity or jokingly.
>
> It is venially sinful out of curiosity to observe animals mating if no sexual pleasure is caused.

In itself it is not lawful to use women and girls as models with only the genital organs covered. But if young artists in their training are compelled to attend art academies they do not sin by sketching such models. They must, however, not consent to any commotion that may arise and they must try to render the danger remote by prayer and renewal of their good intention. If women and girls have no other means to keep them from grave need they may serve as models, provided they employ the necessary precautionary measures.

To consider attentively and for a length of time nude pictures and works of art, giving special attention to the genitals, may easily become a serious sin, especially if they are modern works that are made to arouse sensuality.

It was good to have that cleared up, especially in a seminary where the authorities doctored library art books by covering the "indecent" parts of nudes with white paint—"diapers" we called these safeguards.

The trickiest area was mental sins of impure thoughts or desires, mortally sinful always if one "took pleasure" in the thought or desire. An interesting subdivision here is that of *delectatio morosa*, "morose delectation," defined as "the deliberate complacency in a sinful object presented to the imagination." The forbidden character of morose delectation remains even though the object will later become lawful or if it was formerly lawful: "Engaged persons, therefore, may not imagine their future marital relationships as present and take pleasure therein, even though they do so only mentally. The same may be said of the widowed concerning past marital relations."

Sex, obliquely referred to as "De sexto" ("Concerning the sixth"), was the central concern of much of what we were taught and, almost perforce, so much of what we thought about. That ours was such a womanless world added to the tension. The Rector, in a mysterious lapse, once hired a young woman secretary in the ground floor office of the Mansion. She stayed only a few months, and I forget her name, but I recall various seminarians finding some excuse to visit the office, merely to have a look at a woman. We were, most of us, total innocents, though sometimes the remarks of older seminarians, men who had served in the war, for example, betrayed a more knowing state of mind. Roy Aycock, a fifth-year man during my first year, a war veteran and Southerner from New Orleans, made a remark that has stayed with me for five decades. On Rogation Days, praying for good crops, we had to walk around outside early in the morning before Mass chanting the Litany of the Saints, one of the entries being *A spiritu fornicationis, libera nos Domine,* "From the spirit of fornication, deliver us, Oh Lord." Aycock's comment: "At five-thirty in the morning?" I will end this quick summary by recalling that in our Latin moral theology manual, the work of a man named Noldin, who died in an insane asylum, if you looked up the word *Mulier,* "Woman," in the index, you found the entry *Vide peccatum,* "See under sin."

I have saved for last Father John M. Mahon, Director of Students, or the seminary disciplinarian, the one human whom I have truly hated. Perhaps that may sound timid of me—there should have been more than one. In fact, there would be another eminently despicable person in my life, Father John Hewetson, later my boss for one year; but as he was certifiably insane, pity crept in on my part, though admittedly not very far. Of him, more later. But John Mahon had no such excuse. As Director of Students, his whole purpose consisted in sniffing out infractions of the Rule, issuing dire warnings of expulsion, and grudgingly dispensing permissions. It was said of him that years earlier, as a seminarian, he had never once broken the Rule, but if this were true he would have been an outright loony, which he was not. In any case, I despised the man with a deep, one might say even religious, malice. He saw to it that his beloved Rule formed the basis of seminary life. The Rule came before everything else. Mahon loved to quote that glorious triad of adjectives, the warning that any *incorrigible, refractory,* or *seditious* seminarian would be dismissed. He earned the name "Nagasaki Jackie," for his having announced that the perpetrator of some Rule infraction would be absolved were he to come forward and confess his guilt. The person did so, whereupon Mahon kicked him out of the seminary, or so at least the story went. We used to say, in language that would be inexcusable today, things like "Mahon Japped me." We were remembering Pearl Harbor. Then, too, Mahon had thick, round glasses, which gave savor to the nickname. He relied on informers. One of the rules required that seminarians report serious infractions by others to the Director of Students, and Mahon would smugly declare to us that "good students come and tell me things."

Even more than his petty enforcing of the Rule, his refusal to grant permissions and exceptions enraged us. A fellow seminarian in my time, Jack Catoir, had, and still has, a serious eye condition, and he was instructed by his doctor to read only by a strong light. Mahon refused to allow him to have more than the regulation forty-watt bulb in his desk lamp. Catoir, conscientious to a fault, rigged up a reflector so that he could read by the dim light. On another occasion I was one of a group of five Paterson men let out for a day to run a "Vocation Rally" in Franklin. It happened that, because of delays at the church, none of our making, we came away so late that we felt justified in stopping for dinner (at a place on Route 23 called Jurgensen's Inn, where we didn't have enough money to pay the bill and the owner graciously picked up the rest of the tab). We arrived back at the seminary just after night prayers, but our "senior man," Dick Rento, was nearly expelled. Mahon had Rento into his office three days running, and only when it looked like the dispute might go all the way to the bishop of Paterson did Mahon relent. As Rento reminded me recently, he, Rento, was twenty-eight at the time, he had telephoned ahead and left a message of the problem, and we had had no alcohol. We just got back late.

At times, while we were down at the classroom building, Mahon would conduct surprise inspections of our dormitory rooms, looking for seditious material, anything from secular reading to food. On one occasion he carried out a raid on the "magna aula" or great hall (the former ballroom of the mansion), where the large combined two-year "cycle" classes were taught. He ordered us out of the room and conducted a search of the books left behind. One of books seized was Graham Greene's *The End of the Affair*, condemned as "obscene" and prompting Monsignor Baker, the elderly spiritual director, to announce during his weekly homily, "If anyone has a book like that they should depart this place tonight. The demons of hell are under our roof." Greene even then was considered, along with Evelyn Waugh, one of the two foremost Catholic novelists of the century.

In a development I almost can't believe, Mahon later deserted the priesthood, left from the Newark Chancery Office where he had held some position after his years at the seminary. Actually, if we are to believe the story, he went off with a woman. This last I find even harder to credit, but, as we had drummed into us on countless occasions, *Contra factum non valet ullum argumentum*—against the fact no argument is valid. Various priests and former priests have told me that Mahon became the warden of a prison in upstate New York. One version of the story had him a prison *guard*. Alas, Ed Ciuba, the classmate of mine who eventually became the progressive rector of Darlington, tells me that, howsoever appropriate the rumors, Mahon did not work for a prison but for some office at the University of Syracuse. I do wonder what he did there.

Why did I hate him so? He was caught up in the system. He bought the boloney, so to say. He was just following orders. And the orders came from a formidable tyrant, the rector, Monsignor Joseph M. Brady, called "Paw Paw" because he seemed to begin every sentence with these words. Brady, a stiff, cruel, self-important man, must have made the lives of his underlings painful. Mahon, an ordinary man, not particularly talented but harmless enough, had been placed in a position that required tact beyond the reach of most men and worlds away from his own poor abilities. It is a sad story. My friend Jim Tierney tells me that Mahon had been a likable priest at St. James Church, Springfield, Jim's home parish, before being tapped for the position of Director of Students at Darlington. The Rule and Paw Paw did him in. Still, I detested Mahon. He made our lives miserable for so many years, and though it was all long ago, I cannot "forgive" him.

That's enough about the faculty. As for us students, we dealt with the place in different ways, as I suppose happens with inmates in prison. Some few pious and conscientious types adhered to the Rule and studied hard at all times. They also did extra prayers. The 1950s were the zenith of what is now viewed by many Catholics as a time of embarrassingly intense "Marian" devotion, and one group of seminarians, members of the de Monfort Society, calling themselves "The Slaves of Mary," could be seen praying during recreation in front of an outdoor shrine. As Bob Call put it, "These guys are praying on their own time." Most of us went mechanically through the prayer routines, put in a modicum of study, and found other outlets. The gay seminarians, known in those times as "flits," spent their free time in the outdoor "Grove" or in the rec rooms gossiping and smoking. (Nearly everyone in the place smoked except the best athletes, the extremely religious, and, perhaps not surprisingly, myself.) The "jocks" comprised another clique and gave over every free moment to playing or talking sports. Others took to hiking, or playing music, or working in the book bindery. Bob Call made himself into an expert bird watcher and good billiards player. I played some sports, but always in the "B League," for the less accomplished players. Whenever possible I gave myself over to enthusiastic but haphazard reading. During my last two years I was supplied with paperback books by an easygoing priest, Donald Zimmermann, who came from the chancery to teach Canon Law. He ignored many of the strictures of the place, and, in a little intrigue that could have had him fired by Brady, ordered books for me in his own name, for which I would reimburse him.

Reading alone, however, could not have kept me going for six years. Friendship and camaraderie did that. One had roughly fifty classmates, three hundred fellow students in all, most of them decent, intelligent young men, some "religious," others not, but almost all of them filled with good will. From this three hundred one naturally made a handful of close friends—although "particular friendships" ("pf's") were expressly forbidden. The word "homosexuality" was avoided as if too ghastly to be mentioned, but that was what the authorities feared. The worry was not so much about outright sexual acts as about dangerously exclusive and ardent friendships between two seminarians. In my estimation, during the 1950s at Darlington the number of gays, whether given to "particular friendships" or not, added up to something between twenty and twenty-five percent of the student body. Every one of these seminarians was of course "closeted"—he had to be. I suspect that even among themselves, talking and smoking in the Grove, they never mentioned homosexuality. It was something be to blocked out.

(I am told that today in some seminaries, called "pink palaces," the majority of students are homosexual. There is no reason why a homosexual man cannot be as celibate as his heterosexual counterpart. Indeed, it has been argued that homosexual men are better suited to the celibate life than heterosexuals. But in November 2005 the Vatican officially banned homosexuals from ordination to the priesthood—the joke has already become old about the Pope announcing to a large group of priests that homosexuals cannot be priests and having to add quickly, "I meant from now on." The ban follows the Vatican's recently launched "Apostolic Visitation" or investigation into homosexuality in American seminaries, with the avowed purpose of weeding out homosexual seminarians and priest faculty members who support them. Both moves can be interpreted as a late and faulty response to the child abuse scandals, which, the Church is implying, are exclusively homosexual problems, even though experts in sexual behavior distinguish between homosexuality and pederasty. Additionally, the Visitation unrealistically expects the hunted to hand themselves in for dismissal, whereas in most cases it will drive them "underground" or into some kind of unhealthy mental self-deception about their own identity. The ban and the investigation prompt many to question how a Church that harbors innumerable homosexually-oriented priests and bishops can conduct such an investigation. I won't mention the "blasphemous" suggestion that Jesus himself had homosexual tendencies, something various New Testament scholars see implied in the Gospel of St. John. Safer merely to invoke Juvenal's famous question, *Quis custodiet ipsos custodes?* "Who will guard the guards themselves?")

I fell in with a group largely but by no means exclusively heterosexual. Although we played sports, most of us were not very good at them, and our chief activity, when not complaining about our education, was reading and talking about what we were reading. It sounds rather too grand to say we were interested in the things of the mind, but in fact we were. What we lacked was even a semblance of focus. We had no system or organization. We passed books around among ourselves, and I would be reading *Crime and Punishment* one week, Joyce's *Portrait* the next, then Silone's *Bread and Wine*, then Salinger's *Catcher in the Rye*, then Kerouac's *On the Road*. I read Mauriac, Bernanos, Pasternak, S. J. Perelman, Shakespeare, Max Lerner, Sophocles, Waugh, Greene, Hemingway, Faulkner, Plato; books about jazz, art history, church architecture, the American Civil War; I even had a go at *Art and Scholasticism* by Jacques Maritain. We were too uncentered, too scattered in our interests, to be well informed about any one thing. For that matter, we were not focused even in our formal theological studies, owing to the catechism-like nature of our instruction. Theology could indeed be intellectualized—those countless distinctions, the eight varieties, for example, of the causes of grace—but all the careful analysis was in the service of answers already in place. Our theological studies were, at bottom, intellectually dishonest, and we sensed this keenly. Our course work served to convince us that things must change. We grew more and more "liberal." We read and admired those few Catholic writers who played down literalism in Scripture, who questioned papal pronouncements and the whole *de fide* system, who challenged the interdiction of "unnatural" birth control and divorce, and who argued for liturgical reform through more participation by the laity and the elimination of Latin in the Mass in favor of the vernacular. Our circle ached for reform.

My close friends included Bill Giblin, my pal from Seton Hall; and it was in his car that we took summer vacations that proved, for me at least, liberating. Dick O'Donnell, who went on these trips with us, was a great laugher. He was what Max Beerbohm called "amusable," a quality much to be valued among people who, like me, enjoyed seeing the world as a funny, even absurd, place. O'Donnell readily accepted the nickname I gave him of "Chief" for his habit of addressing unknown people—waiters, store clerks, gasoline attendants—as "Chief." He smoked altogether too much, always Camels, and he never quit laughing at the possibilities I had opened for him by telling him that the animal figured on the package was in fact a dromedary: "What am I going to say, 'Pack of Dromedaries, Chief'?"

Vince McCluskey, in spite of his name, was Polish. His father had a name that began with M, and shortly after he arrived here from Poland, a railroad foreman gave him the name McCluskey when he hired him. What joined me inseparably to Vince was music. He might have become a professional musician, for he was a superb trumpeter; he could read music well, he could play by ear anything he heard once, he could improvise endlessly, and he sounded like Bix Beiderbecke, whom he idolized. I used to tell him—as Eddie Condon said of Beiderbecke—that when he picked up his horn and played those first notes it was like a girl saying yes. Not that I knew what that sounded like. Every Saturday night McCluskey and I and a few others went to a spare room in the dormitory basement and listened on a primitive stereo set to jazz, New Orleans music, King Oliver, Louis Armstrong, Kid Ory, Bunk Johnson, and my favorite, clarinetist George Lewis. During vacations, Vince and I haunted New York record shops and the 52nd Street jazz places, where we heard the likes of the Dukes of Dixieland, whom we thought "good but too slick," and Wilbur de Paris, whom we judged "the real thing." Together with three others we formed a little jazz group, my clarinet being the weak link, that entertained at various seminary functions, such as the occasional Saturday night movie. (We were shown movies rated "Unobjectionable for all, including children" by the Legion of Decency, such as *The Song of Bernadette* and *Joan of Arc*. The most worldly films we saw were *The Quiet Man* and *Shane*. The movies were shown by a professional operator who made his rounds working the projectors at various institutions. He told us that our audience clapped, stamped its feet, and cheered at exactly the same places in movies as did the inmates of mental hospitals.)

McCluskey did me the great turn of introducing me to his pastor, Father Chris Haag, of St. Monica's parish in Sussex, who became my vacation-time confessor and, with his sensible approach to the priesthood, replaced the fanaticism of Scully. It was Haag who eliminated the last vestiges of my scrupulosity with his earthy and humorous analysis of my spiritual bearings: "To commit a sin, for God's sake, you've got to do more than think about the girl." Though I did not see him often, he would, over the years, play an important role in helping me keep my mental balance. Scully never forgave my defection.

Two other friends, Jerry Pindar and John Harrington, the first very close, the other admired from a distance, modified my thinking and behavior. Pindar was among the brightest persons in the class ahead of me, then in my class, and then in the class behind me. He kept getting spinal meningitis and losing a year. That he lived each time made him a medical freak. If O'Donnell was amusable, Pindar was amusing. Our court jester, he was always—and he still is—playing practical jokes. On his first morning in the seminary, he got up five minutes early and lay down on the floor, telling the deacon (a sixth-year seminarian) who came to fetch him that by sleeping this way he was atoning for his sins; he went down the hallway to chapel during the great silence wrapped in toilet paper and shaving; he skipped night prayers and removed into a nearby utility closet all the furniture, including the bed, from a deacon's room; he sneaked into Przezdziecki's room on Halloween and soaped his glass-fronted bookshelves; he got hold of the Brooklyn diocese letterhead and typed a letter to Giblin telling him that, as records showed that he was illegitimate, he must get a special dispensation before being ordained. Pindar was blessed with photographic recall and wonderful powers of mimicry, and I can still hear Koenig when Pindar "did" him: "Take for example, fellers, a burning log. First you have a burning log, then you have ashes. The substantial form has changed, but the prime matter has remained. It's *perdured.*"

At a swimming meet at the river Pindar got on the public address system and announced that this was Monsignor Mc-Nulty from Seton Hall, that the immigrants had come to South Orange, had dug deep, and so on. Everyone thought it was Mc-Nulty. Curious bits of information came to us through Pindar: he learned that the much respected Dominican theologian Garrigou La Grange in his old age would wander his monastery garden muttering, "There is no God, there is no God," and that the same revered La Grange on his hospital death bed kept goosing the nurses.

Pindar once passed around mimeographed copies of the ethics exam before Koenig entered the room, frightening many who thought it was the real thing:

I. Trace the history of dueling— Germans, French, Turks, etc.
II. Solve syllogistically the Vietnam quandary [this was 1955].
III. a/ Give Puffendorf's opinion of the liciety of the useful lie (Bring in Jeremy Bentham, Levy Bruhl et al).
b/ State Schleiermacher's opinion of organized religion.

IV. Discuss duties of conscripts, legislators, riveters in factories, sergeants, corporals, petty officers, generals, cabinet ministers, and policemen when war is declared by their nation. May a man whose draft notice is in the mail volunteer?

After Pindar's third bout with meningitis, Dr. Johnny Petrone, overruling the New York experts, had him discharged from the seminary. He was picked up by the Archdiocese of Washington—which had almost no homegrown priests— where he was ordained in 1960. In Washington, Pindar put a pair of Playboy Bunny ears on the rear bumper of the archbishop's limousine. He later served as a chaplain in Vietnam and was awarded two Bronze Medals and the Soldier's Medal; he eventually became a lawyer and a New Jersey assistant attorney general. His larks may read as silliness now, but in their day they helped me greatly.

With these friends I made two long vacation trips, one to Miami Beach and another to Mexico City. Pindar brought along a bottle of bourbon; and at our first overnight motel stop on the way to Florida, in South Carolina, shortly after I had been given a ticket for speeding, I had my first illicit drink. If you were proved to have had alcohol, it meant expulsion from the seminary. But drinking on vacation—none of it particularly excessive—became for me henceforth a form of keeping my self-respect and independence.

The following summer on the trip to Mexico City we drove around the clock for days, having fitted the backseat area of the car with a small mattress for the one who would drive next, an arrangement that drew many laughs and comments in *macho* Mexico. Occasionally we would stop overnight in a city, the first of which was Monterey. Here McCluskey sat in for a few songs with the band at a place frequented by prostitutes and fell in love with one of them. Vince and she did nothing except talk, but for a year he was starry-eyed and loved to play "It Happened in Monterey" on his horn, although nothing in fact happened.

He had his memories of "stars and steel guitars," but nothing else. This little non-incident was typical of us sex-starved yet well-behaving seminarians. I myself was "in love," most platonically, with the sister of a friend who later joined the Franciscans, David McBriar. I saw her briefly half a dozen times while visiting him. When I talked with Agnes, I seemed able to make her laugh. Recently I had dinner with David, still a Franciscan, and confessed my fondness for his sister in the 1950s. She knew it all the time, he told me.

On the way home from Mexico City we made a long detour so McCluskey and I could see New Orleans. We were so exhausted from driving that on arrival we lay down for a late afternoon nap at the St. Charles Hotel. I was the first to awaken, at 4 A.M. I got up and went out onto closed-down Bourbon Street and learned that we would miss George Lewis, whose week-long engagement had just finished. The next night, after dinner at Antoine's (of all places), we heard music till everything closed, the best of the jazz being at the Paddock Lounge, where famous old trombonist Bill Robinson explained to me that Vince could not sit in with the band because it was illegal in the state of Louisiana for black and white musicians to perform together in public. We got home all the more devoted to New Orleans music and with a new drink with which to flout the Rule, tequila.

John Harrington, the person who most helped alter my mind-set, was a friend but not an intimate. But Pindar was an intimate of his, and I came by much of John's wisdom secondhand. He was an enormous influence in making me take the Church's party line with a grain of salt. He gave legitimacy to my skepticism. John, who was "ABD" or "All But Dissertation" in English from Columbia, was hands-down the quickest and most erudite person—student or professor—at Darlington. He was kind, decent, honest, generous, and completely cynical. He began most of his sentences with "Oh!" and, though an atrocious dresser, was possessed of many ladylike qualities. John insisted that he joined the seminary to avoid the draft. "Oh!" he would say, "It's better than Fort Dix." We never knew when to believe him. He told us he was going to go to confession to Dougherty and say that he had committed adultery with Mrs. Baletza, the ancient Polish woman who dusted the hallways. When Pindar told him how Przezdziecki had confiscated his anthology of philosophers, Harrington had no sympathy: "Oh! You went to him, you chose the Enlightenment."

John's great interest in those days was the theater, especially Tennessee Williams and Eugene O' Neill. He became mentor to any of us interested in the theater. I remember leaving the original Broadway production of *A Long Day's Journey into Night* and running into John, who was re-seeing the play: "Oh, I'm glad you are going to the good stuff. All the Catholics are over at *The Potting Shed* [a play by Graham Greene]." He inspired Bob Call to take me to the New York premiere of *Waiting for Godot*. John knew Bette Davis, and when he learned she had gotten a bad review, he went, without asking for permission, to the forbidden public phone and tried to call her. Mahon caught him red-handed, but John kept saying, "Oh! Don't you see I'm calling Miss Davis? Oh! I'm so depressed. I *must* call Miss Davis. Don't you see? Oh! I'm so depressed." Another time Mahon found John alone in the recreation room, smoking and listening to the radio during compulsory study: "Oh! I'm sorry. Is there some kind of rule?" John was too much for him; he was the one student Mahon couldn't intimidate.

Harrington had little regard for our teachers: "If there ever were a persecution, you'd see—these people, they're just *posing* as Christians. If the Church wants celibate priests, they ought to ordain married men." As for what was being taught, Harrington belittled it so continually that he provoked some anonymous "good" seminarian who followed the Rule to report him to the rector, Paw Paw Brady, who called John into his office. Admittedly, we have only John's account:

> Brady: "Paw, paw, it has been reported to me that you are not orthodox in your beliefs."
> Harrington: "Oh! I subscribe to the Christian mythos."

Brady: "Paw, paw, but I am told you have no interest in theology."

Harrington: "Oh! a glance at my record should suffice to disprove *that* charge."

Brady: (Getting out and examining the record) "Dogmatic Theology, A."

Harrington: "Not guilty!"

Brady: "Moral Theology, A."

Harrington: "Not guilty!"

Brady: "Canon Law, A."

Harrington: "Not guilty!"

The Rector had to concede the point, but went on to another problem:

Brady: "Paw, paw, it has also been noted that you have an unnaturally high speaking voice."

Harrington: "Oh! what would you suggest? Cassels [the speech director] or hormones?"

John left the seminary when he was in "minor orders"—acolyte, porter, lector, exorcist—and was told that by resigning he had "lost" them, but that they would "revive" should he return to the seminary. "Only Rome could do that," he remarked. Afterward he would regale us with stories of the students at South Side High in Newark, an almost entirely black school, where for one semester he attempted to teach Latin: "Oh! the girls in my Latin class say things to me like 'Hic hac hoc. Kiss my ass' and 'Amo amas amat. Latin teacher has no twat.'" After that, Harrington joined the English faculty at Seton Hall, a place he loved and hated. "Oh," he would say, "Seton Hall faculty, Seton Hall College, Seton Hall University—it's perfectly incestuous." When President Kennedy reintroduced the draft over the Cuban missile crisis, John's reaction was "Oh! Does this mean I'll have to take the veil again?" In the early 1970s, a time when so many priests and nuns were opting out of the Church, John's comment was "Poof, there it goes."

Late in life I came to know him well when he conducted at Seton Hall a hugely successful program called Poetry in the Round, for which he hired literary celebrities to give readings and talks. And whenever there was someone coming to speak whom he thought I would like to meet, he asked me to "chauffeur" him or her from New York to South Orange. In this way I had the pleasure of meeting John Updike, Seamus Heaney, Ted Hughes, Tom Stoppard, Elizabeth Hardwick, and Mary McCarthy. In October 1986, when the Mets were playing Boston in the World Series, I had the satisfaction of explaining to Mary McCarthy, at her request, baseball's designated hitter rule. The time I drove Hughes, with Pindar along for the ride (Harrington having told me "*Don't* let Pindar mention Sylvia Plath!"), I illegally parked my Toyota Corolla directly in front of the Student Center where Hughes was to speak. Pindar printed a sign for the campus police: "This vehicle is transporting the Poet Laureate of England. Please do not tow." I don't know what the campus police made of the sign, but the car was still there three hours later. When John Harrington died a few years ago—he ate entirely too much of the wrong food, thinking nothing of downing two or three enormous sundaes while out for "a cup of coffee"—the memorial service in the Seton Hall chapel was overflowing with friends and former students who positively loved the man.

Early 1958 brought me a great frustration. Darlington, which was affiliated with Catholic University in Washington, D.C., had a practice of sending a handful of candidates to Washington during their last year to study at and receive a theology degree from Catholic University. Four of us were chosen, called into Paw Paw's office, and told that the arrangement had been changed and that we would remain at Darlington and take a special exam at the end of the year. "I expect you are disappointed," he said. He had no idea how disappointed I was. To have lived in a city, in the nation's capital, to get away from Darlington for my entire last year—here was something beyond the dreams of lust or avarice. But that dream vanished, and we four, like good soldiers, took our orders. I was also saddened that my assigned chateau mate that year, Eugene Kasper, was not named among us four singled out for the degree. He had a good mind and worked very hard. In our early years at Darlington, we had had to take at least a half year of Hebrew, and those who did well were expected to take another half year. Kasper, who mastered the course, sat next to a fellow Pole, John Paprocki, who never opened the book and would have failed the exam but that he persuaded Kasper to give him the answers: "Come on, be a pal." The result, almost as bad as failing, was that Paprocki did so well that he had to take the second half of Hebrew. Kasper also helped me. With patient coaching he taught me to say two Polish sentences that I could use to feign knowledge of the language:

> Rozmawiam po Polsku bardzo mało. "I only speak a little Polish."
> and
> To dosyć po Polsku. "That's enough Polish."

Thirty years later a visiting medical student from Poland told me I was the only American he had met who spoke Polish without an American accent.

In May 1958 our class was ordained to the subdiaconate, a "major" order, since abolished by the Church. Only Rome could do that. Subdiaconate brought with it the obligation of lifelong celibacy. Pindar, from Washington, told us to keep our fingers crossed during the ceremony. Our class, which had numbered nearly fifty when we entered Darlington, was down to forty, in spite of additions from the diocese of Trenton. We lost Donald McCormack, the former midshipman and a deeply religious man; we lost Tom Morris and Clem Rieger, smart, affable fellows who happened also to be our best athletes. Dick Cummings, who struck us as the perfect, balanced, hardworking seminarian, defected during the fifth year; and Eugene Sanzo, a potentially fine priest by temperament and disposition, disappeared stealthily in the night just before subdiaconate. Whenever a classmate departed the place, a pall descended on us, and we grieved. It was as if there had been a death in the family.

We seminarians, unlike candidates in the military service academies, never used the term "washed out," which carried the implication of having failed to make the grade. With us, candidates simply "left." In my six years at Darlington, as one class was ordained and another entered, I came to know some five hundred fellow students. More than ten percent of these dropped out at one stage or another. But in all this time I knew of only one seminarian being dismissed for academic reasons, for failure to make the grade. Those who left (except for Pindar, dismissed for bad health) chose to leave, and they did so almost invariably because they feared or knew they couldn't manage celibacy. Many left on the occasion of one of our weeklong retreats, that of September 1957. The retreat master was a Vincent McCrorry, S.J., who had been told that there were some "rotten apples" in Darlington and that he should shake the tree. Shake it he did. He talked of nothing but sins against chastity for seven days, and it was said that our own faculty in their role as confessors had all they could do to keep the place from emptying out. McCrorry's central thesis was that any single, completed physical sin against purity, no matter how sincerely repented of, anything from illicit sexual intercourse down to masturbation, meant one was not called to the priesthood. But by this time I had completely overcome any overseriousness, much less scrupulosity. Moreover, for good or ill, I would have passed muster, even with McCrorry. And in any case I had learned to disregard much of what was said by our pastors and masters.

I was clearly situated within the liberal camp. For my friends and me our longing for change within the Church was matched only by our eagerness to get out of Darlington. The deadly Rule had become a joke. We twenty-five- and twenty-six-year-olds bravely talked in the hallways and courageously visited at the doors of fellow seminarians without permission. On vacations we ordered wine with our dinners in New York. I even taught my parents to drink wine with meals, something they had never done. At Darlington we repeated with glee the mantra "seditious, incorrigible or refractory." But we were still careful. There was little sense in being booted out at this late date. A close call came on a Saturday night when Vince McCluskey and I together with a handful of others sneaked into the Speech Lab, a house near the dormitory building, and drank tequila while listening to mariachi records. Being caught would have meant summary expulsion. A face peered in at us through the outside window, and I thought we were finished. But it was only Jim O'Brien, a fellow seminarian.

Our subdiaconate retreat was preached by the priest we liberals considered the foremost theologian in the country, John Courtney Murray, S.J., the man who a few years later would write the Declaration of Religious Freedom for the Second Vatican Council. More than anyone else, Murray was responsible for the sensible shift in the Church's relations with Protestant Christians, Jews, and other non-Christians. In 1958 his advice to us was to make a *rational*, sensible effort to do what we believed we should do. He also told us that when we said "Adsum" in the ordination ceremony, we should intend it to mean "Such as I am, here I am." This retreat made for a good start to our last year. The year was also to be more relaxed and sane because Mahon was removed—sent "upstairs" to the Chancery in downtown Newark—and replaced by Bob Gibney, who had been a deacon when we were juniors. We were not about to take any nonsense from a former fellow student. We were an uncooperative group, and I know that he and the rest of the faculty were glad when our class was gone. Gibney once called us together and asked us to tell him frankly and off the record what our problem was. He wanted to know, he said, why we were not proud of Darlington. No one said anything. Then I, still shy about speaking in public, got up nervously and told him. I don't remember what I said, but after me everyone spoke up, jumped all over him, and I marveled at how manfully he took the beating. At a recent class reunion, the forty-fifth, I asked George Mader, our "first man," what I had said. Mader claims to have remembered some of my very words—"We are the mediocre products of a mediocre institution." Not a terribly refractory or seditious sentiment, at least as seen from this distance.

We knew well in advance the exact day of our ordination and escape from Darlington, May 23, 1959. (Ever since, "May 23" leaps out at me whenever I encounter it in print: Savonarola was hanged and burned by the Church on May 23, 1498; the painter and poet Dante Gabriel Rossetti died on May 23, 1882; clarinetist Artie Shaw was born on May 23, 1910; Italy entered World War I on May 23, 1915.) I started the countdown toward our target date at least a year in advance, heading my notebooks each day with the number of Days-To-Go. Sometimes someone would write the number on the blackboard before classes began.

I was nearing the goal, having made it through the six years at Darlington by pushing aside questions of faith, never mentioning my doubts to anyone, and making only the prescribed "generic" confessions. The seminary's grueling schedule, coupled with my own random but busy reading and my interest in jazz music helped keep my mind occupied. And, by acting as if I believed everything demanded of me, I seemed to be reviving my faith, slowly increasing it upward from the "half faith" of my Seton Hall days. If you are worried about being in the state of grace, we were told, act as if you are in the state of grace and you will be. Theater people say that performance generates feeling, not the other way round. I performed, and I believed more.

Then, in 1959, as the end came into view, serious doubts flared up again. They centered around Pius IX's notorious Syllabus of Errors. To myself I used to say that it was indeed a syllabus of errors because it made eighty-eight stunning errors in holding that its eighty-eight propositions were errors. A crowningly reactionary document, it censured "rationalism," insisting that reason must always be subject to the teaching of the Church; it ruled that philosophy had to be guided by the Church; that the Church had never impeded the "true" progress of science; it condemned "indifferentism," the belief that man may find salvation outside the true Church and that Protestantism is "another form" of the true Church; it dismissed socialism, communism, biblical criticism, and secret societies as "pests." The Syllabus asserted that Church authority was in all regards superior to civil authority; that the Church has the power to use force; that where ecclesiastical and civil laws conflict, the ecclesiastical must prevail; that popular education pertains to the Church, not the state. One particular "error" was expressed succinctly: "The Church ought to be separate from the State, and the State from the Church." In 2000 Pope John Paul II beatified Pius IX, the step immediately prior to canonization. (The canonization of Pius IX will be controversial. Not only did he promulgate the infamous Syllabus of Errors, he proclaimed the doctrine of the Immaculate Conception in 1854, and that of Papal Infallibility in 1870, neither of which endeared him to Protestant Christians. But his behavior was if anything more repugnant to Jews. In 1858 the Vatican learned that a Catholic servant girl had secretly baptized a six-year-old Jewish child, Edgardo Mortara, and the papal police took the boy from his Jewish parents. It was nothing short of kidnapping, but Pius IX, in spite of an international outcry, refused to return the child to his parents. Instead he "adopted" the boy into the papal household, where he grew up to become a priest.)

But why did I trouble about the Syllabus of Errors, a document important in its time (1864), but easily ignored in New Jersey in 1959? It would perhaps have been easy except for something called the Oath against Modernism, which contained much of the same irrational foolishness. The Oath, promulgated by Pius X in 1910, had to be sworn to by all clergy, confessors, and seminary professors before entering into their ministries. It is not as long and by that measure not as bad as the Syllabus of Errors, but for a person who took oaths seriously, here was torment. For me, it brought back to the surface those conflicts that had begun at Seton Hall with my reading of Madgett's *Christian Origins* in Furlong's fateful course in Apologetics. We were made to swear that we believed that the one supernatural God can be known by the "natural light of reason alone"; that "divine acts and especially miracles and prophesies" as revealed in the Scriptures are the surest signs of the divine origin of the Christian religion; that we rejected "the heretical misrepresentation that dogmas evolve and change"; that we rejected rationalism and textual criticism of the Bible; that we believed that all Catholic dogmas were revealed to the Church in Apostolic times and did not change or grow "according to what seems better and more suited to each age"; and that "the absolute and immutable truth preached by the apostles from the beginning may never be believed to be different, may never be understood in any other way." The oath was demonstrable nonsense, and I could see how many simply ignored it. But I could also see how our seminary professors, who were required to retake the Oath annually, may have felt themselves bound by it and tethered to these ridiculous restraints upon common sense. My classmates, as far as I could tell, never gave it a second thought. Something to sign? One more thing, let's get on with it. Indeed, among the many priests I have spoken to in regard to this book, most of them cannot remember taking the Oath. They have blocked it out. The Oath was eliminated in 1967 in the aftermath of the reforms of the Second Vatican Council, but in May 1959 my classmates and I had to kneel, swear, and sign this oath. It was coerced perjury.

We also were made to swear an oath "on the sacred thirst of Jesus on the cross" either to drink no alcohol for five years or to drink only beer and wine for the rest of one's life. I took the beer and wine. Seize the day. Some confessors held—a probable opinion?—that as we were forced to swear under pressure, the oath was invalid. In any case, the American Catholic Church had many alcoholic priests. In my experience they all seemed to be older Irish pastors. But clerical alcoholism was a problem which, unlike child abuse, the Church hierarchy at least attempted to face up to and cure, although they did so only in regard to the younger clergy, who were not the offenders, and in this heavy-handed fashion. I don't see that the oath helped. In time no one paid any attention to it.

But whatever the distress of being forced to take oaths, I was, after ten years of working toward ordination, about to join the company of American priests. Will Durant (that scandalous Seton Hall Seminary dropout and apostate), writing of his experience half-a-century earlier, had spoken about the "unquestionable sincerity" of priests in their religious beliefs. Indeed, in my view, *all* the priests mentioned anywhere in this book, the saintly and the immoral, the hardworking and the lazy, the sensible and the fanatic, the sober and the drunken, were sincere believers. They had come to ordination in their mid- or late-twenties, by which time their minds had lost any openness or suppleness in regard to religious belief. Durant credits the seminary training. The strenuous life of the seminary, as experienced by young men in their early twenties—the age of religious doubt for some few—left little time for skepticism:

> One believed because one could believe without thinking, while doubt demanded thought. In those formative years the mind of the future priest took on the habit of belief; and all the assaults of later experience would hardly dislodge the dogmas there absorbed. The seminary saw to it that barring an occasional alcoholic deviation, these men should be faithful sons of the Church to the day and hour of their deaths. It was a remarkably thorough operation.

It was just as thorough an operation in my day as in Durant's, and although the seminary regimen had not altogether worked its spell with me and had not completely resolved my doubts, it had tipped the scales, so to speak, toward belief. This became more and more the case as the years invested in the belief system accumulated. It was easy at this late date to allow my skeptical misgivings to be swept aside in the excitement of what was to come.

The months prior to ordination resembled nothing so much as a young bride's preparations for her wedding. Each of us had to make arrangements for the restaurant and food at the celebratory dinner following his first Mass. For me it was Donahue's in Mountain View, where I had eaten for years and where my father had once pointed out Babe Ruth, talking with his friend Jimmy Donahue in the outside diner-like section. Then there were the printed invitations, the list of invitees, and place cards. Each of us also had "holy cards" commemorating our ordination. Mine was a Christ by Georges Rouault. New clothes had to be bought, especially cassocks, not the old button-style, but the flashy "Jesuit" sash kind. A car was a necessity to be paid for in installments—a priest's credit was good. We were encouraged to buy unostentatious cars, and I ordered a black two-door Plymouth, stick shift, for just under $2,000. But the most special item was one's chalice. The rage in our time among progressive seminarians was the so-called tasillo-style chalice, labeled the "egg cup" by its detractors, and about as far as one could get from the elaborate, pointed-cup Gothic chalice that represented the traditionalism we were in revolt against. My chalice came from Holland, the work of a famous Dutch silversmith named Leo Brom, who had once made a filigreed sword for presentation to Dwight Eisenhower, from "the grateful Dutch nation to the liberator of their country." This chalice cost a whopping $620, and I felt guilty because, after it had been ordered, my father, who was paying for it, was let go by DuMont when its manufacturing division changed hands. My parents, however, felt that no sacrifice was too much for their son, the priest-to-be. Father Scully, in whose church my first Mass would be celebrated, thought my chalice hideous.

Our official seminary photographs were taken by Fabian Bachrach, photographer of celebrities and presidents.

As the days at Darlington came down to a few, tension replaced the insufferable boredom. Would I be in good health on ordination day? Might I sprain an ankle or break a limb playing ball in these last weeks? Would I catch a cold that weekend? May 23, 1959, was the end of a six-year quest, eight if you counted Seton Hall, and it all came down to this Saturday. After a sleepless night we seven Paterson men were chauffeured down to the city, to the Cathedral of St. John the Baptist. The sun shone brightly. It was all quite magical. Through the imposition of hands by a successor to the Apostles, Bishop James A. McNulty, a mild-mannered man we called "Gentleman Jim," we were about to be ordained "other Christs" with the formidable powers of saying Mass and forgiving sins. The quiet in the sacristy before the ceremony was broken only when the noisy dean of the cathedral, gruff old Monsignor Walter "Bunker" Hill, responded loudly to the question of a young seminarian: "Where is the tabernacle key? It's in the god-damned tabernacle."

The moment came. And we, who until that day had remained locked up in Darlington in the wilds of northwest New Jersey, under house arrest, treated like adolescents, allowed no privileges, no life to speak of, were suddenly on top of the world. Everything had changed. The very priests who at the seminary had lorded it over us knelt for our blessing. Hundreds of people, known and unknown, flocked to the next day's first Mass, to the blessing at the altar, to the great ordination dinner, to the reception in the parish hall that evening, always complete with Father's first blessing. "There is something special," Scully told his parishioners, "in the blessing of a newly ordained priest"— though he had his doubts about this new priest, who earlier had jumped ship on him. Everyone slipped envelopes of money into the young priests' hands.

One sobering note and one only was struck. I had invited our Canon Law professor, Walter W. Curtis, a sensible man who had for some years been my confessor at Darlington, to give the sermon at my first Mass. He had recently been made an auxiliary bishop of Newark, but in spite of his busy schedule, he graciously accepted. In later years he became bishop of Bridgeport, Connecticut, where I am told he was much liked by his priests. One of his innovations was to see to it that his priests were the highest paid in the country. He loved vanilla ice cream and was overweight. But the sermon he preached at my first Mass—unlike other first-Mass sermons—didn't mention me by name and instead dwelt on the weak, unworthy vessels that God chooses to do his work.

7

A SAINT AND A MANIAC

M Y FIRST PARISH, St. Michael's in Netcong, New, Jersey, made me into an honorary Italian. I had known a few Italian-Americans in school, but none had been close friends. I believed that Italian restaurants were the best buy, and I had been in Montclair in the 1940s when "La pizz" came into fashion in our part of the world. But Netcong was the real thing. It could have been a village near Naples. Indeed it was a village near Naples, transported to northern New Jersey, a place named Cesa after a fourth-century martyr, St. Cesario. Netcong had a population of 2,500, which included a handful of Protestants and one large Irish clan, the Grogans. Everyone else was Italian. They ran the place. For example, the elected public school board was all Italian, even though its members sent their sons and daughters to St. Michael's grade school. The public high school was practically a Catholic school. The people who were to be my parishioners and friends all had names ending in a vowel: Amendola, Barbato, Balzano, Benvenuto, Esposito, DiLallo, Lamberto, Pichi, Stracco, Togno. Just about everybody was working class. My closest friends—people with whom I stayed in touch even after being transferred—were Julius DiRenzo, a carpenter; Gus Rampone, a shoemaker; Mike Romano, an A&P butcher; Dominick Arbolino, a welder; and Johnny Phillips, another self-described honorary Italian, a house painter. Nancy Patri, an English teacher at Dover High School and the daughter of a shoemaker, was the one well-educated person in the parish. It was she who, along with Mrs. Mary Johnson, née Benvenuto, helped me commandeer every teenager in the town into an active Catholic Youth Organization or CYO. St. Michael's parish, this little Italian enclave, was situated at the far edge of the diocese, and Chancery officials in Paterson treated the place with benign neglect.

The parish had had the same pastor, Father—later Monsignor—Edwin E. Lange, for nearly forty years. His only curate or assistant had been there for a mere three years in the late 1930s. This was the newly ordained Father Jimmy Doyle, who was rumored to have been removed because all the women in the parish were in love with him. St. Michael's had not had another curate till I was sent there in 1959, precisely twenty years after Doyle's departure. My first evening on the scene, Monsignor Lange told me I was to come with him to inspect the parish hall, and here I was greeted by hundreds of people and a great homemade buffet of Italian-style food. Everyone was happy to greet their new priest. From the diocesan newspaper they had got hold of my picture—that Fabian Bachrach photograph—and somehow enlarged it to about four feet square, and hung this image beneath an even larger sign saying "Welcome Father Hall." And one of these people, a Mrs. Fiorella from Stoll Street, insisted I join her family for afternoon dinner the coming Sunday. Monsignor Lange thought it a good idea for me to eat at parishioners' homes, and so began my engagement with the people of Netcong over their dinner tables. I was forever eating out, and eating as few people did except in other Italian parishes. Each woman had her reputation for certain dishes—Mrs. Fiorella for a light lasagna, Mrs. Togno for her braciola, Mrs. Verdi for her sauce, and so on. Others were known for their homemade bread or pasta.

If the women of the parish were distinguished by their cooking, the men were divided according to the religious society to which they gave allegiance, St. Cesario or the Feast of the Assumption. The two groups were fierce rivals, the division going back to some distant feud that may have begun in the Old Country. On the last Saturday in July and the second in August their annual celebrations took place. The festivities started with Mass, and I put together a short sermon, had a parishioner translate it into Italian, and to the delight of the old people did my best to deliver it in their mother tongue. Next came bidding of money for the privilege of carrying the society's banner. Fireworks were shot off, and a procession of members walked behind a small old-world band—one such as is seen in the Sicilian scenes from *The Godfather*—and wended its way down every street, stopping at designated spots to have people bid money to "shoot," that is, to send up a firecracker in honor of St. Cesario or the Virgin. All along the route people would throw bombs and pin money to the banners. The town erupted most of the day, and then in the evening the feast continued with a great fair that drew hundreds, maybe thousands, of out-of-towners, to food and games-of-chance stands, and to the day's climax with what were said to be the largest fireworks displays in New Jersey. I am told that this Netcong no longer exists and that the feasts are rather pathetic. The old immigrant Italians have died, and younger generations have for the most part moved away or lost interest. The airport where St. Cesario held its fireworks has given way to Interstate Highway 80 and a trade center. New, non-Italian residents complained of the noise and the bombs going off in the streets, and today everything connected to the feasts is much curtailed. For myself, I loved those earlier times, the noise, the food, the fireworks, the primitive piety.

That first summer was the start of four happy years among Netcong's Italian people. Or perhaps it was only three. For a curate's happiness, in any parish, depended in large measure upon his boss. Pastors exercised complete control over their curates, whose lives they could render pleasant or miserable. Young priests and priests-to-be knew most pastors by reputation. Some were regarded with well-earned contempt as tyrants, crazies, or alcoholics. Another failing, though we had no single word for it, was the pastor who operated under the rule of his housekeeper, or secretary, or "aunt," a woman who lived in the rectory and had over the years made herself indispensable. Here was an argument, though not a conclusive one, against celibacy, this need of many priests for the companionship of a woman. There was the old joke about the man who rang the rectory bell at 11:00 in the evening, only to have the housekeeper poke her head out of a window and call down, "You're too late. The pastor and I are in bed." But the pastors I knew and knew of were not, I believe, involved in physical relationships with their women; however, they were in thrall to them and dependent upon them for emotional support. Had these priests been married to their housekeepers, the word *uxorious* would have suited. And a young priest entering one of these rectories as a curate was in a poor position, for certain. He had of course Holy Orders, and the housekeeper could not say Mass or preach or hear confessions, but she was in all other regards his superior, unofficially deputed as such by the pastor. Crossing her meant crossing him. If the curate were unhappy, he could go to the Chancery Office and complain, but the authorities would unfailingly take the pastor's side, and, come the following June, the complainer would be transferred. It was indeed a hierarchical Church though few lay people except those working closely with the priests in the affected parishes knew of this special category in the chain of command. While these housekeepers and secretaries were sometimes derisively called "priestesses," they by no means constituted what liberal Catholics have in mind when advocating the ordination of women.

When I received my letter of appointment, I had never heard of Monsignor Lange, but inquiries made on my behalf brought back the story that although he was a kindly old man, I was in for a rough time. A woman named Irene Grogan was rumored to run the place. I asked my mentor, Father Chris Haag, what he thought of my prospects. He said little and urged me to do my best. I could tell he feared for me. Irene had for many years been a source of contention in the parish, and in the early days tongues had wagged, and wagged, I am certain, erroneously. But that had been long ago. Still, up to the last, she was testy, short-

tempered, and despotic with the authority ceded to her by the
pastor. I was to learn how she relished turning people down. To
give one slight example, youngsters who wanted permission to
play basketball in the parish hall would always get the keys if
Father Lange answered the rectory door, but if Irene answered,
she would send the boys away. In a more critical matter, she ran
the First Communion arrangements, rehearsals, uniforms, everything, much to the annoyance of the nuns of the parish, who
traditionally saw this as one of their most important functions.
Her dictatorial presence was said to be among the causes for
the Benedictine nuns walking out of Lange's school some years
before I arrived. He got replacements from the Sisters of Christian Charity, the German order that had tormented my mother
in Jersey City half a century earlier.

Monsignor Lange, pastor of St. Michael's since 1926, was
loved by many people. In most respects he was a model priest, a
sensible, generous, cheerful, gentle man. I think the word sweet,
in its best evocations, nicely describes him. Still, the Irene factor had long troubled his career. Her influence, for example, led
to the mistaken policy by which her elderly aunt, who played
the organ most ineptly, and her niece, a young woman with
an execrable singing voice, were accorded a monopoly on "doing" church weddings. Lange adamantly refused to allow other
organists or singers to perform even if payment were offered
to the Grogans. Irene's status as housekeeper, cook, secretary,
confidant, and companion had made her his partner in running
the parish. It was all human enough. The life of a parish priest,
especially if he has no curates, is a lonely existence. Irene was an
enormous help to Lange, and only certain very active parishioners, the nuns, and those about to get married suffered. But to
be a curate in a place like this looked tricky. So it was with trepi-
dation that I stepped into the rectory at 89 Main Street, an old,
wood-frame house on busy Route 46, a block from the church
itself. I did my best to be friendly to Irene, this celebrated local
despot, who viewed me with suspicion and distrust from the
first. But she was seriously ill, and within a few months of my

arrival, the local doctor, a man named Gianni, having bumped into me at a Netcong High School football game, told me she was "filled with cancer." May God forgive me, I said nothing but breathed more easily. I would take her place as assistant pastor, friend, and confidant of this delightful man.

Father Lange was the only pastor anyone there ever knew. He had faced down criticism of Irene's authority, and over the years his good will and gentleness prevailed with just about everyone. Nobody's perfect. Irene Grogan aside, he was a saint. Stories of his kindness abounded and reached back to the thirties and forties. He helped struggling people with money; he was generous with his time; he had no interest other than St. Michael's; he turned down diocesan offers of bigger, more prestigious parishes. He personally gave every child in the school a gift at Christmas; he took the children to Bertram's Island Amusement Park at Lake Hopatcong and supplied them with pocket money. When he handed out report cards, he always had a kind word for each child, regardless of grades. I was told how in the Depression years, he would, after daily Mass, give the altar boy a dollar to buy for him two packs of Luckies at fifteen cents each and a five cent *Daily News* and "Keep the change." Now, in 1959, Irene was gone, and only good memories seemed to survive among his parishioners.

My own memories are all of that sort, too. I had him all to myself for three years. But in February 1962 he suffered a mishap that changed everything. Lange liked to say the early 7 A.M. daily Mass, and I had the 8 A.M. It was snowing one morning, and I looked out of the window and saw him floundering in the snow, unable to extricate himself from a fall. I went down and rescued him and thereafter always drove him to the church and remained there reading my breviary between 7:00 and 8:00. But he thought he was being a burden. He retired, the first active parish priest to do so in the diocese—for all I know the first in the country, as it was customary in those days for priests to die "in harness," in the rectory. Lange retired to make my life easier, whereas in fact nothing could have been worse for me. After three happy years I knew I was spoiled and sensed some real unpleasantness headed my way.

Father John Hewetson, Lange's replacement, came to Netcong with an egregious reputation. He was rumored to be the most "impossible" pastor in the diocese—with the exception of Monsignor Carlo Cianci, an old-world Italian tyrant at St. Michael's in Paterson, who among his other sins was a slumlord who made his curates collect rents and evict people unable to pay. (Years later the city of Paterson named a prominent street after Cianci.) Hewetson proved himself a for-the-most-part reformed alcoholic, as when, on his first afternoon in the rectory, he and I together visited the home of Mrs. Verdi, who lived on the other side of the church and cooked our dinners. "Got to keep on her good side," he crudely told me. She asked him to have some wine, but he said that no, he was a drunk. This was forthright, even if meant to seem jokey, and I rather admired him for it. Nothing else was admirable. I couldn't help looking at him and seeing the very antithesis of Lange, a slight man, modest, soft-spoken, refined, and mild mannered. And here was Hewetson, an extra large man, six-foot-three, more than three hundred pounds, loud, vulgar, and, as I learned soon enough, given to fits of screaming rage against laity and assistant alike. He had a German shepherd, "Shelley," always by his side, not quite on the altar steps, but in the sacristy when he said Mass. In the rectory he had a large, loud, squawking parrot, which he caged only when he left the rectory with the dog. At meals he would sit at the head of the table, I to his left, the cage filthy with droppings placed opposite me to his right. He had the parrot trained to sit on his shoulder, but of course the bird shat continually on his master's black cassock, Hewetson all the while talking loud sweet talk, as if the parrot were deaf, and the bird emitting persistent and piercing squawks. It was a madhouse, a scene from an English farce. After a month I gingerly asked Hewetson if he would please cage the parrot during meals that we took together, on the grounds that the bird made me "nervous." He did so, but shortly thereafter he retaliated with a frenzied tirade for my having the effrontery to take an occasional beer during dinner, as had been the custom with Lange and me. Earlier I had asked him if he minded the beer, and he had said, "No, of course not, not at all." Now, however, after the parrot incident, he went berserk, and I discontinued the beer but ate out at people's houses more frequently than ever.

The man was crazy. Only in the Church would the likes of him have been allowed to hold a position of authority over people or over money. Like so many pastors, he had a mania for spending parish money, especially on building projects. He never forgave me for having completed, just before his arrival, two undertakings. I had renovated the old "Union Hall" opposite the church into an auditorium-gymnasium, for a mere $14,000, and had built in the unfinished part of the school a large library, entirely on donated labor and material. All that was left for Hewetson was to "redecorate" the church and make alterations in the rectory. He imported an enormous Persian rug for the sanctuary, replaced the simple hanging sanctuary lamp with a whole string of elaborate Venetian-looking things, bought new candelabra and accoutrements of various kinds, and, cruelest of all, he had the plain wooden statues painted in gaudy colors. For the rectory he was forever calling in the parish builder, Julius DiRenzo, to have him make changes. Hewetson would enlarge the kitchen, install a large professional grade refrigerator and stove, move this wall back a few feet, "open up" some other room, change the back entrance. Once he moved a staircase across a room and then a month later had Julius put it back again. In this way he quickly went through the $50,000 in the parish treasury that Lange had saved over many years. I was told Hewetson had done the same thing in other parishes. How did he get away with it? Partly because of the Chancery's way of thinking that no senior priest was ever in the wrong, and partly because he had a protector at court. Hewetson's brother, Monsignor Joseph Hewetson, held some high-ranking position in the Chancery Office.

John Hewetson needed this cover at headquarters, for in addition to drunkenness, ill-usage of people, and reckless waste of parish moneys, he was rumored to have sexually abused altar boys. I knew no eyewitnesses (I'm reminded of the old line asking how many eyewitnesses are required to prove adultery on the part of a Cardinal of the Roman Catholic Church), but the rumors were plentiful among the priests of the diocese. Later I did hear from an eyewitness, Father Tony Franchino, who had served under Hewetson in Lincoln Park for one year back in 1950. Franchino told me how he, newly ordained and enthusiastic, had run bursting with some important news into Hewetson's bedroom one afternoon (priests were much given to afternoon naps or "studying the fathers of the Church"). There he found Hewetson naked in bed with an altar boy. Much shaken, Franchino went immediately for advice to the nearest parish priest, who happened to be none other than my old pastor, Father Scully in Mountain View. Scully, who had been a 1930 ordination classmate of Hewetson, told Franchino to "forget it." That, of course, had long been the Church's practice in this matter. Had the bishop known of the incident, Hewetson would have been called down on the carpet, told to behave himself, and, if it happened again, been transferred to another parish. But blowing the whistle was like ratting on a fellow police officer. That I should have known of only this single instance of an abusive priest attests to the effectiveness of the hierarchical cover-up. Still, when Hewetson arrived in Netcong, I knew that I should keep an eye on him. For one thing, I, like all curates, was in charge of the altar boys. But one time Hewetson stopped me in the living room of the rectory and announced:

"Well, I'm up to my old tricks."

"Yes, and what's that?"

"Taking the altar boys on a picnic."

He was testing me, trying to discover what I knew. With an aplomb that surprised me, I showed no sign of surprise or recognition. I think I fooled him into thinking I knew nothing. But of course my watchfulness increased, and, truth to say, I found no evidence of his sexually abusing altar boys at Netcong.

Perhaps Hewetson saw himself as too old for that sort of thing. Would that he had been too old for nonsexual abuse. During Mass he would scream the Latin responses at his server if the boy were late with them. If the lad tinkered with the bell and sounded it at the wrong time, Hewetson would turn round and bark out a whopping loud "Quiet!" Conversely, if the boy neglected to ring the bell at the precise moment of consecration and the raising of the Host, Hewetson, unable to turn around, would roar out "Bell!" and kick viciously at the altar boy, his huge leg springing backward and to the side, rather as a horse or mule kicks, a sight for gods and men. Just awful. The little fellows would then come crying to me. Many of them quit being altar boys.

During these Netcong years—especially during my three-year honeymoon under Lange, I was, I believe, pretty much what the authorities at Darlington and in the Chancery Office at Paterson wanted: a conscientious, obedient, hardworking parish priest, with his feet on the ground. The fanaticism of my early days was gone. I had settled down to earth, while keeping a genuine sense of mission. I worked night and day, six days a week, a one-man peace corps. I baptized hundreds of babies, married scores of couples and attended their receptions, heard thousands of confessions (by far the most boring of all a priest's duties), anointed the sick and buried the dead, tried to help with domestic disputes, taught religion four mornings a week in the regional Catholic high school in Denville, and instructed converts coming into the Church. I built up a CYO that had all the teenagers in the town coming to Monday night religious instruction followed by a dance, every young person in town except Paul Fiorella, from the family with whom I had first dined out on Stoll Street. His father, a janitor at the high school, had become a friend of mine. But young Paul refused to attend CYO. I talked to him, and his parents talked to him, but he would have none of it. He had homework, he would tell his parents, and they wisely decided there was no sense in trying to force him. Today I admire him for his stand.

As part of my work with young people, I attended every home football and basketball game that Netcong High played. Surely Netcong was the only public high school in New Jersey to have, as it were, a chaplain, a Roman Catholic one at that. Some years after my time there, the tiny borough of Netcong drew brief national attention when its board of education, which included friends of mine, attempted through various shrewd shenanigans to allow prayer in this high school by having a voluntary gathering of students meet in the gymnasium, before the school day officially began, to hear a student volunteer read, from the *Congressional Record*, passages from prayers said by congressional chaplains at the opening of Congress. The Netcong policy was challenged by the New Jersey State Board of Education, and the case went all the way to the U.S. Supreme Court, which in December 1970 let stand a 7 to 0 New Jersey Supreme Court ruling that declared the practice unconstitutional.

The Netcong High football coach, the son of my close pal Gus

Rampone, was much amused when, after a game in which he had gone for a win and lost rather than settle for a tie, I told him that a tie was like kissing your sister, a notion hardly original with me, but he had never heard it and went around delightedly telling people what I had told him. Besides immersing me (from the sidelines) in sports, my work with teenagers brought on one curious train of events. Inspired by a Pete Seeger concert heard during my first vacation from Netcong, I purchased a guitar and, in a reprise of my eighth-grade dance-band phase, taught myself to play folk songs. I bought this guitar at a place in Manhattan called Noah Wolf's, and was delighted by the coincidence that Seeger himself was in the store at the time. At my request he played a few chords on the guitar I was buying, and then volunteered his opinion that it was a good instrument. Back in Netcong, once I had acquired a little facility on this guitar, I led youngsters—eighth graders and high schoolers—in hootenannies. Today the thought of my having done so is embarrassing, but things were different in the folksy 60s.

More importantly, I developed into a competent speaker, a preacher of a lighthearted, low-keyed, even whimsical sort. My sermons were short and humanistic. In one of them I told how the children in the third grade sent me individual, handwritten Christmas cards, one of which said: "Dear Father Hall, On Christmas I am going to pray for you and all other sinners. Sandra Puco." I introduced a homily on free will, a concept essential to Catholic thought, by offering up the Jewish wisdom of Isaac Bashevis Singer on the subject, "Of course I believe in free will—I have no choice." The great influence on my public speaking was Monsignor Ronald Knox. I loved his unpretentious, homely eloquence, whether he was giving talks to schoolgirls or retreats to priests. So immersed was I in his writings that I derived a style modeled on his. I borrowed ideas from him and quoted him. I drew, for example, on his words about the resurrection of the body—always a troublesome business—where he says that theologians are only guessing about this, especially when they say that we shall all be thirty-three years of age, Christ's supposed age at his death, and good-looking, "which is good news for some of us and makes us wonder how our friends are going to recognize us." At Easter I read my listeners this passage from Knox, in which he speaks of the tug-of-war between Life and Death:

> Every autumn, Death can say to Life, "You'll excuse my saying so, but I seem to have made you look a bit of a fool. What's become of all your spring fashions now? Where are your geraniums? where is your honeysuckle? where are your artichokes?" Of course, there are a few evergreens which confuse the reckoning, ivy and holly and aspidistras in peoples' front windows; but for practical purposes Death can claim, every autumn, to have swept the board. And Life has no answer, except to say, "Just you wait." And they wait until spring comes; and then Life can point proudly to the battlefield of nature and say, "There are my geraniums! There is my honeysuckle! There are my artichokes! Did you think you killed them? More fool you, if you did." And so the old business begins again, year after year. It's like a perpetual deuce-game of tennis; vantage-in every May, and vantage-out every November.

I led into one sermon with Knox's story of the little boy who goes to confession and begins, "I threw mud at busses and don't believe in the Holy Ghost."

The regard and affection shown me by many of Netcong's parishioners could easily have made me more spoiled than I was. It's not everybody who can resist the self-satisfaction attendant upon visiting a family for the first time and finding a picture of oneself, that same Bachrach photo, cut from the diocesan paper, framed and sitting on the mantel. When a minstrel show (it was still the days of minstrels in Netcong) was put on at Netcong High, I attended and at the end was called up to the stage—although I had had nothing to do with it—to be enveloped in thunderous applause. In those times priests, particularly newly ordained priests, were given respect, privileges, and prerogatives all out of proportion to what they deserved. Nothing was too good for Father. Driving up to a restaurant, he would be told, "Park right there in front, Father," and on finishing his meal he would be informed, "You can't pay here, Father." Of course the object of such respect will not be the first person to question the flimsy premise of that respect. It would be ridiculous to say that being on the receiving end of such adulation was not pleasant, especially after having been treated like a near-felon throughout six years of seminary.

During my stay in Netcong I did not have space, so to speak, for religious doubt or theological questions or introspection. Such worries were swallowed up in the excitement, the newness, and the continuing wonder of it all. I couldn't waste time cross-examining myself as to whether I believed in the Holy Ghost. Moreover, I must have been unconsciously caught up in the success of the Catholic Church. My Netcong years coincided with the apogee of the "Church Triumphant" in America, the early 1960s. Catholic parishes, schools, hospitals, seminaries, and universities thrived as never before. Then, too, these were the Kennedy years. At long last, there was a Catholic in the White House. His presidency seemed to help validate my decision to become a priest. It was funny to learn later that on being elected Kennedy had privately complained that now he would have to go to Mass every Sunday for four years.

Hewetson, annoyed at my popularity and my reluctance to eat with him and his parrot, drove down to the Chancery Office and complained to the chancellor, Monsignor Bill Lewis, that I was never in the rectory. Lewis, who knew Hewetson for a maniac, and who later told me the story, went to the bishop and said, "We had better get that young man out of there." They did, and in June 1963, to my mingled dismay and relief, transferred me from Netcong. I was sent to Morristown, the Morris County seat, where there were two big parishes. My assignment was to St. Margaret's, on the poorer side of town, with a largely Italian population. I was glad for that.

8

GIFTS OF FORTUNE

AT ST. MARGARET'S I got off to a shaky start. The boss was the senior martinet of the diocese, Monsignor John J. "Hank" Sheerin. He was a tough old bird, notorious for his gruffness and his temper. But no one accused him of not doing his job with zeal. The bishop of Newark sent him to Morristown in September 1930 to make a parish out of a tiny mission on the north side of the town. Sheerin arrived by train and from that time on hardly took a day off from his parochial duties. He built a combination church and school, converted a large old house into a convent, and put up a handsome rectory. He knew every Catholic, practicing or not, in what grew to be a large parish. The people of St. Margaret's had never known another pastor, and in spite of his strictness, they came to admire and some even to cherish him. He had a rough charm. One of his favorite expressions was "Don't you know how to take No for an answer?" If a parishioner had a brother who was a priest, might that priest come and baptize the parishioner's child in St. Margaret's? No. If a woman now living in St. Margaret's wanted permission to be married in her former parish, she got the same reply. And if she pleaded special circumstances, she heard, "Don't you know how to take No for an answer?" But in the wake of any argument he had with parishioner or curate or town official, when it was over, it was over. You always started again from scratch and were bound to be treated fairly, according to his lights. In Morristown he was always on hand. He knew every politician, sympathetic or otherwise, in Morris County. And although Sheerin was vicar general of the diocese, second in authority only to the bishop, he seldom ventured down to Paterson. His half of Morristown was everything to him.

For the last thirteen years Sheerin had had a faithful assistant, Father Tony Franchino. Having served his initial year as a priest under John Hewetson in Lincoln Park, Franchino came to Morristown in 1950 as Sheerin's first and only curate. A buoyant, upbeat, unpretentious person, Franchino was much more approachable than the pastor. He had a winning smile, and was one of those persons who, when you spoke to him or told him your troubles, seemed to enter into the matter as if yours were his sole concern in the world. Of course his being Italian-American gave him a cachet with that half of the parishioners, but he was popular with almost everyone. He prided himself on being an ordinary guy, a down-in-the-trenches working priest, whose delight on his day off was to go to the track with some like-minded parishioners. He would also place small bets in an illegal lottery down in the Hollow, the black quarter of town. Franchino and Sheerin functioned as an effective team, a version of good cop, bad cop. Then Franchino, while still in his early forties, suffered a severe heart attack. He recovered but was instructed to curtail his activities. And so Sheerin, with some misgivings, asked the bishop for an additional curate and was quickly obliged.

Sheerin and Franchino both distrusted me at first. They blamed me for having my heart still in Netcong. People from there would call me, and I would sometimes return to perform a wedding. These things annoyed the powers at the new place. You are expected to leave your former parish completely, and go, soldier-like, to a new theater of operations. I tried not to show my old attachment, but clearly I did. Then I had it out with Franchino. He had treated me coldly, and then balled me out over some little mix-up about the altar boys. We talked it over. He told me how both he and the boss felt about my lingering feelings for Netcong. I learned, too, that Franchino had been told by an older priest from Sussex County just what a villain I was. This priest and I had quarreled after he debarred

St. Michael's girls' basketball team from playing in his CYO league—my girls had always beaten his. Franchino laughed, and we made up and shared Hewetson stories.

Next I went to Sheerin and told him I understood his concern, but that in the future my loyalties would be entirely with St. Margaret's. He accepted what I said, and that was that, and we got on well afterward. Once I did incur his wrath, when I crossed Elizabeth Gallagher, his secretary and confidant. Elizabeth was a force in the rectory, but she was not a priestess as Irene Grogan had been in Netcong because Sheerin was too strong a personality to share any real power. On this occasion, however, she told some people whom she considered pests that I was unavailable, and I questioned her jurisdiction, so to speak. Elizabeth went and complained to Sheerin, who called me in: "You do that again, and you'll be out of here the next morning." But it ended there. With Hank Sheerin, you knew where you stood.

As for Franchino, he and I became fast friends and a year later I was able to do him a service. Appointments to pastorates, although at the favor of the bishop, followed almost automatically from seniority in years of service. In June 1964 Franchino was next in line for a parish, and we knew that the current pastor was vacating St. Joseph's in Newton. Unofficial word said Franchino's appointment to Newton was as good as done. Then we heard, also on solid intelligence, that there had been a change in plans at headquarters and that Franchino was to be skipped over for the time being, perhaps for as long as a year or two, until another parish opened up. The news devastated him. After fifteen years as a hardworking assistant, the first under the appalling Hewetson, and the next fourteen under the difficult Sheerin, Franchino desperately wanted to be his own boss. He and I had him packed to leave when this later rumor reached us. Without telling Franchino, I asked to see Sheerin on an "urgent and private matter." He received me in the stark front parlor, which was furnished with nothing but three chairs and a telephone next to the priest's chair. I angrily told him it was Franchino's turn—what did he have to do to be promoted, I asked, go to bed with an altar boy? Sheerin, who just may have told the bishop that Franchino was indispensable to him, listened and then dismissed me: "All right, Father, I'll think about what you have said." The moment I left the room, he was on the phone. I stood in the hallway and heard him say, "Well, Bishop, I know Franchino should not have had his heart set on it, but on the other hand..." It worked. When the June reassignments came out, Franchino was named pastor of Newton.

The man who replaced him at St. Margaret's was Tom Coletta, four years my junior. He had been one year in Blessed Sacrament Parish, Paterson, under an Italian-born, aged despot named Pasquale Mele. Monsignor Mele did no work and never entered his church, and when the bishop tried to get him to make his Easter Communion, as was required of all Catholics, by having Coletta bring an Italian priest to the rectory to hear his confession, Mele refused. Much else of what Coletta experienced was equally frustrating. He was newly ordained and full of energy, but found himself under what amounted to house arrest, assigned always by Mele to "cover" the rectory. Unhappy throughout his first year, Coletta requested a transfer and was sent to Sheerin. He brought with him a reputation for unconventional behavior, and when he arrived at the front door of St. Margaret's, Sheerin met him with a snarl: "You are to use the side door, Father, and there'll be no monkeys or fish in this house." Sheerin had heard that Coletta had kept tropical fish and a pet monkey in his room at Blessed Sacrament. In spite of this suspect start, Coletta was soon in the good graces of his new boss. Sheerin, who went on periodic drinking binges, once set out by car while still tipsy to visit his relatives in Kingston and crashed his Cadillac, a gift from the parish on his fortieth anniversary. The call came into the rectory on my day off, and Coletta went after him, got the car towed, took care of formalities with the police, put Sheerin into his own car, and convinced him that the best course would be for him to allow Coletta to drive him on to Pennsylvania. Sheerin, I believe, never forgot this generosity, and Coletta became a kind of son to him. But such was Sheerin's sense of justice that I was never conscious of any favoritism on his part.

I discovered the distinct advantage in working with another curate, in the camaraderie of someone close to my own age, and I found myself just as happy in Morristown as I had been in Netcong. It was as pleasant an assignment as Netcong under Lange, but many times more pleasant than Netcong under the impossible Hewetson. The parishioners here included many Italian-Americans, who had their Italian Society, St. Gerard's, which held an annual observance and the pinning of money on the banner, though nothing like the Netcong celebrations. Morristown also had many highly educated parishioners, Italian and otherwise, some of them new to the parish, whom both Sheerin and Franchino saw as my responsibility. When Franchino, who affected a kind of anti-intellectualism, was dividing up between us the parish societies we would be in charge of, he said of a radical lay group called CFM—Catholic Family Movement—"Yeah, you take them. You'll like them." And I did enjoy listening to these liberal, forward-thinking lay people, for that was my role, and I was in no way to "lead" them.

Not all the tasks Franchino deputed to me were as choice as working with CFM. My duties were to include, for example, providing "Benediction" after the Holy Name Parade. Benediction is the practice of blessing a congregation by making the sign of the cross over them with a large, consecrated "Host" or Communion wafer—the bread that, in the Mass, through transubstantiation, had become the body of Jesus. The Host is placed in a "monstrance," a two-foot gold-plated sunburst on a stand, with a two-inch round glass compartment in the center, behind which the consecrated Host (usually called "the Blessed Sacrament") can be seen. The Holy Name Societies comprised the male backbone of each parish, and once a year, on Holy Name Sunday, the leading men of all the parishes in the county would parade to martial music through the streets of Morristown. Many of the marchers wore tails and top hats. These demonstrations of strength and respectability by the onetime immigrant Church were to be discontinued after 1964, but we did not know this at the time. The parade ended up with a crowded assembly at the football field of Morristown High School, and hence St. Margaret's was the home or host parish, and I had to bring the Blessed Sacrament to the field for Benediction. "You do it," Franchino told me, "I ain't doing it *one more time*." And so, with a police car escorting my black Plymouth, with an altar boy and his bell in the back seat and the monstrance placed beside me on the passenger seat, I convoyed the Blessed Sacrament to the field. There, arrayed in cassock, surplice, and an immense Benediction cape, I carried the monstrance to the tinkling of the bell up to the front of the crowd, and, while everyone knelt, made the sign of the cross over them with the body of Jesus Christ. A whiff of magic from the Middle Ages. Then the reverse procedure till Jesus was safely back in the tabernacle. (Catholic teaching and practice in regard to the Eucharist has for centuries been one of the fundamental grounds of Protestant dissent from Rome. Here the Church of England or "Anglican" position as set forth in the Thirty-Nine Articles of 1563 is typical of practically all Protestant denominations: it condemns transubstantiation as "repugnant to the plain words of Scripture" and as having given "occasion for many superstitions"; the Sacrament of the Lord's Supper is not to be "reserved, carried about, lifted up, gazed upon, or worshipped.") When I later told the amused Coletta about my having brought the Blessed Sacrament to the football field, he told me that I should learn to regard my car as "an extension of the tabernacle."

Some added assignments came down from above, that is, from the Chancery Office, and, as in Netcong, I was again appointed to teach religion four mornings a week in a nearby regional high school, this time at Bayley Ellard in Madison. This work appealed to me—I interpreted "religion" very broadly—and at this time there arrived an opportunity to become even more involved in teaching. Our new bishop, James J. Navagh, formerly of Ogdensburg (Gentleman Jim McNulty having been promoted to the bigger diocese of Buffalo), was a whirlwind of ill-advised expansionist school building. He insisted on erecting grade schools in parishes that could not bear the expense, places that would never graduate a single student. His most grandiose plan was for a "minor" or high school seminary, and he sent out invitations to his younger clergy to study for graduate degrees so that he might staff this school with "teacher-priests." I went for advice to Father Chris Haag, up in Sussex, and he encouraged me to sign on for a degree: I had enjoyed teaching at Morris Catholic High School and at Bayley Ellard. I had long ago fallen in love with books, with English and American literature, and had initiated Great Books programs at these schools. Why not accept the bishop's offer? Doing so would involve taking one course a semester at Seton Hall. The degree and the actual full-time teaching assignment would be years in the future, and even then I would still function as a parish priest on weekends and later on would become a pastor, and so the bishop's program amounted less to a career change than an added dimension to what I was already doing. Haag, a consummate ecclesiastical tactician, also pointed out that if I didn't like the Seton Hall classes, I could simply drop them and tell the bishop it didn't suit. Sheerin, who had once taught Latin at Seton Hall and had a soft spot for the place, made no difficulties. And thus I found myself going down once a week to South Orange. The MA courses there were lively and thought-provoking, not at all like the insipid seminary classes I had sat through for six years. My chief instructor was an elderly Benedictine, Father Virgil, a Johns Hopkins Ph.D. and a stimulating teacher. He could be tough—I got only B+s at first—and he had a cruel streak in him. Once, when we had read Jonathan Swift's "Modest Proposal," he asked the class if anyone "didn't like Swift." One young woman raised her hand (there were now women on the South Orange campus). Virgil looked at her, shook his head, and said, "He's the test of intelligence, you know." On another subject, Virgil privately told me that his idea of hell was an interminable faculty meeting, a view with which I would later come to sympathize.

The Seton Hall course met weekly for two hours. My chief concern remained the people of St. Margaret's parish. And of all the many hundreds of parishioners I dealt with over the years, the most remarkable and memorable were two Morristown couples, who were often together as a quartet, the Logans and the Betzels. Ralph Logan, a quiet, steady man with an impish side that surfaced unexpectedly, was a Columbia Ph.D. in physics who worked in "pure science" at Bell Labs, where he developed the first light-emitting diodes (LEDs), the green and red lights that glow at us everywhere today. His wife, Ann, "Sweet Annie," or "Mother," as we called her, thought the best of everyone. Something of a mystic, she was the most loving person imaginable. She and Ralph had met at Columbia and were married there by Father George Ford, an early ecumenist and progressive who incensed Cardinal Spellman by saying from the pulpit that the Church would one day canonize Martin Luther. Ann was Irish-American, Ralph French-Canadian. He had a brother who was a priest, a Jesuit given to telling off-color jokes in mixed company, something Ralph would never have done. One of the jokes was about a wealthy old man getting an erection for the first time in years and being asked by his servant if he should tell the Mrs. "No," the old fellow said, "order the car. I'm taking this baby downtown." Ralph and Ann later told me that his brother was jealous of their being on such close terms with a priest other than himself.

Hank Betzel, who also worked for Bell Labs, on radar and high voltage, was much more extroverted than Ralph; he was one of the most optimistic, jovial persons I have ever met. Hank and his wife Betty were Hungarian-Americans. Betty had a cheerful personality and an amazing generosity. She was forever bringing other people's children—like the nine Logan children—gifts that she could hardly afford. When a friend of hers was diagnosed with TB after giving birth to a daughter, Betty without a moment's hesitation took the baby, for the first six months of its life, into her home, where she had her own half-dozen kids. Both Ann and Betty belonged to the generation of women who did not "work," but stayed home and managed children, in their case fifteen between them. Both families were gracious, relaxed hosts. I remember particularly the goose dinners Betty prepared for big holidays, and how Hank, the enthusiast, would run out and bring home special ingredients, praise the food to the skies, and cheer on the whole grand production. To enter their house was to be met by this bear-like man, happy, joking, inquiring, serious only when circumstances required. When we took trips to New York as a fivesome, the exuberant Hank led the way to restaurants, plays, and music. But our socializing took place for the most part at their homes, where I was treated weekly to evenings of talk and food and drink. It was as though these two couples and their numerous children formed an extended family to me, and they have continued to do so for many years.

In regard to Ann Logan, I kept her from extending her family any further. Birth control remained an enormous problem for devout Catholics and a quandary for their priests. This was still a time when Catholics—especially American Catholics—made what novelist David Lodge has called "a kind of existential contract: in return for the reassurance and stability afforded by the Catholic Metaphysical system, one accepted the moral imperatives that went with it, even if they were in practice sometimes inhumanly difficult and demanding." Lodge is talking specifically of the Church's prohibition against artificial birth control. That prohibition formed an important part of the Catholic "system," and "it was precisely the strength of the system that it was total, comprehensive, and uncompromising, and it seemed to those brought up in the system that to question one part of it was to question all of it." Catholics were not to pick and choose among the moral dictates of their Church. This "all or nothing" attitude has by now completely changed, but in the late 1950s and early 1960s I had distraught mothers tell me in confession that their doctors had told them that another pregnancy might be fatal. I have heard women say, "I am not afraid to die, Father, but I can't leave my other children." At first, still feeling I owed loyalty to the Church that employed me and gave me status, I was too straight-laced to say much more than "Well, do your best" and gloss over it. But in time I came to tell penitents that even the Church teaches that in the long run one was bound to follow one's own conscience. This was salutary advice, sometimes literally lifesaving. Ann Logan, after being sick in bed for many months with her latest pregnancy, had given birth to another child (to be named Thomas, in part because of my joking suggestion that he be named after Coletta—they already had a son named John). At home were her other eight children, each born about eighteen months apart, and now her health had given way. I visited her in the hospital, where she told me that her doctor had unequivocally warned her against having more children. And I said, "Yes, this has got to stop. You must use birth control from now on." Interviewed last year, some forty years afterward, she beamingly told me that I had saved her life. When I protested that this was a bit strong, she said, "No, no. You truly did. I'm not exaggerating." From none but a priest would she have accepted words licensing behavior contrary to Church teaching.

The biggest influence in my life at this time was Tom Coletta. A complicated man, he was dedicated and devout, but equally brash and irreverent. The propriety of St. Margaret's rectory amused him no end: the formal dining room, the buzzer under Sheerin's foot to summon the next course, Sheerin always to be addressed as "Monsignor," even as he always called us "Father." Coletta, a good mimic, took to calling me "Father"—and does so to this day. Tall, good-looking, and dark, he'd say, "I'm no light-haired 'golden Guinea,' Father, I'm the real thing." He was a dandy, a talented artist, a constant framer of prints, a purchaser of fancy drapery, and an admirer of Edith Piaf. I came to call him Cologne Colette, because in those days he always smelled like one of those cologne advertisements inserted in magazines; and although he was losing his hair, which annoyed him, at least he still had his Canoe, or whatever fragrance he liked at the time. Today he no longer uses cologne and seems not at all the dandy, but he does sport an almost imperceptible gray toupee. And he loved, as he put it, "to cocktail." When I was going to Seton Hall, he insisted that on the way home I stop at The Famous, a deli in South Orange, and buy two pastrami sandwiches. I'd arrive back at about 10 P.M., and Coletta would have Edith Piaf blaring on the stereo, glasses and ice out, and the scotch ready to pour. He was especially fond of scotch. On one occasion he was given an odd-shaped bottle of a special forty-year-old Chivas Regal in a purple velvet pouch. When this expensive stuff was gone, he kept filling up the bottle with cheap scotch, which he would with great fanfare bring out for "special friends, Father," and take satisfaction in hearing it pronounced "so different, so much smoother" than ordinary Chivas Regal. "You get what you pay for," he would tell them.

In his devotion to art he arraanged with the nuns to supply framed prints of classic Catholic subjects for the walls of the school classrooms and corridors. Sheerin would never have allowed money for such fripperies, so Coletta and I would steal from the collection, which the nuns counted on Sunday mornings after each Mass. Coletta would volunteer to help them, and I would come in with CYO money in rolled coins and ask for fifty dollars in bills and he would give me a hundred, and in this way he was able to get the cash to pay his framing expenses.

With Coletta everything was easy come, easy go. If I admired some Michelangelo reproduction of his own just back from the framer, he'd give it to me: "You seem to like it so much, you'd better just take it, Father. I'll do without." If someone were in trouble, he would give the person that month's pay check, $100. (A curate's $100 salary was supplemented by "stipend money," donations people made to have particular Masses "said to their intention" for the release of souls from Purgatory; the amount

given to a priest varied from parish to parish and ranged anywhere from $50 to $150 a month.) Coletta would befriend
unusual individuals, people whom other priests might have
written off as too irresponsible or too crazy to be helped.

And, even more than I did, Coletta liked to keep on the
move. When I knew him, he was always "running." He didn't
need much sleep and almost every night at 10 P.M., his parish
duties completed for the day, he would put on his "play clothes"
or "mufti" and go visit friends. Sheerin was getting too old to
enforce nighttime curfews, and Cologne Colette would sneak
back into the rectory in the small hours. On his official night off,
he attended drawing and painting classes at the Art Students'
League in Manhattan.

What Coletta, a man with whom I, a straightforward heterosexual, developed a kind of "homosocial" friendship, added to
the mix of my life was his peculiar humor and iconoclasm. Like
every other human being, I think of myself as having a sense of
humor, but clearly that gift comes in degrees, and I was not his
equal. I can imagine him laughing at my writing this, and saying, "You're one hundred percent correct there, Father." But I
was capable of catching on, of picking up attitudes from him.
For Coletta everything, grave or frivolous, was worthy of comic
treatment. It was not that he was not a serious and, after his
fashion, a religious man. He was that, and generous to a fault,
but he could not help but see the fun and the absurdity of it all.
Later in life, after years spent directing various Catholic high
schools, he operated a drug rehabilitation center in Paterson,
and then became pastor of the poorest of Paterson's inner city
parishes, Our Lady of Victories, home of the National Shrine
to St. Jude—the Patron Saint of Hopeless Cases. Coletta thinks
the famous St. Jude Novena there a scream but goes along with
it, though when in the company of certain select parishioners
he refers to the saint's relics as "chicken bones."

Sheerin's rigidity and formal manners were a fountain of
merriment for Coletta, and, in turn, for me. Just to have Coletta admonish me in Sheerin's voice, "Don't you know how to

take No for an answer, Father?" turned what could have been frustration into mental balm. His laughter at "Lizzie" Gallagher and her undue influence with Sheerin turned that abuse into a running joke. To Coletta the rectory at 6 Sussex Avenue became, because of Sheerin's political contacts—like Governor Richard Hughes—"the hub" of Morris County; Bayley Ellard High School was "the zoo"; St. Margaret's grammar school children were "all exceptional, Father." Even Sheerin's getting blind drunk for a few days every couple of months was a subject for amusement: "It's just the curse of the Irish, Father." Coletta worked assiduously in all aspects of parish life, but he believed that his free time was his to do with as he pleased, whether it was late night parties or art classes in New York. For a time he worked nights at a restaurant as dishwasher, salad man, and even bartender to get cash for someone in difficulty. That kind of nerve I never had. But I got the idea. Coletta helped very much to loosen the ties that bound me.

Coletta and I performed together under Sheerin during times of great upheaval in the Church. Like most younger priests of that era, we welcomed change for its own sake. The reforms of the Second Vatican Council were in the air. Pope John XXIII had convened this meeting of all Catholic bishops for the purpose of "renewing" the Church and positioning it better in the modern world. Coletta and I oversaw the introduction of laymen—not yet laywomen—as lectors, who read the epistle and gospel during Mass; we conducted the change from Latin to English in the liturgy; we installed a new altar facing the congregation and rigged up sensitive microphones so that the people could hear the words of the Mass. Sheerin, who was old-school conservative, accepted these developments grudgingly. And although he followed orders from the Chancery, he made it a point to have Coletta and me effect the changes. We also began having "dialogues" with Protestants and Jews. Coletta and I participated in a civil rights march of some one thousand people in sympathy with the Selma march. The Morristown *Daily Record* of March 14, 1965, had a front-page article and picture showing the two of us, alongside a black minister and the mayor, holding a Morristown banner and leading the march to the nearby town of Madison.

But some things remained decidedly old-fashioned. Once a year there was still the mania for "getting your ashes" on the first Wednesday of Lent. Even after the latest evening distribution at the altar rail, when you had recited the formula "Remember man that thou art dust . . ." for the thousandth time that day, as you were locking the church someone would come running up and plead for ashes. Savvy priests like Coletta and me kept an envelope containing ashes on our persons till late at night when people would come to the rectory, all excuses, but hoping to be reminded that they were dust. The "sacred ashes" were the burned remains of the previous year's palms—Palm Sunday being another day when church attendance went through the roof. Something for free. In another matter, the puritanical and guilt-inducing attitude toward sex, the Church remained unbending. In Morristown I even ran into a case where the rule for priests and religious sisters applied: *Numquam solus cum sola,* "Never a man alone with a woman alone." A nun at St. Margaret's came down with what looked to be a serious illness, and I drove her and her sister companion to the local Catholic hospital, All Souls, which was about five miles away. Once there, we learned that the sick sister had to be admitted to the hospital. At this point the other nun pointed out that she could not travel back alone with me to St. Margaret's convent—*numquam sola cum solo*—whereupon I drove back to the convent, picked up two more sisters, returned to All Souls, and took the three back to the convent. Coletta's comment, "That's just as it should be, Father."

My mental struggles with belief have been put on the back burner in these last chapters because that in fact is where they were in my life during these years in Netcong and Morristown. Caught up in the everyday goings on in the parish, with the constant stream of expected and unexpected busyness, some of it petty, some of it important, but all of it for the moment urgent, I was absorbed in my work. I didn't waste energy worrying about substance and transubstantiation, the existence of angels and devils, or, come to that, the existence of God. In Morristown I mellowed. I "believed" less, but troubled myself less about not believing, and I was getting more and more out of myself or at least out of harmful introspection. My special friendships with the Logans and Betzels and, most particularly, with Tom Coletta, were especially helpful. Like many a young person, I was much influenced by the people I worked with and for. Thinking Catholics are fond of taking a "sacramental" view of the material world, seeing everything, from bread and wine to other people, as manifestations of the immaterial, spiritual world. "Outward signs of inward grace" was commonplace Catholic parlance. I viewed these five charming, generous people not as graces from God but as gifts of fortune. I was lucky to have them.

In the spring of 1965 Sheerin was operated on for cancer of the stomach. He recovered somewhat, but was suddenly ordered back to the hospital. Coletta and I were having lunch at the New York Tea Garden, a Chinese restaurant off the square in Morristown, when the housekeeper called us with the news. We hurried to All Souls Hospital and were given gowns and masks, and allowed to watch this second operation. Sheerin never recovered, and, after a week unconscious on a respirator, he died on June 1, 1965.

It fell to Coletta and me to run the funeral. I, as senior curate, was in charge of the parish and the purse strings until a new pastor was named. Sheerin's send-off, we determined, would be a good one. He had founded the parish and run it for thirty-five years. Costs be damned, and I let Coletta loose. He had a definite "flare" for this kind of thing, and we put on a good show. First he arranged for flowers for the viewing in the rectory and in the church. Morristown, which a hundred years earlier had been the wealthiest community in America, still had good florists; and Coletta, who knew his flowers, ordered flowers such as I had never seen. He ran over to New York to get new vestments and a special lace alb from Ireland for the laying-out and burial. We hired the parish electrician, Paul Schlosser, to put in a new line and install air conditioning in the front parlor. Coletta and I, with brushes and rollers, then painted the room ourselves because we could find no workmen available. And, of course, new drapes were put up. A contingent of Sheerin's Pennsylvania relatives arrived, along with their bishop, George Leech of Harrisburg. The night before the burial, the coffin was transferred from the rectory to the church, where the bishop and other clerics recited the Office of the Dead. Parish societies kept an all-night vigil. The seminary choir director, Jack Carroll, was a friend of Coletta's, and we hired him and professional singers to augment the choir for the Mass. Rather than let parishioners squabble over who would be pallbearers, we hired professionals. We lined up the best caterers in Morris County for the post-service "repast," which had to be carefully prepared because the day was a meatless Friday. The funeral ceremony was attended by New Jersey Governor Hughes and Congressional Representative Peter Frelingheysen, the mayor of Morristown, dozens of civic leaders, together with seven bishops, scores of priests and nuns and hundreds of parishioners. We had to set up outdoor speakers to accommodate the overflow crowd. Paterson's own volatile Bishop Navagh celebrated the solemn high requiem Mass, which ended with the organ, choir, and many in the pews roaring out Martin Luther's "A Mighty Fortress Is Our God," at which Navagh became incensed. This was ironic enough because, as it happened, Sheerin had been very fond of the hymn.

New assignments were due out a week later, and we learned that Chris Haag, my old mentor and friend, the priest who had rescued me from Scully and perfectionism, was to be the new pastor. Haag later said he had not wanted the promotion from his small church in Sussex, but that Bishop Navagh had insisted that he take the larger parish. The prospect of working under

Haag enthralled me. I was among the many younger priests who would flock to him and sit at his feet—Coletta came to call him "Granny"—and although in recent years I had only occasionally visited him in Sussex, he was still someone very special in my eyes. Haag was liberal-minded, progressive, articulate, charming, and savvy. A hard worker, an accomplished storyteller, a gossip, and a man with a sense of humor, he loved to socialize and host drinks parties for priests. I told the Logans and Betzels what a wonderful man he was and how I was looking forward to his arrival.

Then there came a letter from the Chancery Office informing me that I was being transferred to St. Mary's in Paterson. I was panicked. Thinking there was still time, I went to see Haag, who was making a priests' retreat at the Jesuit house outside of Morristown, and pleaded with him to intervene with the bishop to keep me at St. Margaret's. He said there was nothing he would like better in all the world than to work with me, that he would do his best in urging the bishop to change his mind, but that in such matters he would probably have little influence. Still hoping against hope, I asked Bob Tracy, a parishioner who was postmaster in Morristown, to expedite any mail I might receive from the Chancery, the letter I hoped would cancel the earlier one. None came.

It was rumored that I was transferred because of the funeral, that it had been too lavish and too expensive, all of it topped with the singing of that notorious Protestant hymn. The rumor was untrue. I learned in due course, from an unimpeachable Chancery source, that Haag had in fact asked for my removal. Why he did so I still have no idea. Perhaps, like the Turk, he could bear no brother near the throne.

9

TWO ENTERTAINERS

PEOPLE are fond of alluding (as I did earlier) to St. Paul's words to the Romans that all things work together for good with those that love God. But things can work out well for those who don't love God or even believe in him, and the move to Paterson, so utterly against my wishes, put me on course for the change that would bring me the happiness I mentioned in the first lines of this book.

St. Mary's was a storied old parish in the Totowa, or western, across-the-river side of town, with one main commercial thoroughfare, Union Avenue, and scores of small one-way streets. These streets were lined with narrow two- and three-story early twentieth-century wood-frame houses, most of them covered by now with aluminum siding or imitation brick facing. It was here that many of Paterson's policemen and firemen lived. The Great Falls themselves were in our parish, the power source that had inspired Alexander Hamilton to develop Paterson into the nation's first planned industrial city, America's initial engagement with the Industrial Revolution. It became a city of textile mills—the "Silk City"—and of locomotive works and armament plants. In the first decades of the twentieth century Paterson was the site of historic (and mostly unsuccessful) labor strikes over issues of hours, safety, child labor, and minimum wages. Paterson also produced the transportable railway car diners that dotted the country in the 1920s and 1930s. Hinchcliffe Stadium was within our borders, as was the very large Public School 5, and the new Kennedy High School. I still have a copy of the "Benediction" I gave at its dedication, including words about how JFK wanted us to see ourselves and our country, "young, brave, civilized, tolerant, rational, questing," some of my adjectives borrowed from Arthur M. Schlesinger, Jr. When the mayor told me how he admired my words, I admitted to him my debt to Schlesinger, but he, ever the politician, came back with "Well, at least you knew where to look." St. Mary's boasted a beautiful golden brick, basilica-style church with a campanile, and a large comfortable rectory next to it on Union Avenue. (In speech Patersonians always shorten "Avenue" to a nasal "Av.") A block away, the parish had a grammar school, convent, and small high school.

My new boss-to-be was an elderly Irishman, Monsignor John F. Brady, said to be affable and noninterfering toward his assistants. There was another curate, John Heekin, whom Coletta had instructed to greet me with a scotch and a warm welcome. Heekin, a veritable disciple of Coletta, did so with a bottle of J & B. The parish, which had once been almost exclusively Irish, was by now more than half Italian. These parishioners, all working class people, showed themselves generous, helpful, and receptive of their new priest.

St. Mary's being even bigger than St. Margaret's, and the pastor virtually inactive, I was busier than ever. One barometer of the size and health of a parish is the number of weddings performed yearly—each requiring lengthy "instructions" in marriage from a celibate priest—and at St. Mary's during the wedding season we had as many as three or four a Saturday. Couples had to reserve a date for the church well in advance. One young Italian fellow, who had made arrangements under my predecessor, came to see me with the news that he and his fiancée had broken up: "But if you still have the date, I have a new girl." The number of teenagers in the parish was staggering. I ran Friday night CYO dances in the school auditorium, dances which attracted so many hundreds of youngsters that we had to turn many away for fear the floor would collapse. Another indication of a robust parish was the revenue to run a grammar school and its own high school. Working with high school students had become a specialty with me, something I did with enthusiasm, and here, in effect, was my own high school. Its enrollment was only two hundred and its building much smaller than the grammar school, which had a cafeteria and auditorium. The high school, at one time a parish center and bowling alley, comprised nothing more than eight classrooms, four to a floor. Still, it was a spirited and lively place. I was again teaching my liberal version of religion to high school students, and I was more than ever involved in high school sports because as senior curate my duties included being the school's athletic director.

The most memorable part of my high school connection came in working with Jerry Molloy, a legendary coach and professional Irish funny man. Molloy, Hoboken-born and still a resident of that city, had been basketball and baseball coach at St. Mary's since 1933, the year I was born. He had also worked as a basketball referee in Madison Square Garden, something he never tired of telling people about. His other occupation was that of public speaker. He claimed to give three hundred Communion breakfast talks a year, an exaggeration because these breakfasts were usually held on Sundays. But he was always on the rubber-chicken circuit, and every time I met him he would tell me where he had spoken last week, how he had introduced the governor at some state function, how he had told the story about the porter asking to carry his bag, or the one about his son being the only child in Hoboken to flunk recess, or the one about the minister who asks the three drunks if they wanted to go to heaven. He had literally thousands of old jokes and one-liners stored in his memory, from which abundance he would draw gags to suit any occasion or circumstance. He would tell people how a former player of his named Comerford had once hired Jerry's archrival, Ace Molinari, as a coach:

Comerford: "What shall I pay you?"

Molinari: "Just pay me what you think I am worth."

Comerford: "Well, I want to pay you *something*."

And of course Molloy loved to speak of Irishmen who drank: "I have an uncle who when he gets drunk walks around with his head back. He doesn't want to spill any," or "I have an uncle who gets drunk on one glass of beer. He keeps filling it up." Molloy, in small doses, was wonderful. Introduced by me to my friends from Netcong, he said "Yes, Netcong, I know the place. The only cemetery anywhere with lights."

More for the fun of it than from duty I went to every home and away basketball game, where my job was to restrain this funny man's ungovernable temper. I even went to some practices at our "home" court, the gym of Public School 5, which the local Catholics on the Paterson School Board effectively gave to St. Mary's. During practices I've seen Molloy so upset at a player's performance that he'd pull his tie over his head as if strangling himself while screaming "I'll kill myself! I'll kill myself!" He became infuriated at players missing foul shots and announced that no one could go home until everyone on the squad had made five in a row. Many of them couldn't make five in a row, and it was getting late and Jerry himself had to get back to Hoboken, so he hollered for the ball, stood at the foul line, and banged the ball hard against the backboard into the net ten times in a row, whereupon everyone, himself included, laughed and went home

But practices were private, and it was at the games themselves where I was supposed to calm him down. I was no match for him. For one thing, he had been through more than a dozen young priest athletic directors over the years. They had come and gone, while he remained the spectacularly successful basketball coach of tiny St. Mary's High, for which he had created continually winning teams. In the thirties he had taken St. Mary's to Chicago for some national Catholic championship. During my tenure as his "director," he won his five hundredth game at the school and was recognized as the "Dean" of New Jersey high school coaches. One of his protégés in my time was Bob Hannan, who in a late-season game was knocked hard to the floor with what looked like a serious injury. Molloy and I—for all the good it would do—rushed to his side. After a scary moment he got up and scored his one thousandth career point, a high water mark in those days. Hannan was offered a number of college scholarships and whittled them down to two, Army and Georgetown, whereupon I, at the height of my antiwar feelings, prevailed upon him, with Jerry's approval, to go to Georgetown.

During games, with me sitting next to him on the bench, Jerry screamed and carried on. At bad calls or mistakes he hurled his jacket onto the court and ran around in small circles howling. He'd leap up and kick over chairs. He took off his shoes and threw them at the scoreboard. The referees were intimidated by his reputation and his knowledge of the game, and ejected him only when he became particularly egregious or personal, as when he yelled at a referee by name in words audible throughout the gym, "You're a lousy coach but a lousier referee." I soon realized that I should just sit back and enjoy the spectacle, as objectionable as it was, as bad an example as it was for the kids. For the youngsters seemed to understand that he was a peculiar phenomenon, to be respected but not imitated. Molloy was a true choleric, and minutes after an explosion he would be calm, apologetic, and joking. Some of his treatment of the players was endearing. When his star pitcher decided to quit, Jerry told the rest of the team to forget it: "So we won't win that many games. What does he expect me to do, make a novena?" When his third baseman made three consecutive errors in one inning and in effect threw away the league championship, Jerry put his arm around the kid and said, "It's all right, Bruce, we all make mistakes. I make mistakes. I got married. Bruce, I still love you, but I have to tell you, from now on you're excluded from my prayers."

Molloy as entertainment I dealt with fifty or sixty times a year. My other delight I met twice a day. This was Monsignor Brady. If Molloy was a professional, got-up Irishman from Hoboken, Brady was the real thing. He had come to this country from Dublin to study for the priesthood at Seton Hall and, having been ordained in 1918, he had become more Irish with

each year. He kept and cultivated a brogue, which together
with his small stature, leprechaun demeanor, and mischievous
eyes, made him the preeminent Irishman in the diocese of
Paterson.

He had two failings, neither of which affected me. He had
been a pastor with a priestess, a woman famous in the diocese,
whom he referred to as his "Aunt." But she had been seven years
dead by the time I arrived at St. Mary's. The senior curate back
then was Vincent Puma, formerly one of "Scully's boys," but long
since liberated. Puma was a whirlwind of involvement with the
city. To Brady he was "Oh, the man about town, the Politician."
Puma had been instructing a black woman to become a Catholic—something Irishman Brady couldn't fathom—and then a
black friend of the would-be convert broke into the rectory,
opened doors looking for things to steal, and burst into the
bathroom where Auntie was taking a bath. She screamed, had a
stroke, and died on the spot. True story. In Brady's eyes, though
he never mentioned the incident, Puma the Politician had been
to blame. In any case, Auntie was no longer around to tyrannize
over the curates, and Brady never replaced her.

His other fault was drink. The same Vincent Puma was
once asked by Bishop McNulty, "Can you keep Brady sober for
six months so he could be made a Monsignor?" But by the time
I came to the parish Brady's drinking was no longer a problem, for he had evolved into a strictly periodic drinker, twice a
year, the week after returning from short vacations he took to
Ireland. He would arrive by stealth back into the rectory, say
nothing to anyone, put up on the hallway bulletin board a note
saying "The Pastor Is Out," and go to his room. The sexton, a
man named Jim, knew the drill and would supply him with
drink and food for exactly one week. Then after seven days of
oblivion, Brady would turn up at the table for lunch, fresh as
paint. The week "out" formed part of his vacation. For years he
had not drunk on the job, except, I was told, during the weekend of the Kennedy assassination. This catastrophe for Irish
Catholicism was too much for Brady. His custom, between

Sunday Masses, was to direct cars in the parish parking lot, an entire square block in back of the church. This jovial behavior was an instance of his eccentric charm, but on the Sunday following Kennedy's death he directed traffic in his cups, wearing a bathrobe and a fedora, weeping and repeating, "They killed my friend, they killed my friend." But I myself never saw Brady the worse for drink.

I talk about him here not only as the man who made my two years in Paterson enjoyable and whose antic talk diverted me from worries about belief, but also because he was a voice of the old and dying Church, the Church we younger priests could not help but secretly admire, although we were all the time, as Brady said, "shouting" for change. Between him and me were nicely poised the old and the new in the Church. He was in some ways reprehensible. For example, he found it dismaying that his parish should have changed from Irish to Italian: "My God, not a white man on the block." When I told him how in these ecumenical times some Church theologians were trying to wiggle out of the plain fact that the Gospel of Matthew blames the Jews for the death of Jesus, Brady thought about it for a moment and said, "Maybe the Puerto Ricans did it." He came from a time when "Father" knew best, did his work, took his orders, tried to laugh his way through difficult times, and was permitted, by virtue of his office, a good deal of quirkiness, or worse. I doubt the Church has his likes today. I fear, too, that on paper Brady comes out less benign than he was in person, for his playful and ironic voice never betrayed the slightest touch of anger or malice. Only he could get away with telling the children preparing for confirmation, "Miss your answer to the bishop, and you'll be turned into a rat."

I had not been in the parish twenty-four hours before I realized what a treasure his talk was and decided to write some of it down. Three days into my new assignment, grammar school graduation took place. Brady sat in a big chair in front of the altar while I stood on his left, handing him the diplomas. Each graduate knelt before him just long enough to be given a diploma. Brady kept up a quick chatter from beginning to end, something different for each silent child:

"I knew you'd make it.
Away we go. Do you know Jackie Gleason?
Sorry to see you leave.
A nurse? You can hold my hand.
Don't get hit. Watch the traffic.
You're the best looking of the bunch.
Last but not least. I knew all the time you were out-standing."

But as a rule I saw him only at table, lunch and dinner, in the formal old-fashioned dining room, fitted out, as had been the case in Morristown, with a Persian or "Turkey" carpet and a buzzer under the Monsignor's foot to call the cook to bring in the courses. Meals began promptly at the ringing of the church Angelus bells at 12 noon and 6 in the evening. He would be first to arrive, wearing a dirty maroon smoking jacket, a black shirt front and full Roman collar, standing at his place at the head of the table and waiting for us. He would mutter a garbled grace, make a swipe at himself for the sign of the cross, and begin talking. He didn't use greetings. In fact I never heard him say hello to anyone. It was a curiously impersonal style, and I sometimes doubted that he knew my name. Anything not to his liking or that he thought silly was "yours"—your bishop, your mayor, your new liturgy, your athletes, your school, your graduation. His talk was laden with favorite words and phrases: "Yeah" and "Hah" and "Oh my God" and "I don't know," this last pronounced "dunno" and always implying that you didn't know. After meals, in my room, I would jot down bits of his conversation.

Like most workers in the field, he distrusted diocesan head-quarters, especially the bishop:

"Oh my God, your new bishop is in the paper again. Says the Holy Ghost sent him to Paterson. From Ogdens-burg. Oh my God. Yeah, he says the Holy Ghost sent him here. I dunno. My God, you'd think the Holy Ghost would have kept him in Ogdensburg. Yeah, well, he'll be wanting to come here for confirmation. Great day that will be, oh a big day. The nuns will have the kiddies all lined up."

We curates looked upon the nuns as martyrs of the Church, locked up in their convent with a mother superior who just might be a tyrant or a lunatic. Assistant priests were at least free to run about and get away from their pastors. But Brady thought the nuns were not working as hard as they once did and were being given too much freedom of movement:

> "Oh my God. Your nuns. You'd think they would teach the kids something. I was rehearsing your students for confirmation the other day, 'Sonny, who made you?' 'God.' 'Terrific. You're the best in the class. Next. Who made the world?' 'Christ.' 'I don't think he did. Next. What's confirmation?' 'We didn't get that far, Father.' My God, you'd think the sisters would teach them what confirmation was just in case the bishop asked them. And the Seven Capital Sins. 'Can you name the Capital Sins?' No answers. Do they have Capital Sins anymore?"
> "Deadly, I think they say 'Seven Deadly Sins' now."
> "Seven Deadly? What are the Seven Deadly Sins?—anger, hatred, lust, greed, — my God I forget them myself. Your nuns don't teach religion anymore. Theology. Catechism isn't good enough. You'd think they'd teach the children to say the Act of Contrition. At least that, but oh no. Driving around in a big car. Going off to college Saturday mornings to become professors. I dunno. Do the sisters do anything now? Some do, I suppose. Wouldn't know it to look at the kids at Mass—squirming around in the pews, heads darting around like rabbits. Don't know what the Church is coming to."

While my circle of liberal priest friends was avid for change

in the Church and in society, Brady opposed any change, ecclesiastical or otherwise:

"Paper says they're protestin' again. Oh my God, yeah,
students. Youth. Oh my, bad. My God, you'd think they'd
study their lessons. Don't have to. Your youth. In California. You read about it? Don't you look at the papers?" [He
himself read every word of the *New York Times* and the
Paterson papers, each morning in his study.]
  "What are they protesting?"
  "Dunno. Wasn't there. Dunno know what the country's
coming to. Your youth. Their fathers slave and work and
scrimp and send them to college and what do they do?
Protest. And get married the day they graduate. Never a
cent for the old man. Ingratitude. Hah! It's a funny country. Well, isn't it?"
  "Well, yes."
  "Oh indeed, don't I know it. Been seeing it for a hundred
years. Oh my God, where is she? No soup today? Yeah,
don't know what the country's coming to. It's in the papers all the time. They want their rights. Yeah, everybody
wants their rights. Everybody's protestin', even the priests.
Yeah, everybody shoutin' and hollerin' about their rights.
My God when I was ordained, a priest didn't have any
rights. He just did his work. Worked hard too. And played
golf. Very important to play golf. I should know. My God,
I played every course in the state."

For John Brady, even midnight Mass was an innovation:

"Yeah, what time is midnight Mass, Father? Ringing
the damn phone. Then showing up at midnight, right out
of the bars and into the church, 'goin' to Mass.' Your parishioners. Look at the ones who come to midnight Mass.
Never see them all year. Then there they are in the front
pew. Oh, we used to have a lot of trouble with midnight

Mass. Right from the tavern. Goin' to Mass. Hah!"

Brady thought ecumenism a mistake. Most younger priests, like myself, thought ecumenism was crucial to the future of the

Church. I told him I had met the minister of the Baptist Church across the street:

"I dunno him."

"Seemed kind of shy. I was going by, and I went up and accosted him."

"You accosted him?"

"Well, these are ecumenical times, Monsignor."

"Oh indeed, I should know. I've sent enough people over to his place on Sundays. I've sent them, but they never go.

They would rather stand in back of my church. Or on the stairs outside. I don't know why they bother coming to Mass at all."

"The minister's name is Henry Seidel."

"Dunno. There have been some good ones over there in the past. Nice lads. Wanted to discuss *religion!* Hah! Some of those fellows are good preachers. Preaching is important in the Protestant church. And singing. Oh, indeed. Singing is important. It's one of the requirements. Nowadays we're supposed to sing, but we can't do it like them. I don't know about this fellow across the street. Never see much going on over there."

"Oh, they have people coming to church."

"I dunno. We're changing. We're all the same now, regardless of race, color, or creed. I hear there are less converts each year. Oh, it's a great country. We're all the same. Yeah, ecumenical. Not long ago if a Catholic married a Protestant here it was in the little room where you fellows fill out the forms. They didn't even get into the big office. Now they are married right in the church. Sure, no difference. All the same. Can Protestants get married at Mass? Someone said they could."

"Yes, they can. That's the new liturgy."

"My God, I never heard of that before."

The new liturgy, especially the change from Latin to English in the Mass, was all the rage with the younger clergy. We were making Mass more "meaningful" by putting it into the vernacular. Only later would some worry about throwing out the baby with the bath water, about exchanging mystery and grandeur for everyday words and guitar-accompanied folk hymns like "Kum Ba Ya." Brady was adamant:

"Your new liturgy is no liturgy. Do whatever you feel like out there—that's the new liturgy. I can't see that with all the shoutin' anything got any better. And having Mass for the kiddies at Hinchcliffe Stadium, giving out Communion like chocolates. Your new liturgy. They made a mess of it. Tried to go too fast. If they wanted to change to English they should have thought it through and did a decent job."

"Well, that's your bishops' committees."

"I dunno. Wouldn't know who did it. I don't see where it made people more devout. I mean I would like to see evidence of some progress. I think it's getting worse. Oh, your Catholicity is dying out. Used to be a time when people said their prayers and went to Mass. At least they went to Mass. I always say if somebody goes to Mass, there's hope. Well, is that right?"

"Yes, I suppose it is."

"And they used to make missions. Oh, indeed. Everybody had to come. People hanging out the windows, sitting all over the steps, even on the altar. Your men came out. Tough old birds too. [He had the notion that too much religion in a man—like going to weekday Mass—was a bad sign. Daily Mass was fine for women.] Oh, you had to make a mission. And they got hell from the missionary. Now you don't hear about hell any more. It's not in the new liturgy."

As curates, we had little concern with parish finances, which were always the responsibility and worry of the pastor. But we younger priests believed that, as part of Church reform, the laity should be more closely involved in parish finances. I told Brady that one of his trustees, old Doctor Schultz, had just died:

"Oh, did he? I'm surprised he lasted as long as he did. This weather did it. Hot weather is bad for old birds. I'll have to make old John—what's his name?—a trustee."

"D'Arienzo."

"Yeah, whatever it is."

"He'd take it as a great honor."

"It's not anything. Your trustees are nothing. It's state law. Every parish has five trustees. Your bishop is president, your Vicar General vice president, and the pastor secretary treasurer. And then the two lay trustees. They're nothing because it's three to two. Or four to one. Hah! My God, they've had trouble in the past with lay trustees. Take over your church. Yeah, they would. If you let them. My God, I'll never forget the time at Hopatcong when I built a rectory or some damn thing and this lad comes in and wants to know why he wasn't consulted. He says he's a banker—he wasn't a banker, he worked in a bank. He says that from being a banker he knows the duties of trustees and they are to be consulted. I said, 'Sonny, since this is so onerous a responsibility I am happy to relieve you of it. Your services are no longer required.' Hah! My God, was he mad.

"Everything is money, Catholic or not. You take that parking lot out back. All those houses I had to buy to get that parking lot. The damn thing cost me two hundred thousand dollars. For a parking lot. That one house still out there. They knew I wanted to buy it and they were going to make money out of the Church. Father was going to get them a nice house in the suburbs. Well I fixed them. I surrounded them with macadam. Hah! The lassie came over here ten years ago screaming that I was ruining her beautiful property. I said, 'Yes, it's all gold inside, I know.' And now the husband comes around the other day asking if I was still interested. I said 'Sonny, who are you?' I knew damn well who he was. 'Don't you remember me?' 'Yeah, a very valuable house.' Would I like to come in and see it? 'I don't have to,' I said. 'I know all about it, it's all gold inside.' Hah! Money."

When the bishop ran a campaign to put up new schools, all the pastors in Paterson "came running" to a parishioner of

Brady's, a successful builder named Ottilio. Here was something pastor and curate could agree on:

> "My God, Ottilio came in here and said Father I want to give you something for the campaign. I said my God you do enough. But he gave me a check. I wouldn't even open it. Oh some priests, terrible. Always buildin' and shoutin'. And hitting up on the same old people. Four or five collections. People trying to go to Mass and ushers keep shoving baskets in front of them. I don't allow it here. Seems too much. And the penny-ante stuff, dinners and lunches and raffles and bingos, it's not Christian. One collection is all. And if they don't give, let them at least go home with a smile on their faces. No wonder some people don't go to church."

And, finally, everything about Paterson intrigued Brady—and me:

> "Where's your new mayor from? Is he a Catholic?"
> "Yes, I understand he is."
> "I wouldn't know. A good one? Goes to Mass? Maybe he goes *now*. I dunno, seems a nice enough lad. I knew your old mayors. All the old people have moved out of Paterson. Oh, good people, too. Oh, indeed. Yeah, they moved to Wayne or Bergen County or Ridgewood or somewhere. Don't blame them. Well, would *you* like to live in Paterson if you didn't have to? My God, there was man in here from Brooklyn said they were moving in and he wanted to send his kids to the school. I said I didn't know about that, it was a matter for the Department of the Interior. Told him to see your principal. But he's coming here from Brooklyn. Owns a tavern there. I said, 'What the hell do you want to come to Paterson for?' And he says, 'My wife wants to live in Jersey,' and I said, 'But this is not New Jersey, this is Paterson. It's different.' Yeah, the people here are different. Oh my God, don't I know it. Nowadays they don't even know

how to talk on the phone. 'Are you there?' That's how they answer the phone, 'Hello, are you there?' 'No I'm not. I'm somewhere else.'"

Not everyone caught on to him. It is the ironist's privilege to allow his ironies to go undetected. One evening I was "instructing" a young couple for marriage. They were seated before me in one of the little front offices. Brady, passing by and wearing as always his maroon smoking jacket, poked his head into the room and said, "Marry the girl. I would. It's the only solution," and disappeared. "*Who* was that?" the young groom-to-be demanded. Just Monsignor Brady, I explained. The man who helped make my time in the cathedral city so enjoyable.

10

A PARTY

I HAD NEVER been to Europe. When an opportunity
came in July 1965, soon after I was sent to Paterson, the
visit changed my life. And although my trip took place
forty years ago, I recall it as vividly as anything I have ever experienced. My determination to go to Spain rather than, say,
London or Paris, had taken hold back in 1955, when some seminarian classmates, including Bob Call, went to the Fiesta of San
Fermín in Pamplona. The festival was originally a religious holiday honoring the fourth-century bishop and martyr; but over
the centuries the feast has evolved into a week-long earthy and
exuberant celebration of wine and song and bulls. The stories
Call told on his return made me yearn to attend these festivities.
Like many young men of my generation, I all but worshipped
Hemingway, and my favorite Hemingway novel was *The Sun
Also Rises*, the work in which, one might say, he definitively described the fiesta. I have not looked at his book in fifty years, and
I hope that what I put down here is not secondhand Heming-
way, than which there are few things worse. Here's the way I
remember Pamplona.

Call, or "Mr. Call" as I always referred to him, like myself a
priest of six years' standing, agreed to "do" Pamplona with me in
as Pamplonican a style as possible. He met me in the Madrid airport, where a Hertz rental car was waiting for us. We arrived at
Pamplona the next morning, July 6th, in time for the opening of
festivities. Like other *sanfermineros* we wore the regulation costume for the fiesta, white shirts with red pañuelos or bandannas
tied around our necks. Call, so as to make us look less like foreigners, insisted we have plain red pañuelos, "not touristy ones

184

decorated with brown bulls." This worked somewhat to our advantage, but his fluent Spanish proved a much greater help.

We drove through the city past swirling crowds of people. White and red were everywhere. Not just the white shirts and red pañuelos of the men, but white dresses and red neckerchiefs of the women, and similar outfits on the children. As we came into the Plaza del Castillo, the center of the fiesta and our home base for the coming week, a policeman in a white coat, white pith helmet, and white gloves directed traffic with a white baton. The large square had a concert bandstand in the center surrounded by an area for dancing, which was in turn ringed by grass and trees, paths and benches. The broad sidewalks were occupied by café tables, while the actual walkway was under a colonnade which fronted the tall buildings—banks for the most part—that bordered the square. Flags of Spain, Navarre, and Pamplona jutted out from balconies and windows. We found a parking spot and then a table at the Bearin Café. Like the plaza's two other enormous cafés, the Iruña and the Txoko, the Bearin had black-and-white striped awnings that extended out over the sidewalk. We had time for a croissant and coffee before joining the crowd moving toward the Ayuntamiento, or City Hall, where at twelve noon the fiesta was about to explode.

As you neared the Ayuntamiento the crush of people was immobilizing. Noon struck, a skyrocket went up, and the fiesta began. Everybody started shouting and dancing to music that came at you from all directions—from military bands, fife bands, string bands, all dinning away and leading people back to the plaza. And now there appeared peñas, or young men's social clubs, each with its own street band and led by men carrying large white banners on which were painted cartoon figures. All week long you would encounter these dancing and singing youths, called *mozos* (literally "youngsters"), performing traditional Navarran music.

We were washed back up to the square and down an alley to the Rincón, a bar where natives, mostly old men, were seated at tables drinking wine from glass porróns and eating bread and cheese. A glass of red wine, *vino tinto*, cost the equivalent of two cents. Call asked directions for a shop selling leather wineskins, or "botas," and we were directed to a place upstairs two doors away. The proprietor listened patiently as Call explained that we wanted wineskins with leather straps and not red nylon cords as on tourists' botas. The man had to make them up special, fifty pesetas each. Back at the bar we found that everyone had a suggestion for breaking in a new wineskin. At length it was decided that the new botas be filled with cheap brandy and let stand for a few hours before discarding the liquor and rinsing the bota with wine.

With our brandy-filled wineskins we drove the car to 14 Calle Amaya, a few blocks away, where Call had arranged for us to stay in the house of the Widow Zabalza. Our pension, three flights up a winding staircase, was a dark little room on an air shaft and furnished with two sagging beds, a ladder-back chair, and a large plastic crucifix. The bathroom was down the hall and had no hot water. But who needed home amenities when we would be practically living in the streets? We left our luggage in the room and headed back downstairs. The street is the stage for the fiesta: you dance in the streets, you sing in the streets, you eat and drink in the streets. The San Fermín celebration is as open and as public as the streets. Even the central aspect of any Spanish fiesta, the bullfight, had here its street component in the *encierro*, the running of the bulls through the town streets.

I poured the brandy into the gutter and had the wine skins filled at a bar. Call and I had our share of wine from various botas, our own and others', as we took to offering and receiving wine from strangers at every street corner. Four Spanish youths stopped us and spoke to Call. "They want us to come with them to the Club de Natación and dance with the whores." "Tell them later," I said. "I did, I told them we wanted to see the fireworks."

The Rincón bar was crowded, but we were invited to squeeze into a corner table where four men and a dark young woman were seated before two large pitchers of sangria and small plates

of olives and cheese and bread. Everyone was clapping hands
and singing, and people kept jumping up and toasting in song
San Fermín, Pamplona, the festival, the bulls, even (with a broken chorus of *The Battle Hymn of the Republic*) the two Ameri-
cans. The girl at our table, who came from Tangiers and whom
the men called "La árabe," was a charmer. She now had six men
in tow. We seven all left the Rincón together, and then another
Arab stopped her in the street. He wanted to take her picture:

"It's too dark, it will never come out."

"It will be all right. There is a flash bulb built right into this
camera."

Some of the Spaniards did not believe it.

"Put that shawl over your head. Look like a real Arab."

"She looks like the Madonna."

"That's the first time anyone ever said I looked like a virgin,"
she said.

Everybody laughed, the bulb went off, and a cheer went up.
In the Plaza Mr. Call and I each had half a dance—if it could be
called dancing—with her before the little group got separated.

The fireworks started. Call was enthralled as he explained
which were Japanese and which were European in origin. Little
pieces of debris and ashes floated down on everyone. Nobody
cared. Delirium was general, and we were part of it, and, for all
I knew, it meant more to us, more to me for certain, than to others. Because in my case (Call's too, though this is my story) it was
happening to a priest. As a priest, I had been to parties, and had
on occasion had more to drink than was good for me, but Pamplona was very different. Most of the revelers drank only wine,
and, more importantly, paced themselves; they became celebratory or happy or thoughtful, but not really drunk. I marveled
at this mass, controlled, semi-inebriation, something I could
not imagine taking place back home in the States. And this
party was going to last eight days. My joining-in required some
daring, given my background of self-abnegation and restraint.
But now, for the moment at least, the priesthood, to which I
had dedicated myself for sixteen years, man and boy, seemed

far away, much farther than the 3,500 miles to Paterson, New Jersey. Part of me remembered that one is a *sacerdos in aeternum*, a priest forever, one from whom the sacerdotal character never departs. In an emergency even a defrocked or apostate priest can validly effect the sacramental miracles. In fact, even in the absence of emergency, the powers remain. I thought of the French story—the French will write or eat anything—about the ex-priest who at dinner with carousing friends consecrates a bottle of red wine into the blood of Christ, whereupon one pious man at the table slowly and reverently drinks the entire contents to prevent further blasphemy. Nothing so dramatic was to happen at Pamplona, but I had for a time surrendered my ties to the clerical state. No one had the slightest idea that I was a priest. I was posing as an ordinary person, not so much running from my life's "vocation" as merely allowing myself to slip unnoticed into this pagan and revelrous scene. I was venturing into a week-long *dies non*, a time when no rules obtained. Some of the rules from which I was disassociating myself would take longer to dissolve than others, but the process had taken hold.

Each day of the fiesta revolved around two events, the encierro and the bullfight. At six-thirty the next morning Call and I were among those who got up, or those who had not gone to bed at all, to witness the encierro through the town streets to the bull ring. All along the route of the encierro, crowds of spectators congregated at the street corners where barriers were erected. Lucky people with passes or connections watched from balconies, the iron gratings of which were covered in white bunting, put there, we were told by some natives, so that men in the streets below could not see up the dresses of the women above them. That first morning we got to the corner of Estafeta Street early enough to perch on top of the restraining barricade. Beyond this point the men who would run loitered in the street and tried to appear relaxed. We didn't run. We were superannuated, for one thing. But, what was more important, we were foreigners. This part of the fiesta was reserved chiefly for young local males who were out to prove their manhood. We heard the rocket go off and the roar from the spectators further up the route, and then eight bulls and a few steers came galloping past us, along with young men running to keep ahead of the animals or diving off to the side and covering up. It was over in a minute.

The bullfights themselves began promptly at five in the afternoon, every day for a week. Call had gotten us good tickets, *sombra,* or shaded seats. The fact that we were priests, something known only to ourselves, added to the edge of the thing. We didn't bother inquiring, but I was sure there was some Church prohibition against clerics attending bullfights; indeed, for a time Rome had officially forbidden priests, under pain of excommunication, from attending operas or other such "spectacles," as Canon Law called them. But here we were, and the bullfight, reprehensible in many ways, captivated me. I did not try to rationalize or defend it, but found myself bedazzled by a phenomenon that is more ritual than sport. That first afternoon a relatively unknown bullfighter named El Piero turned out to be the hero and was awarded two ears and a tail. The next morning's *Diario de Navarra* said that El Piero had been good, but not *that* good. The reporter considered this overly generous award a by-product of the fiesta spirit. He added that through the intercession of San Fermín no one had been killed in the encierro, although there had been some serious injuries, all of them to foreigners.

After the first full day the fiesta became blurred almost as it was happening. I experienced it as a jangled maze of early morning encierros and late afternoon bullfights, of tilted botas and porróns of red wine, of bars that offered, gratis, trays of *bocadillos,* hard-boiled eggs in olive oil and chunks of salami and bread, bars that served glasses of Fundador brandy for about a dime. At one such haunt I borrowed a guitar and surprised the assembled merrymakers—could an American do this?—by being able to play the fiesta's theme song, "Uno de Enero." I remember walking the ramparts of the city and hearing Mr. Call point out the very spot, or so he claimed, where Ignatius

Loyola was hit by a cannonball in 1521 before going off to found the Jesuits; I remember having lunch at a bar called the Caballo Blanco on the edge of town and falling asleep outside in the grass where sheep grazed. But mostly there come back to me nights at the Café Iruña in the Plaza del Castillo, nights alive with wine and talk and the music of wandering peñas. I remember a rocket that hit a balcony, a celebrating French soccer team than had just won some championship cup, a young woman who accompanied them but wandered from table to table making conversation, a German motorcyclist arrested and thrown into jail over night for arguing with a policeman about a parking spot (one didn't quarrel with the authorities in Franco's Spain). Call and I would sit late into the night at this western side of the square, drinking and talking, as the three big cafés slowly emptied out, and groups of survivors came together to form new, fleeting friendships at 2 A.M. It went on like this for days. People got tired and clothes became dirty. The Fiesta of San Fermín looked worn.

By the sixth day I needed a rest. I told Call I was taking the car for a day and a night to San Sebastián:

"Are you pooping out on the fiesta?"

"Not exactly, I just want a little change. I'd like some swimming and beach and a hot shower. That damned cold water."

"Okay, but it's part of the fiesta, living in this pension. You're living like a native here."

"Yes, I know, but a rest and some hot water will be nice."

"You don't like the room. The dirt and all."

"It's fine, but once in a while I need a change. And they say San Sebastián is one of the most beautiful cities in Spain."

At San Sebastián I could look from my hotel window across the bay and see the graceful half circle of shoreline with green mountains at either end. The beach was edged by a high colonnade supporting a boardwalk in front of the grand old hotels that stood side by side for nearly a mile. I changed in the locker room under the colonnade and went out onto the beach and listened for someone talking English. I spread my towel in the sand near three young women, and lay down and began reading a recent *New Yorker* that contained the Salinger story about a precocious boy writing home from summer camp. The nearby voices were American. Should I, still in a Pamplonican mood, approach them? go up to these girls (as all young women were called in 1965) in what amounted to flirting? It took a lot of nerve on my part. I had never done such a thing. I was thirty-two. It was amazingly easy:

"Hello there," I said, "are you from the States?"

The words sounded conventional and silly.

"From California. We thought you were English."

"No, I'm from New Jersey. A schoolteacher."

The girl who had answered, Fay, the tallest of the three, wore a one-piece bathing suit, and sunglasses that she kept taking off and putting back on as if trying to make up her mind which way she looked better. The shortest girl had a pretty round face with dimples. She wore a red bikini. She let Fay and the other girl, Nina, carry the conversation until she was sure she was interested. Fay told me how she had quit her secretarial job to go on this trip:

"By God, that's the spirit. And yourself?"

The red bikini, Linda, was a schoolteacher. First grade. Her first year of teaching:

"And your pupils think you're the best teacher in the world, right?"

As for Pamplona, they had never heard of it:

"You see those men out there in the water with red bandannas around their necks? That's a sort of badge showing that you are celebrating the fiesta of San Fermín."

"What's it like?"

I did my best. Encierros, bullfights, fireworks; people in the streets singing, dancing, drinking from botas. As I was talking I thought to myself how impossible it was to explain this celebration. But my listeners were persuaded that it would be a shame to have come this close to Pamplona at this time and miss the fiesta. They accepted my offer to drive them there tomorrow for the final day.

That night we four went to dinner. Here I was, on the first "date" in my life, and clumsily enough, I had three girls. The restaurant was up two flights of stairs. Some of our fellow diners looked with curiosity at three young foreign women being escorted by one man. Afterward I guided them to a flamenco bar near the boardwalk and thence to a dance place where a five-piece band was playing American music. I was becoming more attracted to Linda by the minute, and while Fay and Nina danced, Linda and I danced, or rather I did my poor best to follow. Our performance seemed to amuse people—the other dancers, the waiters, the band. I explained to her that I was a terrible dancer, but she didn't seem to mind that I was such a klutz. The next song was very slow. She danced close. She was wearing an orange silk sleeveless dress, and her arms seemed to me soft and round and perfectly tanned. I kept asking myself if I were really here, in San Sebastián, Spain, dancing slowly, even romantically, with a beautiful young woman. She interrupted my reverie:

"And what did you think of my bikini today?"

"Well," I said with a laugh, "I thought it was swell."

"It's my first and I was a little shy about wearing it."

"It's very becoming."

"They have to fit just right, you know. That's the secret."

"Yes, I suppose so. Or I suppose that's part of the secret,".

By way of redeeming myself for my inadequate showing on the dance floor, I asked the band to play a Pamplona street song. They obliged, and people jumped up and clapped their hands and sang. The walk back to the hotel was uneventful except that by then Linda had had slightly too much to drink and the other two were keeping a close eye on her. In the lobby Linda's giddiness mildly shocked the clerk and the elevator man.

The next day I drove the three young women to Pamplona and got them into the Hotel de los Tres Reyes, the best in town, a great contrast to 14 Calle Amaya. The hotel concierge obliged me with three extra tickets to the last of the bullfights. The girls were to meet up with me and Mr. Call at the Café Iruña. Sitting there with him at four in the afternoon and waiting for them, I hoped they would like the fiesta. By the time they arrived they already loved it and had supplied themselves with red pañuelos, the kind with brown bulls on them.

Halfway through the bullfights, sitting in the shade section with Linda—we had separated ourselves from the others—I realized I was trying to explain too much. I had described everything from the little colored ribbons on the bull's neck indicating the farm that bred him to the matador's asking permission of the judges to kill the bull. Then I stopped abruptly and quit playing the apologist. I omitted all mention of boxing, the Chicago slaughterhouses, the Spanish temperament, or, God help us, anything about life and death drama. At one point the blood bothered her:

"Is the blood upsetting you?" I asked.

"No, not really. It's exciting and I'm getting used to it."

"Good. Have some wine. That helps."

She tried to be brave about drinking from the bota, which by now was dirty and uninviting to a newcomer. Once you have been in Pamplona for a time you regarded a grimy bota as part of the mystique of the place, but to her it was merely a foul-looking wine skin. "The wine inside is clean," I said. "Keep the nozzle close to your mouth, head back, that's it."

The bullfights closed with Antonio Ordóñez, a legendary matador who had come out of retirement, being awarded "a seventh bull" because his first two had been poor performers. Ordóñez put this bull through a series of magical and seemingly endless turns that drove the crowd into a frenzy. Then he killed on the first sword. After being awarded two ears, he stood facing the peñas, lined up in the cheap sun seats, as the people showered him with "appreciations." He caught a thrown bota, held it high at arm's length, and with head tilted back drained its contents, the wine squirting without interruption into his slightly open mouth for a full three minutes, a feat that for the crowd equaled what he had just done with the bull. Some few of us among the spectators knew that Ordóñez was the son of the bullfighter on whom Hemingway had based Pedro Romero, the fictional bullfighter in *The Sun Also Rises*.

"Storybook ending," I said to Mr. Call.

He and I took our three "girls" to the Rey Noble, the best restaurant in the city, where we all had gazpacho, paella, and white wine, Bodegas Bilbaínas. Later we went to the plaza and sat on the ground against some trees and watched the last of the fireworks. The fiesta was bubbling over even as it was phasing out. We tried to dance, but this was impossible in the crowd of people. Instead we worked our way to the Rincón bar to which Call and I had returned often and where a week earlier the old men had argued about how best to break in a new bota. Here we found everyone drinking wine and clapping hands to Navarran songs. We got a table and ordered a porrón of wine.

It was two in the morning when Call and I walked the three young women back to their hotel, where Linda asked the night clerk if it were possible to get anything to eat:

"The kitchen is closed, Señorita. The dining room is closed."

"But suddenly I'm terribly hungry. Is it possible?"

She looked beguilingly at him. "In Pamplona," the man conceded, "at fiesta time, everything is possible." He put through a call and ushered us into the empty dining room.

"These Spaniards," I said to Mr. Call, "they will do anything for a pretty face." Presently someone—I don't think the man was a waiter—arrived and asked what we wanted to eat. Call leaned back and spoke to him in Spanish. "Sandwiches would be easiest for him at this time," Call told us. "How about ham sandwiches, ladies?" The sandwiches and red wine tasted delicious at that ridiculous hour.

"We don't know how to thank you," Linda was saying, "It's been the best day of our trip. "Thank you," I said, "Our pleasure." We all five said good night.

That was it. Our three friends were to be off early the next morning by train to Barcelona. Between my favorite, Linda, and me there had not been even one mild embrace, much less a kiss. But these young women, conjoined to the exuberance of the fiesta, had transformed the two of us, myself first, and, somewhat more slowly, Mr. Call, too. (Many years later I told one of his daughters, on her wedding day, that she had me to thank for the whole business, me and that car ride to San Sebastián.)

Call and I walked up one last time through the Plaza del Castillo towards 14 Calle Amaya. The streets were empty now except for small clusters of revelers who refused to give up. A peña, dwindled now to six young men, stopped for our benefit. They lit candles and lay down very still in the street and sang:

> Pobre de mí
> Pobre de mí
> que se han acabau las fiestas
> de San Fermín.

"Poor little me, poor little me, the Fiesta of San Fermín is ending." If it didn't sound trite, I'd say that, for me at least, some things were just commencing. And somewhere in California that year, I suspect that three young women were telling their friends of the man from New Jersey they had met on the beach at San Sebastián and how he had taken them to dinner and then driven them in his car to an amazing festival at Pamplona; and about how, once there, he and his friend had escorted them to cafés, bullfights, a beautiful restaurant, fireworks, and late-night sandwiches at their hotel; and also how these two entertaining young men—I like to think they saw us this way—had simply wanted to be kind and to share with them the fun of San Fermín, how neither of them made any sexual advance, untoward or otherwise. A short, chance episode, diverting but soon enough forgotten and of no importance to them. Little did they know just how big an adventure that casual encounter had been for me.

11

AT LAST

ENOUGH of distractions, of Jerry Molloy's corny jokes, of glorious old John Brady, of Pamplona and its attendant allurements. What of my interior life? my state of mind and my decade-and-a-half battle with unbelief?

My mental state was good, having grown more and more healthy over the years. The scruples and worries had disappeared into the past. They had begun in high school, reached their zenith in my freshman year of college, and petered out over the next few years. Those times, by far the most troubled of my life, were by now more than a dozen years distant.

On the other hand, the problem of faith that had started in my first year at Seton Hall had not gone away. A graph would show my faith slowly recovering itself, or seeming to do so, from the second year of college onward, reaching its high point in the time immediately after ordination, my four years in Netcong. But such a graph would be misleading because even in the best of times my faith was vague and never more than half of what it would have been in an unquestioning believer.

How did I remain a parish priest so long? The answer is complex. Not only was I always busy, always on the job, but my efforts were rewarding in that I was working with and for people whom I liked and who seemed to like me. Furthermore, I made a conscious effort to function in a way that supported belief. Performance generates feeling. I performed well, I behaved like a totally believing priest. I was never careless with religious rituals: baptism, confession, the marriage ceremony, benediction, novenas, the prescribed funeral and grave-side prayers—all these I executed with care and reverence. Even if alone in the church I genuflected before the Blessed Sacrament reserved in the tabernacle. Saying Mass, I scrupulously followed the rubrics, everything from careful "vesting," or putting on of the sacred garments, to speaking the words clearly and without unseemly haste; I handled with reverence the sacred vessels, the chalice and the Communion plate, and treated the Eucharist as if it were indeed the body of Christ. Catholic liturgy was theater that ruled out improvisation. The officiating priest was to follow the script and look the part. Appearance, show, surface were what counted. *La facciata è tutto*, the facade is all, I would tell close priest friends. (I used to claim that this was an old Italian proverb, but in fact I made it up.)

And, of course, I had for years tried my best to practice the negative capability mentioned earlier, the art of remaining, as Keats put it, in uncertainties and doubts without irritable reaching after fact and reason. I had done what I could to quash the logical, reasoning part of my mind and had struggled to be content with half-knowledge, or, in my case, half-faith.

But all these factors—the constant busyness, the affection of parishioners, the careful enacting of forms, the efforts at stifling the reasoning side of my mind—could carry me only so far and only so long. The seed of unbelief had been too well sown back in my freshman year of college. At some time in my second year at Morristown, my faith, such as it was, started to come undone. I loosened the hold I had been keeping over my mind, and just let the matter play itself out. I cannot point to any specific moment. It just happened. The rational side of my mind took over, and after a few months in Paterson the downward trajectory of my faith hit flat zero. I did not believe.

A story that I read during my Paterson years resonated so nicely with what I felt back then that I draw on it here to help explain my mental bearings in the mid-1960s. The parallels are hardly exact, but still, the Spanish philosopher Miguel de Unamuno's novella *Saint Manuel the Good, Martyr* (1931) reverberated with me. In the story, an elderly woman, Angela Carballino, decides that, because Rome has begun the beatification process of the man who had been for many years her parish priest, she will commit to paper what she knew of him. Don Manuel, this "matriarchal man," was an altogether devoted priest in a village in Northeast Spain. His flock, with the exception of Angela's brother, Lazarus, a freethinker and intellectual who had gone to America, were all believing Catholics, and for them Don Manuel worked tirelessly. "His life," we read, "was active rather than contemplative, and he constantly fled from idleness, even from leisure." He salvaged wrecked marriages, forced unruly children to submit to their parents, reconciled parents with their children, consoled "the embittered and weary in spirit," and "helped everyone to die well."

Don Manuel "also worked with his hands, pitching in to help with some of the village tasks. At threshing time he reported to the threshing floor. . . . Sometimes he took the place of a worker who had fallen sick. . . . In winter he chopped wood for the poor. . . . He also was in the habit of making handballs for the boys and a goodly number of toys for the younger children." He helped the local schoolteacher instruct his pupils in various subjects, not only the catechism. Don Manuel even attended village dances and "more than once he played the drum to keep time for the young men and women dancing; this kind of activity, which in another priest would have seemed like a grotesque mockery of his calling, in him somehow took on the appearance of a holy and religious exercise."

Angela, who had gone to school in the city, returned to her village at age sixteen and devoted her life to assisting Don Manuel in his work, making herself into his unofficial "deaconess." When her twenty-fourth birthday was approaching, her brother came back from America. Lazarus made it plain to everyone that he was more than ever a nonbeliever, though he admitted that he respected Don Manuel as a sincere, intelligent, dedicated man, so unlike other priests he claimed to have known. Lazarus and Don Manuel become friends and take long walks together around a nearby lake: "In the village, an uncon-

scious expectancy began to build up, the anticipation of a kind of
duel between my brother Lazarus and Don Manuel—in short
it was expected that Don Manuel would convert my brother."
And sure enough, in due course the brother announces to his
sister that he will take Communion in the church on the following Sunday. Word of his conversion spreads and is received with
rejoicing, and on the appointed day the entire village witnesses
Don Manuel, his hands trembling and tears running down his
face, administer the Communion wafer to Lazarus.

Later that day Lazarus tells his sister that Don Manuel had
appealed to him "to set a good example, to avoid scandalizing
the townspeople, to take part in the religious life of the community, to feign belief even if he did not feel any, to conceal his own
ideas." The two had staged his conversion:

> "But is it possible?" she asks.
> "Possible and true.... In trying to convert me to his holy
> cause . . . he was not trying to score a triumph, but rather
> doing it to protect the peace, the happiness, the illusions,
> perhaps, of his charges. . . . I submitted to his logic,—and
> that was my conversion. I shall never forget the day on
> which I said to him, 'But, Don Manuel, the truth, the
> truth above all!'; and he, all a-tremble, whispered in my
> ear—'The truth? The truth, Lazarus, is perhaps something
> so unbearable, so terrible, something so deadly, that simple
> people could not live with it! . . . I am put here to give life
> to the souls of my charges, to make them happy, to make
> them dream they are immortal—and not to destroy them.
> With the truth, with my truth, they could not live at all.
> Let them live. That is what the Church does, it lets them
> live. As for true religion, all religions are true as long as they
> give spiritual life to the people who profess them, as long as
> they console them for having been born only to die.'"

I entertained no delusion that I was saintly or even more
than ordinarily effective as a parish priest, but I did see myself
and my predicament in this story. I saw the good that religion

could do, saw this in spite of some knowledge of the evil side of the Church's history: crusades, wars, inquisitions, corruption, anti-Semitism, intolerance of other faiths, reactionary politics, cooperation with dictatorships, opposition to science. (The child-abuse outrages were yet to become public knowledge.) But my Catholic education had insisted that the abuses of the past had long ago been addressed and removed. The two real and present evils I knew were the harmful condemnation of "artificial" birth control and the inducement by the Catholic system of an unquestioning—and therefore unhealthy—acceptance of authority. Still, in my view, the good that American Catholicism was doing, including the small amount of good that I was doing, outweighed the evil. The Church ran schools, hospitals, orphanages, universities, charities; we parish priests had a hand in some of this good: we taught in schools; we helped the poor; we encouraged good instincts in young people; we listened to people with a practiced ear; we consoled people in the confessional (I even had one or two follow me from long distances because of my supposed ability to help scrupulous persons); we counseled fidelity and forgiveness and charity; above all, as in Unamuno, like leaders in any meaningful religion, we offered people a sense of belonging to a special community wherein we provided or tried to provide an answer to the human craving for something beyond the usual and the daily, something "transcendental." We did some good. I believed in the good, not in the God.

Precisely thirty years later another fiction, John Updike's *In the Beauty of the Lilies*, presented me with another resonating story of the loss of faith in a Christian minister. On a spring afternoon in 1910 the Reverend Clarence Wilmot, pastor of the Fourth Presbyterian Church on Broadway and Straight Street in Paterson, New Jersey, experiences the "last particles" of his faith dissolving in "a visceral surrender, a set of dark sparkling bubbles escaping upward." (The Paterson location made for a nice coincidence.) In Clarence's seminary days at Princeton the authority of his professors and the solidity of the Christian neo-Gothic surroundings had done their best to mask "the possibility that this was all about nothing, all these texts and rites and volumes and exegeses and doctrinal splits ... [the possibility] that these real-enough historical entities might be twigs of an utterly dead tree, ramifications of no more objective validity than the creeds of the Mayan and Pharaonic and Polynesian priesthoods." Wilmot had brushed aside these doubts and clung to his faith. But now that was gone, fizzled. He has of a sudden decided, once and for all, that the naysayers he had read in order to refute them—Hume, Darwin, Renan, and Nietzsche—were right. Especially did Robert Ingersoll ring true to him. "The God of the Pentateuch was an absurd bully, barbarically thundering through a cosmos entirely misconceived. There was no such God, nor should there be." Wilmot preaches a sermon in which he begins by quoting Ingersoll in order to rebut him:

> One great objection to the Old Testament is the cruelty said to have been commanded by God. All these cruelties ceased with death. The vengeance of Jehovah stopped at the tomb. He never threatened to punish the dead; and there is not one word, from the first mistake in Genesis to the last curse of Malachi, containing the slightest intimation that God will take his revenge in another world. It was reserved for the New Testament to make known the doctrine of eternal pain. The teacher of universal benevolence rent the veil between time and eternity, and fixed the horrified gaze of man upon the lurid gulf of hell. Compared with this, the doctrine of slavery, the wars of extermination, the curses, the punishments of the Old Testament were all merciful and just.

Clarence's "refutation" of Ingersoll falters terribly and does more harm than good. The whole Judeo-Christian system has in his mind come tumbling down. Life has suddenly told Clarence "what he had long suspected, that the universe was utterly indifferent to his states of mind and as empty of divine content as a corroded kettle. All the metaphysical content had leaked away, but for cruelty and death, which without the hypothesis of a God became unmetaphysical; they were simply facts, which oblivion would in time obviously erase." Clarence abruptly relaxes his "mental contortions" and gives in to "facticity." To him, latter-day apologetics in Christian books and journals are now sad pap—"paper shields against the molten iron of natural truth . . . fantastic doctrines and preposterous rationalizations." Credulous people, he thinks, hope beyond hope that death will be the beginning of a new life of some vague kind with God: "For most men this was all religion was, this gamble at the back of their minds, with little to lose but an hour or so on Sunday mornings. But for him, alas, it was a livelihood, and his manhood's foundation."

Clarence stays on in the ministry for one year, at the urging of his superior, who suggests that his faith may revive. It doesn't, and Clarence just barely manages to go through the motions for the stipulated twelve months. He survives by keeping busy in the "ecclesiastical maze, wherein a blameless quotidian industry concealed and overarched the essential unreality." Anyone who has undergone the loss of faith will, I think, marvel at Updike's convincing account, especially remarkable in that Updike himself is, as it were, on the other side, said to be a believer in spite of the attendant difficulties he sees in theism. Unamuno's Don Manuel lived a life of martyrdom because of his unbelief, but Updike's Clarence Wilmot has a sadder fate. His loss of faith, his capitulation to what he sees as the truth, depresses him, unmans him, and, a few years later, kills him.

I realize that on one level it is unhelpful to compare one's actual lot with that of fictional characters, as if these persons in novels were real people of one's acquaintance. But as these two characters compel in me such identification, I feel I should underscore a contrast and assert that in my case the loss of faith, the gradual descent (or ascent) into unbelief, brought with it finally no anguished horror, no abiding sadness or grief. It brought a joyous release, a blissful and mind-freeing deliverance.

I didn't close my eyes to the reality of religious experiences and religious phenomena, but to acknowledge these is quite different from acknowledging a God. I knew too that some intellectuals—not Catholic ones—argue that God is now only a metaphor, or another name for the laws of physics or the movement of electrons, or as Tolstoy is quoted as saying, the object of one's desires. If that was all there was to it, you could have counted me in. But belief for me meant belief in a personal, creating God who was concerned in some way with mankind, the God of Judaism, Christianity, and Islam, and to this I would no longer assent. Once I gave over trying, once I relinquished my longing to believe in God, the distinctive features of Catholic belief showed themselves in an embarrassing light. For Catholics are asked to embrace more irrational notions than followers of any other religion on earth. When I engage with a Buddhist who believes in reincarnation, or a Shintoist who believes in ancestor worship, or a Mormon who believes in gathering up the names of everyone who has ever lived so as to "baptize" them, I remain polite, although in my mind I can't help regarding such doctrines as benighted or just plain silly. But when such beliefs are weighed against Catholic tenets of the Trinity, the Virgin Birth, the Incarnation, the Resurrection, the Ascension, biblical inspiration, Mary's bodily Assumption into heaven (her Immaculate Conception is easier to accept if one believes *everyone* is conceived free from "original sin"), the Resurrection of the Dead, the Eucharist, Baptism, everlasting hell and eternal heaven, angels, devils, papal infallibility, supernatural apparitions, purgatory, holy water, indulgences, First Friday and First Saturday Communions as guarantees against damnation, beatifications, canonizations, the intercession of the saints, miraculous medals, and so on *ad infinitum*—I say that, compared to these fantasies, the beliefs of the Buddhist, Shintoist, and Mormon appear positively enlightened. Mark Twain wrote of the natives of Hawaii before the Christian missionaries got to them, "How sad it is to think of the multitudes who have gone to their graves in this beautiful island and never knew there was a hell."

And to hide all the irrationality behind the shibboleth of "mysteriousness" was really no answer. To affirm that the Trinity is beyond human comprehension sounded now like simple obfuscation. Some things are beyond human comprehension because they are too much for our minds. Light-year distances are an instance. But other things are beyond comprehension because they are absurd, like the resurrection of the dead at the end of time. The problem of evil or pain in human life, in a world said to be created by an all wise, all good, all loving creator, was often—with a little help from the Book of Job—palmed off in Catholic teaching as a mystery, although another fanciful notion, original sin, was also commandeered to help explain the vastness of human suffering. (Animal suffering didn't count.) But to me suffering seemed quite unmysteriously explained by some elementary biology—along with a little help from Ecclesiastes: Time and chance happeneth to them all. And so I found myself a stolid, though silent, nonbeliever. Not merely an agnostic, but an atheist, nasty sounding as the word was.

I never could buy the assertion that philosophically speaking, even scientifically speaking, agnosticism is much more "logical" than atheism. I knew all the arguments: that you could not, for example, prove a negative, and of course you could not prove that no God existed. But in my view the burden of proof was all on the other side. You cannot disprove that there is a guardian angel at my side—he's incorporeal, a "spirit"—but disbelief seems a lot more rational than belief. I understood why most people viewed the argument from design as the strongest "proof" for the existence of God, but even then I knew enough of evolution, of the unimaginable periods of time that made evolution possible, not to be troubled by the line of reasoning set forth seven hundred years earlier by Aquinas. (Today's "Intelligent Design" arguments are really nothing new except in their claim to be science rather than theology, a claim recently dealt a setback when a federal district judge in Pennsylvania ruled that Intelligent Design is merely "creationism relabeled.")

While quietly thinking that at this point in human development smart people ("brights") were more likely to be nonbelievers, I was willing to admit that there were brilliant people in the Church and that these people wrote brilliant books of theology, brilliant except that there was, in the end, nothing to it. I knew, too, that science could not answer certain "ultimate" questions, that these "why" questions were beyond the reach of evidence. But these questions seemed also beyond the reach of philosophers and theologians. A line from my college days persisted with me: There is no belief so foolish that some philosopher or theologian has not embraced it. How was it that the Catholic Church, or any other church or religion for that matter, or, to come to my own case, how was it that I should have the answers? Or even an inside track toward the answers? I would not put it as acerbically as some do, but having been on both sides of the belief divide, having been a "chaplain," I can appreciate these words of Richard Dawkins:

> I once asked a distinguished astronomer, a fellow of my college, to explain the Big Bang to me. He did so to the best of his (and my) ability, and I then asked what it was about the fundamental laws of physics that made the spontaneous origin of space and time possible. "Ah," he smiled, "Now we move beyond the realm of science. This is where I have to hand over to our good friend the Chaplain." But why the Chaplain? Why not the gardener or the chef? Of course chaplains, unlike chefs and gardeners, *claim* to have some insight into ultimate questions. But what reason have we for taking their claim seriously?

Very little, as far as I could see. And the vehemence, the conviction, the sincerity with which the chaplains of the world thought they possessed the answers had nothing to do with the validity of their claims.

As Samuel Butler would have said, "Lord, I do not believe. Help Thou my unbelief." My old friend Father Benedict Groeschel—Pete of my high school years—reminded me recently that faith was a gift. I told him that unbelief was also a gift, a rarer gift. This was not mere jest or word play on my part. It seems to me that humans are more ready to believe and to hope than to look the facts in the face. I can't take much credit for becoming a nonbeliever. That was largely luck. Even though I was born into an America where religion flourished, I knew that in Europe, the cradle of the West and of America, religion was losing its persuasive power. Good fortune also gave me a skeptical temperament—even though it surfaced only when I was nineteen and didn't triumph in me till I was thirty-two. Better late than never.

At St. Mary's I continued my parish duties, though with a difference. I worked just as conscientiously as before, but that work was no longer the point, the raison d'être of my existence. With my head clearing, I was able to look with more delight at the world around me. It could hardly be said I became a hedonist, but I did relish life the more. Often, like a teenager discovering new facets of existence, I would say to myself jejune things like Life is Art, or Life is Music and Wine (I knew nothing of Women). It was the talk of an adolescent, for in many respects I was the victim of a protracted adolescence. And then, at Seton Hall, of all places, where I was nearing an M.A. in English, I encountered, in one of Father Virgil's courses, this time in Victorian Poetry and Poetics, Walter Pater's celebrated rhapsody in the Conclusion of his *Renaissance Studies*. I had never heard this kind of thing verbalized, even as an "adversary" view. But when I read Pater, his message came to me as to one already committed:

> The service of philosophy, of speculative culture, towards the human spirit, is to rouse, to startle it to a life of constant and eager observation. Every moment some form grows perfect in hand or face; some tone on the hills or the sea is choicer than the rest; some mood of passion or insight or intellectual excitement is irresistibly real and

attractive to us,—for the moment only. Not the fruit of experience, but experience itself, is the end.

I won't quote Pater's too often quoted line about burning with a gem-like flame. However, the words about Rousseau's deciding to dedicate what remained of his life to intellectual excitement certainly sounded good to me—though much too exalted. Pater allows for "great passions, the ecstasy and sorrow of love, the various forms of enthusiastic activity, disinterested or otherwise." I had had my passion for God, for religion, for enthusiastic activity whether disinterested or not. But I was innocent, really, of the "ecstasy and sorrow of love," and my life had yielded only a touch of that "poetic passion, the desire of beauty, the love of art for its own sake" that in Pater's view does most toward giving the "highest quality" to the handful of moments that constitute one's interval. Although this last passion was clearly beyond my capacities or even my inclinations, Pater's formulation of it had great appeal. All my life I had been instructed in principles very different from this pagan philosophy. In Catholic thought, everything, not just prayer and worship, and, in my case, priestly work, but all human acts, all deeds of kindness or decency or love, all attempts at learning or teaching, were to be in the service of the Lord. And all art, whether in literature, painting, sculpture, or music, was to delight *and* to instruct.

But now, as my religious beliefs or the vestiges of them fell away, there increased within me, all very inarticulate and nothing as grand or as passionate as Pater's expression of it, a slowly dawning conviction that the good things of the world could be enjoyed for their own sake. I thought of Father Furlong at Seton Hall claiming you must not enjoy a chocolate ice cream sundae strictly for its taste, but had to seek nourishment for the body also, as the Lord required. And among the things that were now ends in themselves, the excitement associated with freedom of thought came first on my list. As for the passion of love: if there was no God, why not fully embrace human existence? Why

put one's efforts into loving and serving a nonexistent super being, regardless of any peripheral good to others or even to one's
self? Of human love I knew little. I loved my parents and my
friends, I had been secretly infatuated by certain women—like
Agnes McBriar—but I knew nothing of the "ecstasy and sorrow of love." Why not, on what Pater called this short day of
frost and sun, give that a try? And thus two new possibilities
were opening up to me, intellectual freedom and sexual love.
(As for art for art's sake, I think I had quietly believed that all
along, as had, in my view, most thinking people, at least since
the Enlightenment, except of course religious fanatics, Marx-
ist fundamentalists, and Jacques Maritain.) The ecstasy and
sorrow of love were not to hand, as yet, but the exhilaration of
intellectual independence came flooding in upon me. In that
regard, my long struggle was over. It had indeed been uphill
work. I surrendered at last and felt not defeated but victorious.
My deliverance—for it amounted to that—was all the sweeter
for having been so long delayed.

12

BEGINNINGS

A SPECIAL GRACE to St. Mary's, Paterson, was its nearness to New York. You had but to take "Union Av'" out to Route 46 East, merge onto Route 3, and in no time you were through the Lincoln Tunnel and into Manhattan. About fifteen miles. I was scarcely settled into St. Mary's when, in the fall of 1965, I started going on my days off to the NYU School of Continuing Education (on Saturday mornings, on company time, I was still attending Seton Hall). NYU held registration in the lobby of Number One Fifth Avenue, and my class met in the Main Building on Washington Square, in the center of Greenwich Village. This was indeed what old Bishop Dougherty had called "that New York thing." I signed up for a course in English and American Literature of the Twentieth Century. The instructor, Walter James Miller, had no connection with the English department proper and would not have been much regarded by them, and I suspect he reciprocated their indifference. He had published criticism, short stories, poetry, translations of Jules Verne, and a book on technical writing; he had a weekly radio book review program on WNYC; and he was one of the most inspiring teachers I ever had. He knew many writers personally. He knew Joseph Heller. He knew Kurt Vonnegut. He knew Auden. Miller's two-semester course began with Hardy and continued on through Pound, Eliot, Joyce, Fitzgerald, and Hemingway—down to Dylan Thomas.

I came over from Paterson every Tuesday evening, and in short order got to know Miller. He was only a dozen years older than I, but seemed altogether my senior and the complete man of the world. He had gone to Columbia and studied

under luminaries like William York Tindall; he had served in
the War; he had been married and divorced three times. At
NYU Evening School he basked in a considerable following,
especially as all his women students were in love with him. He
made no secret of his "interest" in women, and he kept a room
at the Fifth Avenue Hotel for late night assignations. "After all,"
he told me, "I have my reputation to uphold around here." Of
course I wore civilian clothes, but I divulged to him who, or
what, I was. Miller, while regarding me as a prospective convert
to worldliness, never said anything disrespectful of the Church,
but he could read my interest in his secular, free-thinking ways,
and he relished encouraging my "conversion." Besides inspiring
me with a love of Eliot, Joyce, and Faulkner, he told me two specific things that remain distinct in my memory. One was that
society had better start treating women like first-class citizens.
"We cannot go on wasting half the talent of the world" was the
utilitarian way he put it. This was 1965. He was an early "male
feminist," long before any such term was in vogue. Recently I
reminded him of this. "Yes," he said, "I was right about that one."
The other concerned the little cigars I had just taken up. We
were walking across Washington Square Park and he noticed
them in my jacket pocket and addressed me as a strict father
might his son: "You don't smoke those things, do you? Give it
up. They're no good for you." I did not give them up till ten years
later when I developed a touch of asthma.

In February the spring term commenced, and Miller took up
the second half of his course. I sat down in class next to a stunning woman in her mid-twenties. She had the kind of beauty
that made her the most striking woman in any gathering. I said
nothing. She looked at me and at the packet of small cigars in my
shirt pocket: "If you are going to smoke those," she said, "I will sit
somewhere else." These were the days when students and professors smoked in class. Her remark was spoken in a firm but not
unkind way. Still, not a very good start. "Oh no," I told her, "I'm
not going to smoke." Actually, this was true, for I smoked only after dinner and of course "didn't inhale." I scarcely exchanged two

more words with her the rest of the term. Once, during a break, I was standing outside the classroom with another student, a handsome, self-confident fellow, when she walked by us and into the room, occasioning my making some harmless remark to him about how stunning she was. He agreed, but with a determination in his voice as if he intended to do something about it. For myself, I saw not even a remote possibility. In the meantime, Miller, in his enthusiasm and digressions, never got to the end of his syllabus. Accordingly, he told us that if we were around in the summer we could attend, gratis, the summer version of the course when he would take up where he had left off.

Miller's offer sounded inviting to me, for it fitted well with my plans for the July vacation. I had decided to spend the month in Greenwich Village, and the prospect of living there excited me as much as the idea of going to Pamplona had the summer previous. A new and close friend, Joe Giannelli, who taught English at St. Mary's High, joined with me in finding a sublet. We drove into the City, picked up a copy of the *Village Voice*, put through a call, and went to look at a listing for 125 Sullivan Street, near the corner of Prince Street, where an NYU graduate student had an apartment. When we arrived he was on the phone, and I heard him say, "I'll call you back, I think I've rented my apartment." He had indeed. I loved the place—almost because it was dark and dowdy—and took it on the spot for July and August. A railway flat on the second floor in a tenement building, it consisted of a front room, a kitchen with bathtub, and a small windowless bedroom off a corridor leading to a toilet at the back. The front window looked out across Sullivan Street to a Chinese laundry and the convent of nearby St. Anthony's Church. One-Twenty-Five Sullivan is situated in the dead center of what was then "Little Little Italy" at the southern end of Greenwich Village, in the middle of the two blocks where the Festival of St. Anthony is held every June. Being a sentimentalist, I have often been tempted, while walking in the neighborhood, to go in and ask to look at the apartment on the second floor, for no other reason than to see the place again.

My hope for that summer was to fulfill a longtime ambition of trying to write something other than a school assignment. It was to be a "Journal" of my eight days in Pamplona. A busy year had pushed the fiesta out of my mind until now. I reminded myself of Thoreau's story of the Englishman who wanted to be a poet, but went first to India in search of a fortune to support his poetry writing and ended up never writing any poems: "He should have gone up garret at once" is Thoreau's comment. This dingy Sullivan Street apartment would be my garret, its very dinginess suiting my romantic notions about living in the Village and trying to write. I took with me a dictionary, Strunk and White's *The Elements of Style*, and copies of the *Diario de Navarra* covering last year's fiesta. The young man I sublet from had left me the use of a phonograph, so I also brought over records of flamenco and other Spanish music. I had the resources I needed along with another special *aide-mémoire* in the person of Mr. Call, who possessed a nearly photographic memory. I worked mornings and afternoons and went out evenings with Call, whose parish lay just across the river in Jersey City. The first days in July 1966 were incredibly hot, and on the Fourth we visited his Puerto Rican parishioners who were roasting a whole pig in the garage of an Esso station. The temperature had been topping 100 degrees for a few days just then, and the black macadam of the streets was melting, getting little bubbles in it. But back on Sullivan Street, heat or no heat, I slogged away daily and in the end produced a forty-page typescript in which Mr. Call figured prominently. I trust the result had but small resemblance to Hemingway, but I will never be too sure. It was published in a little magazine in 1976.

I luxuriated in the newness of my position, the freedom from responsibilities for a full month, and the utter anonymity of my situation. The location seemed magical, the wonderful feel of the Italian community around me, with its small specialized food shops, a vegetable stand, a tiny market with a few shelves of canned tomatoes and dried pasta from Italy, a butcher shop called Pino Prime Meats, Joe's Cheese Store—"Latticini

Fresci"—and Vesuvio's Bakery, around the corner on Prince Street. At the Napoli Restaurant, on Sullivan and Spring, a dish of spaghetti cost $1.19. There were boccie courts. There were storefronts marked "Private Club, Members Only" where old men sat outside speaking Italian and observing the street life. I moved quietly among my neighbors, a would-be writer.

Meanwhile Walter Miller's class beckoned. It had already started, Tuesday and Thursday evenings on the eighth floor of what was called the NYU Press Building, across from an extra piece of park land next to Washington Square. The class had fewer attendees than usual, and Miller arranged the seats in a circle; and there, two chairs away, was the beautiful young woman from the spring term who had told me she would change seats if I smoked. Here was an opportunity to talk without awkwardness. As veteran Miller followers, we had something in common. (I know the dialogue here is fairly accurate, for I would write it down the next day.) After class I caught up with her:

"Hello. You're taking this course."

"Yes—I think he's marvelous. Last week I sat over near the door, and twice this woman came in *doused* in some awful perfume."

"I know the one. With a crazy hat."

"Yes, that's the one."

We walked to the corner and exchanged names. She spoke with a faint but enchanting accent. Her last name she spelled for me—Gsell—but the first name, pronounced in the German manner, threw me. When she was out of sight I wrote the name on the cover of a notebook as I thought I heard it: "Mah ree ahn nah." It had sounded like a cross between Marion and Mary Anna, but with soft *a*'s as in *father*.

On Thursday night we talked for a long time at the break. She worked at RCA Classical Records and loved her work. And I was a teacher, staying a month in the Village and trying to write. After class she gave Miller some RCA records, and I asked him if he would in due course read my Pamplona journal. Then she and I went down together in the elevator and walked through the lobby. It had begun to rain heavily, and we stood talking in the doorway. I started saying how she could help me learn something of classical music. She interrupted:

"I'm afraid I have not been altogether honest—I must tell you right away that I'm serious with someone."

"Engaged?"

"Well, no. Almost."

"But we can still talk?"

"Yes."

"And if you are really about to get engaged, I think you had better ask that woman from class where she gets that perfume. And those hats, too."

She had an easy laugh:

"I hope that I didn't seem too forward or anything," she said.

"Oh, no."

"It's just that people can be hurt. So it was good to tell you, right away."

"But we can be friends. Shall we make a dash across the park? Will you wear my jacket?"

"No."

"I knew you wouldn't. Okay. To the Loeb Student Center, just across the way. There's always something going on there."

She liked the Student Center, the billboards offering bus rides to the Shakespeare Festival in Connecticut and listing poetry readings and lectures on LSD. I asked at the desk if there were any cafeteria open. No. It was still raining. "This is like Aeneas and Dido caught in the rain," I said, ridiculously. In the auditorium they were having a lecture on how to tell jokes, and members of the audience were invited up to the stage to tell funny stories. They were very bad at it. We stood in the back. I suggested we have a drink and something to eat at McBell's Pub, on Sixth Avenue, about three blocks away and right around the corner, it turned out, from her apartment on Washington Place. As she later told me, my grabbing a cab in the rain—pure luck—to go those three short blocks struck her as pretty impressive. We got a seat in McBell's, under a saxophone that hung on the wall (where it remained for thirty years until the place closed down). When I asked about wine, I was told that they had only "vin rose"—pronounced as in Vince and your ordinary garden rose. She agreed that was funny.

And here we were, both from New Jersey. Well, no, not originally in her case. She had been born in the Ukraine in a German-speaking Catholic village on the Black Sea, and after the War her large family had emigrated to America, refugees from Stalin's terror, in 1951. She had left New Jersey directly after high school and had gone to live for a time in the Evangeline House on West 13th Street. I said hers was a case of God and the

Salvation Army protecting the working girl. (The story I used to tell that I first saw her singing on a street corner with a Salvation Army band isn't true.) She did not, I told her, look like a girl from the Salvation Army residence. I even convinced her to have her picture taken by a professional photographer. (The resulting portrait was not at all typical, being too somber and severe. She was an utterly joyous person.)

And what about me? I was born and bred in New Jersey, and was half German-American. My mother could even speak German, but never did because, as she said many times, "We're always at war with them." I taught at a Catholic high school in Paterson. Was I married? No. Was I involved, "committed"? No. I told her of my plans to write about Pamplona, and of my doubts whether the result would be any good. Of course, what could she say but that I should go ahead and do it. But mention of the writing launched me into rhapsodies about Pamplona. The festival of San Fermín was in fact in progress at that very moment. Why not a little fiesta of our own? Spanish restaurants and music? She did not say no. Nor did she mention the man she was going with, and she later told me that it was our fellow student from the spring class. Her overstating the seriousness between them had been part of a young woman's immediate response, I think, to a man rushing to date her. We walked to the corner—about fifty feet—where she insisted that she must proceed on her own, that she had an appointment. But, yes, she would go out with me on Saturday night.

I had a date. If I didn't count the meals with the three girls in Spain, this was the first real date of my life. I recall the blue-gray sports jacket I wore—every priest had a jacket or two for his days off. I dressed carefully, and then walked up from Sullivan Street to 115 Washington Place and rang the bell for the third floor. She buzzed me in and welcomed me to her apartment, modest but much more pleasant than my railroad flat. It was cheerful, with French windows, a small living room with an arch leading to a similar-sized dining room, and a separate kitchen with no bathtub in it. I sat in the living room while she continued getting ready. She came out in an eye-catching black-and-white dress, and, by God, if she didn't ask me to tie its two bows across her back. She was not being flirtatious. It was a straightforward matter that this dress had to be tied by someone else. With heart beating faster than usual—could I really be this close to the bare flesh of a woman?—I did so. And down the stairs we went and out into the street. I remembered that the man was supposed to walk on the outside of the girl, though where I learned this I can't imagine. The restaurant, of course, had to be Spanish. We walked westward, across Seventh Avenue at Sheridan Square, over West Fourth and down that tree-lined street, past the brownstone houses with their front stoops jutting out onto the sidewalk. There were uneven sections of sidewalk that required careful negotiating for two people walking side by side. At Horatio Street, it was but two short blocks to El Faro, the only restaurant in this part of the West Village, on the edge of the meat packing district, which in those days was strictly the site of meat importing companies.

El Faro, which offered inexpensive fare while carrying a two-star endorsement in Craig Claiborne's *Guide to Dining Out in New York*, was crowded and exciting. "El Faro" means the Lighthouse, I pedantically explained. I also added, however off the point, that Joyce, whom we were reading in Miller's class, said that a pier was a disappointed bridge. She loved El Faro, the funky dark decor and the first-rate seafood. We sat in an alcove decorated by bullfight posters, and I could truthfully tell her that in Pamplona I had seen every one of the matadors listed. (The posters are still there, forty years later.) Again I suggested a little festival of our own. She was, she reminded me, still seeing someone "on and off." "Well," I told her, "I'll be here for the off."

I did my best to maintain a composed demeanor. I was out on a date in New York City with a woman, a charming, smart, funny, absolutely beautiful young woman with an ever-so-slight but hard-to-place accent, who seemed to be enjoying herself and to be interested in what I had to say. After dinner we took a taxi uptown to a place into which I had once wandered

forlornly with Mr. Call, on East 84th Street, where there was
a bar with live music and dancing. Given my inability on the
dance floor, this required nerve on my part. We tried to dance,
and I admitted to her that I had just wanted to dance with her
even though I didn't know how. Of course she lied and said I
was not doing too badly. After our "dancing," Marianne, whose
name I had by now mastered, said she would like coffee, and we
went to Dorian's on Second Avenue and sat at an outdoor table.
She told me she was impressed by my taking her to so many
places. But we were not through. My Spanish fit was in full
force, and we just had to go to the Café Madrid on West 14th
Street, another place where Call and I, two sad bachelors, had
been so often that I had come to know the flamenco singer, a
man named Paco Ortiz. Marianne and I stayed till closing time,
listening to him perform. Paco, awed by her looks, sat down at
our table and told her that where he came from, Malaga, men
would go out in the back and fight with knives to the death over
a girl like her. She laughed, but Paco, with his Spanish seriousness, insisted it was true.

As she and I walked the few blocks home to her place, she
permitted me to take her hand only when crossing the street.
No good-night kiss, not even a peck on the cheek, was conceded
at this stage. It was, she said, all too early. But yes, we could go
out again.

And so it began. To recount how exciting all of this was to me
is impossible. Once more, I will have recourse to a writer who
seems to have suggested my state of mind. *New York Times* book
reviewer Anatole Broyard said of himself that once he had
moved to Greenwich Village after the War:

> I wanted to be young again. I wanted to be ordinary. . . .
> Sex was as much a superstition, or a religious heresy, as it
> was a pleasure. It was a combination of Halloween and
> Christmas—guilty, tormented, clumsy, unexamined, and
> thrilling. It was as much psychological as physical—the
> *idea* of sex offered the major part of foreplay. A naked

human body was such a rare and striking thing that the
sight of it was more than enough to start our juices flow-
ing. People were still visually hungry; there was no sense
of *déjà vu* as there is now. As a nation, we hadn't lost our
naïveté.... The suggestion of a nipple through a sweater or
a blouse ... would have been considered pornographic....
It would be almost impossible for someone today to understand how far we were from explicit ideas like pleasure
or gratification.... One of the things we've lost is the ter-
rific *coaxing* that used to go on between men and women,
the man pleading with a girl to sleep with him and the girl
pleading with him to be patient.... The energy of unspent
desire, of looking forward to sex, was an immense current
running through American life. It was so much more
powerful then because it was delayed, cumulative, and
surrounded by doubt.

Broyard is talking about 1946, but for me it could just as well
have been 1966. I was twenty years behind.

Only four people knew of my romance, Call, Giannelli, Coletta, and Ann Logan, "Sweet Annie," she alone of the Logans
and Betzels, my Morristown foursome. One Sunday afternoon
these two couples came over to the Sullivan Street apartment,
and as we left to go out to eat, Ann and I fell in at the rear of
the little procession of five people. She was the one I could tell.
She had seen pictures I had taken during Pamplona and had
registered not the slightest surprise at seeing a photograph of
California Linda and her friends, identified as girls Mr. Call and
I had escorted to a bullfight. But she anticipated me:

"You've met someone, right? Tell me what she's like."

"Who? How did you know?"

"Oh, I could tell."

"She's very nice."

"Have you made love yet?"

"No."

"Oh, right. Of course. That takes time."

That was the kind of person Ann was. Truly religious, a deeply committed Catholic, with nine children to show for it, but incurably romantic. Hers was a special womanly blessing on my project.

I was in love. I wooed Marianne with dinners, wine, music, and poetry. Together in that shabby tenement on Sullivan Street in what became—so to say—a ritual, we would listen to Sabicas and Montoya, Mozart and Piaf, drink white wine, and read poetry. We read Eliot:

> For I have known them all already, known them all—
> Have known the evenings, mornings, afternoons,
> I have measured out my life with coffee spoons;
> I know the voices dying with a dying fall
> Beneath the music from a farther room.
>   So how should I presume?

And Lorca, for no reason other than his being Spanish:

> Oh city of gypsies,
> who could see you and forget....

And of course Dylan Thomas, the martyred-to-alcohol romantic poet then in vogue, who wrote, or so he said,

> ...not for the towering dead
> With their nightingales and psalms
> But for the lovers, their arms
> Round the griefs of the ages...

The lines strike me today as overwrought, but in 1966 they seemed ineffably good. And Thomas again:

> If it could only just, if it could only just be
> like this for ever and ever amen.

We made a pilgrimage to the White Horse Tavern, where Thomas drank himself to death. We ate again at El Faro, and at El Rincon de España, where we came to know Carlos, the owner, who said Marianne was *muy bonita y muy simpatica*. Our own little fiesta continued to progress. We went as far as Fire Island and as near as that Sullivan Street staple *The Fantasticks*, but left at the intermission, both of us finding it unlistenable.

After I returned to St. Mary's in August, I would go over to the City whenever I could and meet Marianne after work at the RCA Red Seal Division on East 24th Street. Music was her love, and she possessed an extraordinary singing voice. We were once invited to a party at a swank Park Avenue apartment, courtesy of Walter Miller, where the pianist knew dozens of German lieder—Schubert, Schumann, and Brahms—and Marianne was the hit of the evening, as she always was whenever she could be persuaded to sing. We discovered a striking coincidence. While singing in the choir at St. Joseph's Church on Sixth Avenue, she had gotten to know the choir director and church organist, a young man named Michael Miller. "Mitch" Miller? The piano player in my eighth grade dance band? The very same. He had proposed marriage to her, having first, he admitted, checked with his mother. Marianne told him she was not inclined toward him in that way.

But between her and me, there lay my "situation." I falteringly admitted to her that there was a mystery about me, something in my past—and no, it wasn't that I was married, or widowed, or divorced, or going with someone. These, I insisted, would not have been mysteries. And it was something I could not bring myself to tell her. After six weeks something of a stalemate had set in. We would not be intimate, she made clear, until this "mystery" were cleared up. We talked for hours on the phone over a private line in my room at the rectory. (My fellow curate, John Heekin, had encouraged my having this little luxury installed.) Then, in late August, Marianne called me on a Monday night:

"I know what your mystery is."

"You do? Is it really time?"

"Well, I know."

"Don't say it. I don't want to hear you say it."

"Okay."

For her, my being a priest posed no obstacle. A lapsed Catholic herself, she in fact thought it rather wonderful, even funny. Her parents had been upset with her for dating non-Catholics, and here was someone very Catholic. We agreed to go to the Sullivan Street apartment—mine until the end of the month— on the very next day, my Tuesday off. I telephoned Cologne Colette with the news, and confided to him that I didn't know what kind of condoms to buy. "Get Trojans, Father," he told me. I drove into the city, via the Lincoln Tunnel, as usual. It was a clear, sunny, late afternoon. I went down Ninth Avenue, looking for a drug store and praying like a teenage boy that I would be waited on by a man. I spotted a corner place on the left at West 24th Street. I forget the store's name, except that it sounded distinctly German-Jewish. The shop has now disappeared, but for years it stood there, testimony to my initiation. They carried so many kinds of Trojans that in fact Coletta's advice was not very useful. What did he know?

Marianne and I planned to meet at the apartment and go out to dinner first. She told me that on her way there a little boy asked her to cross him over Sullivan Street. She took his hand and then said, "Where are you going now?" and without answering he disappeared into St. Anthony's Church. We went to eat, appropriately enough, at another Spanish restaurant, El Cortijo, located nearby on the corner of Houston Street. We had a bottle of Rioja wine. For me, Dutch courage. We walked back down Sullivan Street. I was thirty-three years old. Of course she would be able to help me. These were the sixties, and she had for some years gone steady with an Armenian—her "five-year plan"—who turned out to be one of those who would marry only his own kind, and she had stopped seeing him.

I do not know how much of this to tell. That I was nervous with anticipation, worried but hopeful, hardly needs saying. Sex the first time is momentous for anyone, but for someone my age who had been brought up and indeed become, you might say, quintessentially Catholic, it was all the more so. In Catholic teaching sexual intercourse was licit only within marriage, but, to give the Church its due, the act itself was not denigrated. It was something mysterious and profound; it was both exalted and dangerous. Seminary textbooks on the Sixth Commandment, remaining always in what was called the decent obscurity of the Latin tongue (even after other textbooks were translated into English), raised the physical sexual act to almost metaphysical heights. And, commonplace as it sounds, and as often as it has been said, I did reflect that this was it, this was what all the stories and songs and poems were about. Virginity is not supposed to have degrees, but I think there are layers of innocence. I had never practiced what Catholics called "self-abuse," had never consciously effected an orgasm. I had never been near, much less touched, a naked woman. Making love was not all magic at first, and I would need time to get the hang of it. Marianne patiently, sexily, lovingly, led me though the steps.

Marianne and I "went together" for a year. Still, I had no intention of leaving the priesthood. But as I no longer believed, my actions didn't seem unreasonable, much less immoral. On the other hand, not wishing to scandalize parishioners who might happen to run into me in New York, I was careful not to be seen in a compromising position—we did not hold hands in public or even appear too intimate walking along the streets. Still, it comes home to me now that, consciously or unconsciously, I was lining up my ducks in a row. Or, in the terms of the Gospel, making friends with the mammon of iniquity. For at this time I did another daring thing for a priest in 1967: I rented an apartment in the Village. Together with Cologne Colette and Mr. Call I took a lease on a studio apartment at 27 East 13th Street, for a monthly rent of $137.50, or about $45 each, considerable money for a priest back then. But the thrill of renting this apartment, the delight that came with having the key in one's pocket, was for me even more magical than Sullivan Street. For this place, on the second floor of a plain, eight-story building grandly named "The Van Buren," was no two-month sublet, but our own. Coletta went to work decorating and bought, on sale, from Hoffman-Koos Furniture in New Jersey, a huge purple and crimson convertible sofa bed, a contraption so ugly that they practically gave it to him. Mr. Call brought over from St. Michael's in Jersey City cases of cognac and Green and Yellow Chartreuse, "borrowed" from his alcoholic pastor. (This was none other than Father Jim Carey, the one-time Seton Hall Athletic Director, who in 1953 had distinguished himself by getting sloshed drinking from the National Invitational Tournament Championship cup.)

This apartment was situated more properly in the Village itself than was the Sullivan Street place, and we felt, or imagined that we felt, the famous Village tolerance and bohemianism around us. We were intensely pleased with ourselves to be renting a bit of this fabled part of New York, which to us represented unconventionality, indulgence, freedom, the counterculture, and the antiwar movement all rolled into one. Here we were, priests in mufti, in the domain of artists and writers, of bars like the Cedar Tavern and Earl's Hotel, of dozens of bookstores, most notably the Eighth Street Book Store and the secondhand shops on Fourth Avenue, of folk-song cafés like the Gaslight on MacDougal Street and jazz meccas like the Village Vanguard on Seventh Avenue. We had inexpensive restaurants like Monte's and Porto Bello in the Italian neighborhood to the south. Even though we couldn't get to these places often, it was nice to know they were there. A few short blocks from the apartment was Washington Square, bordered on all sides by the varied buildings of NYU, a place where I continued to take adult education courses with Miller. But here also I was gaining a surer foothold. Miller arranged that I would teach a course he had designed for himself called "Vocabulary Building and the Nature of Language"—whatever the latter may have meant. "You know those Latin etymologies better than I do," he generously told me. I was to teach the course, which paid $500, on my days off from St. Mary's. Another duck in the row.

More critical still, I applied to the NYU Graduate School of

Arts and Sciences and had done so, marvelous to say, with my bishop's permission. Most Catholic bishops are circumspect, dutiful (the sexual abuse scandals aside), "harmless" chaps who got where they are by being careful. Paterson's Bishop Navagh was different. A slightly nutty, even unstable man, he flew into uncontrollable rages one minute and was kind to everyone the next. He gave generously out of his own pocket to the poor. I was later told on the best authority, his executor, that on his death he had only $400 to his name. The building of schools was Navagh's great ambition, and he called me into his residence and asked questions about small St. Mary's High. I told him I thought he had summoned me about the lavish funeral for Monsignor Sheerin and the singing of "A Mighty Fortress Is Our God." Not at all, he said. What he had in mind was making me, eventually, the head of a large new high school he was planning to build on land the diocese owned in Totowa, the next parish over from St. Mary's. I was to tell no one, but was to complete my MA studies at Seton Hall. What did he think, I asked him, of my applying for doctoral studies at NYU once I had finished at Seton Hall? He thought it an excellent idea, as long as I could pursue the degree part-time while continuing my parish work. He felt it fitting that a "doctor" should head up his new high school. Then Navagh died, in Rome, struck down by a heart attack in St. Peter's Basilica during a session of the Vatican Council. No one ever mentioned that chimerical high school again, and indeed, in a short time Paterson's Catholic high schools, including St. Mary's, would close or contract.

Lawrence Casey became our new bishop, a no-nonsense practical fellow, whom Coletta and I called the Coal Miner, on the disrespectful grounds that he, like so many Irish-American pastors and bishops, should have been a Pennsylvania coal miner. We were thinking of Sheerin, who had family roots in coal-mining Kingston. Casey was good enough to let me finish up at Seton Hall, and even gave me permission to go ahead and apply to NYU. I suspect he didn't want to seem to be contradicting everything Navagh had set in motion. In April 1967 a letter came to "Mr. John Hall," 410 Union Avenue, Paterson, telling me I was accepted at the NYU Graduate English Department for the fall term.

Marianne and I had our difficulties. For one thing, I was available for the most part only on Tuesday evenings, and I had to drive back to Paterson in the small hours of the morning. One time I found that a 12th Street parking garage closed at 2 A.M., and I couldn't get my car out. I had to call a priest-friend, who went to St. Mary's and said Mass for me Wednesday morning. I also got to New York some late Saturday nights, leaving Paterson at 9:30 after confessions and having to be back soon so as to be on deck early in the morning. Also, like most curates, I had a two- or three-day break after Christmas and Easter. Our dating went on and off. Marianne was twenty-seven and was not going to go through another "five-year plan." Twice she broke it off, and in one instance during our separation I naively told my sole woman confidante, Ann Logan, that Marianne had disappointed me by not wanting to make love one more time before separating. "That's not how girls say good-bye," Ann counseled me.

But worse than my unavailability, in the short and in the long term, were my mood swings. In spite of my enthusiasm for our dates and lovemakings, in spite of my self-described liberation, and in spite of my nonbelief in God and the conviction that what we were doing was morally good, afterward I would feel not only tired but moody and depressed. When I had three days off after Christmas, I would be all fervor the first night, but dejected the next. How Marianne put up with me I don't know. I even went to see old Dr. Gross and told him how exhausted I was after a night of lovemaking. He thought I was overdoing it. "You're not eighteen," he said. But my real problem was not physical. It was guilt at the double life—seeing Marianne one night and administering the sacraments back in Paterson the next day. Then, while aware that I was living a schizoid existence, a new worry assailed me. Was I cut out for this "normal" side of life, for life with a woman? Perhaps I had been damaged, rendered unfit by all those years of abstinence and self-denial. And so in July 1967, one year into our seeing each other, I arranged to put my mental state to a test. We went for ten days to Cape Cod. I was fine, a most encouraging sign. We had such a good time that I even wrote a short poem—the sort of foolishness usually committed by young men—but then I was young at this. It closed with the lines:

> The courtesies of love
> in Massachusetts
> in Falmouth
> in July.

In August, back at St. Mary's on Union Avenue, things happened quickly. I found myself running the place alone. Monsignor Brady was in Ireland—"The pastor is out"—and the other curate, no longer Heekin but a young Italian fellow we called "Cheech," had the month off. Even the housekeeper was on vacation, her place temporarily taken by a beautiful young woman from Ireland, a nurse who was planning to become a missionary sister. Her name was Mary, Mary Small or Mary Little, I'm ashamed to say I can't recall which. She was of great help to me when I developed a high fever. After dragging myself around for a few days, I went to see a local doctor named Joseph Black. He told me I had mononucleosis and had to take complete bed rest. Mary insisted there was no such thing as mononucleosis: "I'm a nurse, and I should know. In Ireland they don't have a disease of that name." But she took solicitous care of me. From my sick bed I called around for priests to stand in for me, to say daily Mass and also to take confessions on Saturday. The Franciscans in West Paterson sent a priest to stay in the rectory over the weekend, but he made a pass at Mary and upset her terribly. I got rid of him and phoned the Chancery to line up a different substitute. Then Dr. Black called on me, took blood, and diagnosed hepatitis. I started to turn yellow. The emergency medical workers lifted me onto a gurney and carried me out the front door and down the steps to a waiting ambulance. I didn't look around, but I knew that on busy Union Avenue parishioners were witnessing this.

At St. Joseph's Hospital, in downtown Paterson, priests were treated like royalty, and I had a private room and most attentive care. From the rectory Mary sent a huge bouquet of flowers, but swore me to secrecy as to who had sent it. One of my first visitors, Cologne Colette, put up on the back of the room door a large poster of Sophia Loren standing at water's edge in nothing but an open, wet shirt. Next, in came Bishop Casey. I kept hoping he would not turn around and see the picture. He briskly wished me well, gave me his blessing, and said, "Well, you can put NYU out of your mind." All I could think was: "Not so fast." But I nodded.

Then, quite miraculously, Marianne appeared:

"How did you get here?"

"They have busses to Paterson, you know."

"Oh, yes."

She visited three times, and during one of these occasions my mother walked into the room. With what I congratulated myself on as quick thinking, I told her that Marianne had been sent to visit me on behalf of Professor Walter Miller, of whom my mother had heard me speak.

Lying there in St. Joseph's, in a continuous sweat, my body making the bedclothes and pillows not just moist but "wringing" wet, lying there lost in a physical weakness such as I had never experienced, I decided to leave the priesthood. As it happened, my departure was the first from the diocese of Paterson in that era. I have known many men who left the priesthood after I did, and from my unscientific sampling it appears that all of them defected because they wanted sex and the companionship of marriage. Most of them, had they been allowed to marry, would have been happy to remain priests. In my case I left for two reasons: marriage, yes, but, even more basically, unbelief. Were I believing, I cannot imagine that I would ever have left. Neither would I have left when I did without having a loved and loving woman to go to. Time and chance. And thus everything worked out nicely. I firmly made up my mind, at a time when my body was at its lowest point ever, to get out. I said nothing to Marianne.

After two weeks the doctors permitted me to leave the hospital, on condition that I do little but rest. It was August 31, 1967. Coletta drove me back to St. Mary's, where I packed some things. I went to say good-bye to Mary in the kitchen:

"You're not coming back," she said sadly.

"How did you know?

"I can tell," she said.

Then I knocked at the door of Brady's study—the first time ever—and of course found him reading the newspaper. I told him I was taking a "leave of absence." He said, "Well, good luck. Just don't foul the nest, that's all," and dismissed me with a flick of his hand. I would have enjoyed one more joke from him, but it was not to be.

Coletta drove me to the City and left me at the East 13th Street apartment. I lay there on the gaudy pullout sofa bed. Marianne came in at supper, fed me, and lay down beside me. She was not the type to worry about contagion. I asked her if she would be my wife, and she sat up, smiled, and clapped her hands, just once.

POSTSCRIPT

MARIANNE AND I were married a year later, on October 13, 1968, at the Episcopal Church of the Ascension in Greenwich Village, scarcely a hundred yards from where I sit typing now. Actually, we were married three times. I had engaged Cologne Colette to perform the ceremony, but he called me the day before the wedding to say that Marianne and I would have to be legally married first because he was not licensed to perform marriages in New York State. I telephoned the rector of Ascension, John McGill Krumm (formerly the chaplain at Columbia and later a bishop), with whom I had made arrangements for the wedding. On hearing of the problem, he graciously told us to come in that evening with two witnesses. I then called my closest new "secular" friend from NYU, Bill Graves, explained the situation, and asked him and his wife if they would do us the favor of witnessing the marriage that very night. He said, "Hang on," and called out, "Irene, it seems that Jack was a priest and they need two witnesses tonight—can we make it?" This "rehearsal" wedding went smoothly, as did the ceremony proper the following day. Marianne's family and relatives, who knew nothing of my background, thought it was a Catholic church and genuflected in the aisles on entering and leaving.

The third ceremony took place a year later in our apartment, with my old seminary friend Vince McCluskey officiating, the three of us with glasses of wine in our hands. Father Kenny Lasch, of the Paterson Chancery Office, had obtained a "rescript" from Pope Paul VI releasing me from the obligation of priestly celibacy. The dispensation was granted in a papal audience on July 4, 1969. Marianne and I would, in ecclesiastical parlance, no longer be merely "attempting marriage," but would be validly married "in the eyes of the Church." Our son Jonathan, born in 1973, would now be "legitimate" in those same eyes. (So would his son, also a Jonathan, born in 1996.)

I allowed myself this last bit of Catholic rigamarole for the sake of my parents, chiefly my mother, because my leaving had been hardest on her. My father took it more in stride and was content as long as I was doing something worthwhile, and studying for a doctorate qualified as just that. My mother, more religious than he, and certainly more Catholic, accepted the fact that I had to do "what I had to do." But she was devastated at first. With my rescript from Rome I could at least tell her that everything was right between me and the Church. She had been inordinately proud of having a son a priest. She had carried in her purse always a snapshot-size copy of that Fabian Bachrach ordination photograph. I felt her sorrow keenly. But what could I do? I did not become a priest to please my parents, though please them it did, nor would I remain a priest to please them. The best statement I have seen in regard to a situation like this comes, once again, from Updike. In an autobiographical essay he writes about how, having exited from a marriage and having left his wife and children "more in harm's way than felt right," he had taken heart from his mother's words, "Well, we carry our own hides to market." The debts, the responsibilities we owe our ancestors and descendants, are real, "but realer still is a certain obligation to our own selves, the obligation to live." These thoughts would not have helped my mother. What helped my mother was that she, like everyone else, loved Marianne.

Shortly after I left, Monsignor Edward Scully sent me a letter saying I had "betrayed the only woman in my life, Mary, the mother of Jesus." Monsignor Chris Haag, saying he figured I could use the money, sent me a check for two hundred dollars.

My time at NYU Graduate School stretched from that September 1967 through May 1970. I loved every minute of it.

NYU was so untendentious, so different from anything I had experienced. Professor Gordon Ray, who directed my dissertation, once wrote a letter of recommendation for me that mentioned my release from the priesthood as having "liberated in him an enthusiastic drive for research and study." It was Ray who got me started on Trollope. (Marianne did not know—nor did I—that in marrying me she was also marrying Anthony Trollope and Max Beerbohm, but she never complained. I am not saying she was perfect. She was, for example, often late.)

In 1970 I got my Ph.D. Already having three degrees of a sort, I thought it not worth the bother to attend the NYU graduation, held that year in Madison Square Garden. I now rather regret not going. My parents would have enjoyed it.

In that same year, 1970, the first of open admissions at City University of New York, I was hired to teach English at Bronx Community College, and ten years later was given a joint appointment to the CUNY Graduate Center. My community college teaching is rather like social work, and hence related to my past. At the Graduate Center I give seminars in the Victorian novel to doctoral candidates. These latter students are marvelously talented, but I doubt they enjoy graduate school as much as I did. How could they?

My mother spent the last year of her life, 1982, in a nursing home. Neither her doctors nor we her family told her she had terminal cancer. This unwillingness to inform the patient was not unusual twenty-five years ago. Toward the very end, through the influence of my old friend Father Pete Groeschel, we had her transferred to the Sacred Heart Home in Philadelphia, where the Dominican sisters—in anticipation of the hospice movement—cared exclusively for patients dying of cancer. These nuns had a policy of not charging money for their services, and would not accept any donations from the families of their patients. They relied on Divine Providence. With incredible devotion, patience, and kindness they helped my mother die in peace.

My father, six years later, having suffered a severe stroke, also spent the last year of his life in a nursing home, unable to speak or care for himself. When, toward the end, after a further medical collapse, he showed signs of being in great pain, I got on the phone to his doctor and screamed at him. For what purpose was my dying father suffering? "I hear you," he said. Two days later, my father, his support systems removed, was dead. He had always been such a strong figure in my life; he had, during my first twenty-six years, been forever doing things for me. This was the only thing I was ever able to do for him. In the 1950s and 1960s we were taught that the Church did not require a patient to take "extraordinary means" to prolong life. In this regard the Church has grown more conservative, giving "ordinary means" status to medical interventions, like long-term use of a respirator, which years ago would have been judged extraordinary and therefore not obligatory for Catholics.

In 1984 the Seminary of the Immaculate Conception, its enrollment down to one sixth of what it was in my day, retreated to Seton Hall, and the Archdiocese of Newark sold Darlington, buildings and land, to developers. New roads were cut through and scores of vulgar million-dollar homes were built on the grounds. The Crocker Mansion, perhaps the most exquisite white elephant of its kind in the country, for years lay vacant and deteriorating. But recently the building, all seventy-five rooms, has been restored and at the present writing is on the market for twenty-five million dollars. A steal. The seminary dormitory—now called "Walsh Hall" after the archbishop who laid the cornerstone in 1937—has been renovated into luxury condominiums, and the "de-consecrated" chapel is used for parties and social functions. The situation invites the common-place about the mighty having fallen.

At Pamplona, the fiesta has become more crowded but less un-inhibited. Botas are now out of style or outlawed, and people drink indoors or from plastic cups.

Since my leaving the priesthood, I have not followed theological arguments, except those widely reported in the news. But I am told that the Catholic Church is much changed from the one I knew, that it has become in some respects more democratic, more—as old Monsignor John Brady had predicted—Protes-tant. There was a time, in the early 1970s, when some people thought religion and churchgoing were dying out in America as they had in Europe. Alas, the opposite seems to have happened. But the religious resurgence has been mostly among the Protes-tant fundamentalists and evangelicals (like "your President," as Brady would have said) and not among the mainstream persua-sions. I do think it a shame that the American Catholic Church, which in my time embraced not only a colorful primitivism, but prided itself on running some very good universities and serv-ing as home to many thinking people, is now often lumped to-gether with right-wing fundamentalism, the two drawn to each other chiefly by an opposition to abortion, homosexual unions, and stem cell research. The papers are full of the news that the Catholic Church in America is in crisis, not only because of the sex abuse scandals, but from the paucity of vocations to the priesthood (and to the sisterhood). According to Catholic sources, the numbers of college-level seminarians across Amer-ica are down to fewer than one tenth of what they were three decades ago. Catholic Ireland, which as late as the 1960s sent priest "missionaries" to the diocese of Paterson, has suffered an even more precipitous drop. Maybe some day Paterson will be sending missionaries to Ireland.

Statistics show that Catholics in this country now disregard the interdiction of "artificial" or "unnatural" birth control; they see contraception as no more unnatural than, say, mirrors, which enable us, quite unnaturally, to see what is in back of us. The ridiculous policy that had so troubled my years in the priesthood has become a nonissue, here and of course in Europe, where Catholic Italy has the lowest birth rate on the Continent. Of course in parts of Africa, like Uganda, and other places where Catholic propaganda against the use of condoms still has influence, abetted sometimes by Washington's religiously based promotion of "abstinence only" programs, the Church and our own government are responsible for countless HIV infections and AIDS deaths.

I continue to be a contented and cheerful nonbeliever. I do grow impatient when Christian fundamentalists and other slack thinkers imply that I am less moral than they are because I have no reason to behave myself, lacking as I do belief in a deity who promises me heaven or threatens me with hell. The same shallow people try to corner the market on what they call "spirituality," something they fraudulently oppose to secular humanism and science. I can be just as "spiritual" as the next person. I, too, believe in "things bigger than myself"—generosity, forgiveness, fairness, and so on. I don't want any person, however sincere, telling me that unless I had a "soul" directly or indirectly created by God, I couldn't appreciate these things or comport myself decently. I am "spiritual" enough to relish Shakespeare and Bach and Henry Moore; I can stand in awe at the cathedrals of Salisbury and Wells; I can revel in the language of Milton's *Paradise Lost* and in that of the King James Version of the Bible; I can respect and reverence some of the teachings attributed to Jesus, and delight in the smile on a child's face. The physicist Richard Feynman said that just because he knew something about the stars didn't mean he couldn't see the beauty in a starry night sky. Or, as V. S. Naipaul put it, "I don't need some guru to tell me 'Sky big, me little.' I already know that."

I try not to offend religious people. I remain, for example, quietly attentive and with bowed head—"as if in prayer," as we used to say—when at Christmas and other holiday dinners my relatives have one of the family lead grace, thanking God for their food and other blessings. My relatives know better than to ask me to say grace, but if they did ask me I'd be tempted to give them Swinburne:

> We thank with brief thanksgiving
>   Whatever gods may be
> That no life lives for ever;
> That dead men rise up never;
> That even the weariest river
>   Winds somewhere safe to sea.

But in fact I wouldn't give them Swinburne, wouldn't offend them with these sentiments (or with such overly alliterative verse). In America it is considered bad form to disparage anyone's religious views. We don't have to respect the notion that the sun goes around the earth or that the earth is flat, but we must shy away from ridiculing or belittling absurd religious positions and beliefs. Such reserve seems an abuse of reason or at least of the critical faculty. It would be braver if, after first insisting on respect for all people whatever their religious convictions, we had at those convictions with might and main. But we don't. Besides, for most adults, it's too late. If people have not learned to doubt in their late teens or early twenties, they probably never will. Maybe Unamuno's Don Manuel had it right.

Furthermore, as I've insisted here, there is no gainsaying the fact that organized religion can bring out the best in certain people. Daniel Dennett, a self-professed atheist philosopher, writes:

> For day-in, day-out lifelong bracing, there is probably nothing so effective as religion: it makes powerful and talented people more humble and patient, it makes average people rise above themselves, it provides sturdy support for many people who desperately need help staying away from drink or drugs or crime. People who would otherwise

be self-absorbed or shallow or crude or simply quitters are often ennobled by their religion, given a perspective on life that helps them make the hard decisions that we all would be proud to make.

But at what cost? Religion, it can be argued, also fosters—on a broader scale—guilt, worry, fanaticism, bigotry, oppression, exclusion, tribalism, cruelty, persecution, superstition, ignorance. Everyone is free to weigh the pros and the cons. But what if, whether one be for or against religion, there is, at bottom, no deity, nothing to religion but what could be termed its own external realities?

And thus my thoughts are still troubled by the question of what will take the place of religion when people leave off superstition and wishful thinking—if they ever do. Perhaps the need for something like religion is naturally selected, a component of our makeup. Clearly religion is not going to be superseded by poetry, as Matthew Arnold quixotically envisioned, or by a proletariat state, as some Marxists foolishly thought. And secular humanism doesn't seem to be faring too well, either. Science, with its practical and irrefutable successes, has in the popular imagination moved into a position of authority and prestige formerly reserved for religion. The man or woman in the white laboratory coat has to some extent replaced the bishop with his miter and the rabbi with his tallith. But science has come nowhere near to sweeping the field, as some of its earlier advocates had predicted. Science has not—so far at least—satisfied the human craving for transcendence and for meaning. Nor do most scientists expect it to do so. Harvard biologist Edward O. Wilson believes that if people understood the epic of evolution they would find the story of life on this planet "the best myth we will ever have," and far more enthralling than anything in Genesis. But Wilson's view seems an outside hope because evolution, in addition to its complexities, can't offer immortality to individuals or "divine privilege" to a particular group. I wish them well, the humanists and scientists. It is sad that in this country so many of them stay closeted behind a socially acceptable and vague monotheism or a timid agnosticism. That's a harsh way to put it. Only "facticity" makes me do so. Against the fact, no argument is valid. That much I remember from my old days.

In moments of vanity I like to believe that, had the *Index of Prohibited Books* not been eliminated by the Second Vatican Council, this book would have made the list, if not by name, certainly by category.

I have had a satisfying run—fellowships, grants, research abroad, publications, and such. With an obsessive focus, that legacy from my father, I concentrated my studies on a single author at a time, first on Anthony Trollope and then on Max Beerbohm. They are very different kinds of writers, but both are comic artists. Trollope's comedy is rooted in common sense, the attraction toward which I look upon as inherited from my mother. Beerbohm's comedy is rooted in edginess, something my father cultivated and taught me to admire. My second career, as an English professor, has been a happy one. I feel rather like my colleague Gerhard Joseph, who says, "In my next life, I want to be an English professor."

Sadly, Marianne died in 2003 after a bout with acute leukemia. At the time I said to Bill Graves that if I had never left the priesthood, I would never have experienced such intense loss. Priests grieve, of course, over the deaths of their parents, but such separations are more in the course of nature. The death of a much-loved spouse of thirty-five years is qualitatively different. Or so I learned. Walter Pater spoke of the ecstasy and sorrow of love, and here was my sorrow. But from the start in 1966, Marianne and I had a good time of it. I still have, somewhere at the bottom of a clothes dresser, that black-and-white dress.

Very recently, no more than two months ago, while I was trying to read a book in Washington Square Park, a young man with a "Jesus Saves" button came over to me and launched into his spiel. I interrupted by asking him how old he was. "Nineteen," he told me. "You'll get over it," I said, "just hang in there."

ACKNOWLEDGMENTS

I AM INDEBTED to the following priests for patiently jogging my memory or correcting it: the late Henry G. J. Beck, Jack Catoir, Ed Ciuba, Tom Coletta, Bill Giblin, Jerry Graziano, Benedict Groeschel, the late Chris Haag, John Heekin, Eugene Kasper, Ken Lasch, David McBriar, George Mader, Vince Puma, Dick Rento, Bishop Frank Rodimer, Thomas Trapasso, Jack Wehrlen, and Robert Wister.

Family members Sally A. Hall, Audrey Joan Clark, and James Ehrenberg have also shared memories with me.

Other help, everything from reading the manuscript to tweaking my bits of Italian and Spanish, came to me from Betty Betzel, Gerry Breen, Bob Call, Mary Ann Caws, Jim Crowther, Herman and Marsha Cummins, James DeMetro, Frederick DeNaples, the late Julius DiRenzo, Joseph Giannelli, Stephen Gill, David Gordon, Bill Graves, Mickie Grover, Jan Heissinger, Gerhard Joseph, James Kincaid, Meryl Koopersmith, Francisco Legasa, Ralph and Ann Logan, Daniel Lowenthal, Ray Mazewski, Mario Materassi, Walter James Miller, the late Nancy Patri, Johnny Phillips, Jerry Pindar, and Jim Tierney.

Julia Miele Rodas supplied careful editing and helpful suggestions. I acknowledge generous support from the CUNY Research Foundation.

PHOTOGRAPHS

✝✝✝✝✝✝✝✝✝✝✝✝✝✝✝✝✝✝✝✝✝✝✝✝✝✝✝✝✝

The text of this book was set in Adobe's Brioso Pro
with Bernhard Modern Standard as the display by
the Nangle Type Shop in Meriden, Connecticut.
Lucian Berhard deliberately designed his typeface
not to rely on the ink spread commonly associated
with letterpress impressions for its final appearance,
but on the contours of the type itself. He thereby anticipated the eventual arrival of digital typography.
Brioso was designed by Robert Slimbach, of
Adobe Systems, who endeavored to
capture the "liveliness" implied
by the typeface's name.